25

PLACES *in* CANADA
EVERY FAMILY SHOULD VISIT
JODY ROBBINS

TOUCHWOOD
EDITIONS

Edited by Renée Layberry
Proofread by Cailey Cavallin
Design by Pete Kohut
Cover and interior photo credits listed on pages 367–368

LIBRARY AND ARCHIVES CANADA CATALOGUING IN PUBLICATION
Robbins, Jody, author
25 places in Canada every family should visit / Jody Robbins.

Includes index.
Issued in print and electronic formats.
ISBN 978-1-77151-201-5

1. Family recreation—Canada—Guidebooks. 2. Canada—Guidebooks.
I. Title. II. Title: Twenty-five places in Canada every family should visit.

FC38 R63 2017   917.104   C2016-908152-4

We acknowledge the financial support of the Government of Canada through the Canada
Book Fund and the province of British Columbia through the Book Publishing Tax Credit.

Canadä

The interior pages of this book have been printed on 100% post-consumer
recycled paper, processed chlorine free, and printed with vegetable-based inks.

PRINTED IN CANADA AT FRIESENS

17 18 19 20 21   5 4 3 2 1

For Dan and Eve, who make coming
home the best part of any trip

Contents

Introduction

I caught the travel bug early. In fact, it may have been hereditary. When I was growing up, our family would scuttle back and forth between our home on the prairies and Lake Erie, where extended family lived. Then we'd mosey over to New Brunswick's Miramichi Bay. I'm amazed my parents made this trek each and every summer. I certainly wouldn't be up to the task of taking a sulking child (that was me) to a historic boarding house with no running water, heat, or electricity.

Now that I'm a parent myself, I prefer an easier road. I look for spots that offer something for all members of the family, not just those that cater to adult tastes or kiddie favourites. Still, those summers taught me invaluable lessons—in particular, an appreciation for diversity. It opened my eyes to all that was different and precious across this vast country of ours. My imagination soared as I was forced to get creative and entertain myself in new and unfamiliar places.

Those early years taught me that travel is about more than your destination. Yes, it's a discovery of parts unknown, but it's also about you. Horizons expand both geographically and personally; when discovering new destinations, you discover more about yourself. Why? Because travel tests you. How do you react when things go belly up? Can you take flight delays in stride or do they ruin your day? You're guaranteed to have countless "teachable moments" when travelling with children as they watch you deal with unexpected situations. From problem solving to patience to the importance of preparedness, travel introduces and refines valuable life skills in ways that cannot be replicated in the classroom.

Our perceptions of the world are based on what we've experienced. Taking children out of their little worlds and opening them up to new experiences and ways of life lays the foundation for lifelong learning. Travel can change a person. It's about more than geography—it's a journey of self-exploration that can make you more tolerant, more interesting, and better able to adapt to new situations. It fosters a curiosity that inspires creativity, joy, and discovery. If I can impart this to my daughter, I've done my job.

Fortunately, you don't have to go someplace exotic or fly thousands of kilometres away to learn these lessons; you can engage minds and cultivate rich experiences close to home. 2017—the 150th anniversary of Confederation—is an ideal time to explore Canada: from coast to coast, north to south, community events and celebrations will mark this momentous occasion.

The memories indelibly inked on my brain are those that have shown me the world through a child's eyes. We all lead busy lives; kids and adults alike are overscheduled. But when we remove ourselves from our everyday environment and mindfully participate in new, shared experiences, real and profound bonding occurs. So disconnect from the daily grind and find the best connection of all. If not now, when?

HOW TO USE THIS BOOK

As much as I'd love for you to read this book from cover to cover, I suspect most folks will flip to a destination of interest and go from there. And that's OK. Flip away, skip ahead, and read what tickles your fancy to get inspiration for your next family vacation.

In writing the bonus chapters, I interviewed parents across Canada, plus North America's top travel bloggers and writers, so I could share their travel secrets with you. I wanted to know: How do you plan a trip with children that's easy and enjoyable (and not regrettable)? Many inspiring ideas came forth, and I encourage you to read those additional chapters and share the findings with your friends and family.

DISCLAIMER

Writing tourist attraction, hotel, and restaurant reviews for national magazines and newspapers is challenging. Not the writing bit, but staying current. And when writing a book, a year (or more!) can pass between the time a writer submits their manuscript to their publisher and when it appears in bookstores. A lot can change in that time. Prices go up, companies go out of business, and new ones emerge. Also, ownership changes can dramatically affect visitor experience.

We—the publisher, fact-checkers, editors, and I—have gone to great lengths to ensure the information provided in this book is accurate at the time of publishing. Even so, I want to encourage you to remember that change can happen at any time. If a destination, tour outfitter, hotel, or restaurant mentioned in this book has piqued your interest, it's still a good idea to confirm rates and details directly with the provider of that experience.

Canada is such a diverse country; it was a real challenge to narrow this list down to only twenty-five destinations for fabulous family travel experiences. So I'd love to hear your thoughts on the ones you visited and how your family enjoyed the journey—and, by the way, do let me know if I missed anything in this book, because I undoubtedly did. You can find me on Facebook (Facebook.com/TravelswithBaggage) and Twitter (Twitter.com/Jody_Robbins). I'm looking forward to hearing all about your adventures!

Examining the rib of a grey whale at the Shaw Centre for the Salish Sea.

Senses are quickly revived when strolling through the Sunken Garden at the Butchart Gardens.

Victoria

Canada's Garden City

Set on the southern tip of Vancouver Island, Victoria is a city made for families, foodies, and nature lovers. With lush green spaces to enjoy and enticing pebbly beaches to comb, you'll rack up plenty of outdoor time without even trying. Better still, thanks to Victoria's compact size, you're never too far from kid-approved amusements. Besides the local marine life, there are butterflies, bugs, and farm animals to get to know at hands-on attractions and revitalizing gardens. Whether on the water, up a mountain, or in the city, there's something for everyone to enjoy in one of the sunniest cities in British Columbia.

TAKE TO THE WATER

Vancouver Island is one of the best spots for whale watching in North America, with plenty of species of marine mammals living in the waters around Victoria. Black-and-white orcas and humpback whales are the most frequently sighted, but it's possible to spot minke and grey whales too. Keep an eye open for seals, sea lions, and porpoises, as well as bald eagles and countless sea birds in their natural environment. Your chances for viewing orcas are best from April to November, but marine wildlife tours led by certified naturalists operate throughout the year and showcase an astonishing diversity of ocean occupants.

You don't need to spend much money when poking around Victoria's Inner Harbour, and the sea air will revive those with flagging energy. Wander down to the wharf and admire the tall ships, ferries, and float planes. Water taxis carry passengers from one side of the bay to the other, while harbour ferries cruise to several locations in the inner and upper harbour. Chug over to Fisherman's Wharf, where you can feed the resident seals. Try the famed fish and chips at Barb's Place, or enjoy some ice cream while checking out the funky float homes.

Rent a canoe, kayak, or stand-up paddleboard to investigate the city via its waterways. If you have children over age five, consider a kayaking tour. Take in the rich aquatic life, including jewel-toned starfish, as you glide gracefully in a tandem vessel. Some tours take you to local haunts like the bathing hole up the Gorge Waterway, while others will have you paddling around the Inner Harbour and even out of town.

FOR LANDLUBBERS

About a block away from the Inner Harbour, Miniature World has tiny displays that will pique the interest of those both young and old. There are close to 100 intricately designed dioramas that take you to fairytale lands and iconic events in history. Peer into Dickensian London, First Nations villages, and the construction of the Canadian Pacific Railway.

Nearby, the Victoria Bug Zoo has just enough of a creepy-crawly factor to keep teens entertained. Want to hold a tarantula in the palm of your hand? How about letting a stick insect cling to your arm? Bug guides operate a safe animal-handling experience while revealing the secrets of the praying mantis, the glow-in-the-dark scorpion, and a 1.7-million-member ant colony, all of which await you in this insectarium.

At the Royal British Columbia Museum, wander through the natural history galleries to get a feel for the province's coastal rainforest and Pacific shores. There are enough stuffed critters throughout to thrill a taxidermist; try making a game of spotting the ones that don't exist anymore. Meander through the First Peoples Gallery and take in the incredible workmanship displayed in carvings, masks, and artifacts. On a rainy day, the IMAX theatre is a big hit. And if you're in Victoria over the weekend, be sure to catch a Wonder Sunday, with special tours and activities designed just for families.

Children could spend hours feeding the seals at Oak Bay Marina.

A friendly butterfly pops by to say hello at Butterfly Gardens.

Dip your hands into the touch tank at the Shaw Centre for the Salish Sea.

Baby goats are some of the stars at the Beacon Hill Children's Farm.

Meet ducks and other animals at Beacon Hill Park.

Before or after your visit to the museum, take a few moments to gaze at the totem poles in Thunderbird Park, just outside. Littles can play hide-and-seek around the native plant garden, while caregivers soak up views of the glittering Inner Harbour. In the museum's back courtyard, you'll find some of Victoria's tastiest eats from various food trucks. Sample local treats and keep those blood sugar levels steady to set up your visit for success.

GLORIOUS GREEN SPACES

Beacon Hill Park, which extends from downtown to the shore of Juan de Fuca Strait, will captivate youngsters and refresh adults. And if you time it right, you can catch the twice-daily goat stampede, which sees these adorable, bleating creatures trotting from barn to pen when the Beacon Hill Children's Farm opens and closes each day. There are other friendly critters to make friends with at the farm, including ducks, chickens, pigs, and peacocks. Bear in mind when planning a visit that the Children's Farm is closed just after Thanksgiving Monday until the second week of March. The park's streams and lakes are also a haven for great blue heron, river otters, painted turtles, and crayfish—some of which you might spot.

Human kids can burn off energy at the miniature golfing green, or dive into the water play area. Pack rain boots to keep feet dry when exploring the soggy black cottonwood grove. The meadows of spring wildflowers offer pretty spots for family photos, as do the lofty watering can and the Mile 0 marker of the 4,971-mile (8,000-kilometre) Trans-Canada Highway.

When visiting Canada's city of gardens, you really ought to see its flagship, the Butchart Gardens. You may think that a visit to a garden will be a snooze-fest, but consider how much children love to roam in open spaces. This national historic site offers over 55 acres (22 hectares) to explore. Open all year, there are visual thrills in every season, including summer firework displays, magical Christmas lights, and hundreds of thousands of bulbs in bloom in the spring. The handcrafted carousel inside the Children's Pavilion is an added bonus. With an afternoon tea experience that caters to children, plus another two restaurants on site, families (and their dogs!) can happily spend the entire day in this botanical paradise.

You'll also find Victoria Butterfly Gardens just minutes away. This tranquil indoor garden features lush foliage and beautiful blooms, and is home to many rescued tropical animals, including flamingos, tortoises, and even poison dart frogs. The big draw, of course, is the thousands of free-flying butterflies. Don't be surprised if they like you so much they decide to land on you!

OAK BAY

A ten-minute drive from downtown Victoria will bring you to the charming village of Oak Bay for a laid-back day away from the tourist trail. Check out the independent shops that line Oak Bay Avenue, including an excellent toy store and bookstore.

In nearby Estevan Village, you'll discover that teatime isn't just for old ladies in outlandish hats. Settle down to a children's tea party at Crumsby's Cupcake Café, and watch the littles lift tiny teacups from their saucers and nibble cupcakes lovingly served on a tray—that is, when the young ones aren't investigating the toys in the play area. Grown-ups can admire the framed works of art by local children while sipping barista-made coffee and savouring from-scratch baked goods.

After tea, walk the few blocks to Willows Beach. Against the stunning backdrop of a dormant volcano (Mount Baker) and the Olympic Mountains, families can while away the day in the shallow, protected waters or at the shaded playground.

Then it's a quick drive or walk south on Beach Drive to the Oak Bay Marina, where adults can gaze longingly at the sailboats, imagining what life on the coast might be like, while the kids feed the resident seals frozen fish bought at the marina gift shop.

WORTHY SIDE TRIP

If you've been to Vancouver Island, you've likely passed Sidney-by-the-Sea, the location of both the airport and two ferry terminals.

This unpretentious seaside town has plenty of diversions within easy walking distance, and can provide an affordable base camp for families.

The moment they walk through the doors of the Shaw Centre for the Salish Sea, children will be entranced by the tricked-out elevator that evokes a submarine diving into the sea. The floor rumbles, lights flash, and bells and whistles go off all the way down. This aquarium offers more than the usual tanks and fish-feeding frenzy; here you can interact with the ocean through a number of different stations. See how sharp a killer whale's teeth are, hold the rib of a grey whale, or peer into a microscope to watch minuscule marine life. Especially exciting is the touch tank, where everyone can get their hands wet petting starfish, spotted sea slugs, and hypnotic anemones.

Saunter along Beacon Avenue, the town's main drag, and discover why Sidney is known as Canada's Booktown. (Spoiler alert: it may have something to do with the number of secondhand bookstores lining the avenue.) You'll also find a well-stocked toy shop and the Sidney Museum and Archives (admission by donation).

🍴 TASTE

There are many places to take afternoon tea in Victoria, but the **Fairmont Empress** pulls out all the stops with its Prince and Princess Tea package. Children feel oh-so grown-up choosing their own blend, and there are mini-scones, cookies, and finger sandwiches to nibble on, not to mention crowns and tiaras to don.

Zagat-rated **Pizzeria Prima Strada**, located on Cook Street near Beacon Hill Park, is a good choice for families. Kids will love the wood-fired bambino pizza, while parents will appreciate the high chairs and baby change station.

Using only sustainable, Ocean Wise–recommended seafood, **Red Fish Blue Fish** is a waterfront takeout joint housed inside a shipping container on the Inner Harbour. It's well worth waiting in line for the tacones and tempura-battered fish and chips, served with hand-cut fries and homemade tartar sauce.

Want to cook your own seafood? Pop into **Satellite Fish Co.** at the end of the pier in Sidney for fresh-off-the-boat fish and shellfish. These fishmongers know how to pack for travel, so be sure to stock up before flying home.

NAP

Hotel Zed is an attractively priced, groovy hotel with amenities geared specifically to the younger set. The brightly coloured lobby has board games and old-school typewriters, and plays music on vinyl. The Ping Pong Lounge (complete with Wii stations), hot-pink water slide (the Zedinator), and complimentary longboards are added bonuses. The retrofitted 1967 VW shuttle bus will get you downtown, or you can do the ten-minute ride on complimentary bikes.

At **Hotel Grand Pacific**, overlooking the Inner Harbour, ducks waddle around the grounds, delighting young guests. In need of a sippy-cup of milk and some snacks upon arrival? The staff will ensure that your mini-bar is stocked with favourites by the time you check in. Borrow a cruiser bike and tour along Victoria's many pathways, or make a splash in the large indoor pool.

In Sidney, **Cedarwood Inn and Suites** offers reasonably priced waterfront accommodation ranging from motel-style rooms to kitschy cabins overlooking the central garden. The new addition boasts suites with jet tubs, fireplaces, and balconies overlooking the sea. Request a room with a kitchenette if you fancy preparing a seafood feast with bounty bought from the docks. There's also a communal BBQ and picnic tables outside.

GETTING AROUND

Victoria International Airport is serviced by BC Transit feeder buses that connect you to buses to downtown Victoria, Sidney, Butchart Gardens, and the BC Ferries terminals at Swartz Bay. The feeder buses operate on a limited schedule; be sure to check the BC Transit schedule before you travel.

Victoria Harbour Ferry operates adorable water taxis from March to October, taking you from Selkirk Landing to Ogden Point with numerous stops in between. Victoria's downtown and Inner Harbour attractions are easily explored on foot. But if you want to take it easy on your feet, a fun and memorable way to see the sights is with the Victoria Pedicab Company (your bike chauffeur doubles as a tour guide!). Or splurge on a horse-drawn carriage tour with Tally-Ho.

BC Ferries links Victoria and other spots on Vancouver Island with the Gulf Islands and Lower Mainland. Victoria Clipper is a passenger-only ferry service between Victoria and Seattle. You can also get to and from Seattle with your vehicle on Washington State Ferries and the Black Ball Ferry Line.

FUN FACTS

- **The Fairmont Empress Hotel** serves 500,000 cups of tea annually.
- Over 80 resident orca whales in three pods, as well as 120 transient orcas, visit the waters around Victoria between spring and fall.
- **The Butchart Gardens** hosts more than a million visitors each year.
- **Victoria** was named one of the 15 Friendliest Cities in the World by MSN. ca Travel in 2013.

GET EXCITED ABOUT YOUR TRIP

- *Picklefeathers*, by Aileen Headen, tells the tale of a lost duck and the grandmother and granddaughter who help it find its way back to its family at Beacon Hill Children's Farm. (All proceeds of the book are donated to the farm.)
- *Waiting for the Whales*, by Sheryl McFarlane, is an award-winning story-book about a grandfather and his passion for whales.
- The vivid, evocative art of Roy Henry Vickers is sure to excite both young and old about a visit to the British Columbia coast.

Listen to the waves lap against the shore with a beachfront room at Tigh-Na-Mara Seaside Spa Resort.

Paradise Mini Golf and Fun Park has a super-cute course.

Parksville–Qualicum Beach

Endless Shoreline and Ancient Coastal Rainforests

Making waves with its luxurious sweep of soft sand, Parksville–Qualicum Beach is an under-the-radar region with an endless stretch of coastline. Warmly referred to by locals as Oceanside, it is one of a dozen charming, diminutive communities nestled on Vancouver Island's eastern shore. Here, a motley crew of toothless tykes armed with nets, buckets, and spades relentlessly seek out aquatic treasures. Join the hunt for sand dollars, moon snails, and purple starfish along the 12-mile (19-kilometre) coastline, a geological anomaly from the Ice Age. The extreme tide recedes up to half a mile (1 kilometre) from the shore, and when the Salish Sea swoops back over the hot sand, temperatures can reach 21°C (70°F), making this the warmest seawater in all of Canada. The shallow water and sandy beach make this area a paradise for skimboarders of all skill levels.

Yet there's plenty to do besides beachcombing and skimboarding. "Coming here really works for us with kids," says Darren Hribar, dad of three. "The swimming is easy, there's little risk, and there's kayaking in the bay." After you've strolled barefoot across the wave rippled sand, head to the emerald forests where canopies of old-growth trees provide a tranquil environment. And in town there are plenty of parks and amusements to delight all family members.

CATHEDRAL GROVE

Take a leisurely stroll through accessible old-growth stands of Douglas fir trees, located in MacMillan Provincial Park, about a thirty-minute drive from Parksville. You may find yourself convinced you're walking through an enchanted fairyland when roaming the network of trails laced with giant conifers so tall you have to throw your head all the way back to glimpse their tops. Nobody could blame you for expecting a woodland sprite to appear amid the sprawling ferns that coat the landscape; they don't, of course, but that doesn't mean you won't feel the magic of the park, especially when pressing your palm against the ancient pillars of this coastal forest.

The largest tree in the park, at over 800 years old, predates the arrival of Columbus to the Americas by more than 300 years. This jumbo tree towers at 250 feet (76 metres) tall—a whopping 65 feet (20 metres) higher than the Leaning Tower of Pisa. Wind storms have downed several other massive trees, yet they're still valuable. Supporting the next generation for years to come, they become nurse logs and provide nutrients to their seedlings.

VENTURE UNDERGROUND

There are over 1,600 known caves on Vancouver Island, which makes it home to the highest concentration of caves in North America. Exploring the "Island of Caves" is a cinch with tours operated by Horne Lake Caves and Outdoor Centre. For those over five years old, there are four caves to explore in Horne Lake Caves Provincial Park. It's challenge by choice as each individual decides whether they're up for crawling through the beautiful passages in search of crystal formations and ancient fossils.

Here, the cave ceilings look like they've been sprayed in diamond dust. Referred to as cave glitter, it's actually caused by the light from explorers' headlamps bouncing off tiny water particles. There are stalactites over 35,000 years old, and a terraced cascade of flowstone looks just like an ice cream waterfall. Wear your rubber boots—there's water in these caves. "When you hear the sound of the rushing spring, that's the sound of a cave growing," says cave guide Miles Fullmer.

These caves are open all year round and remain at a constant

The ocean is calm and gentle around Parksville.

The annual sandcastle competition is a must-see event.

There's a whole new world to explore underground at Horne Lake Caves Park.

Skimboarding is one of the many draws to the beaches of Parksville.

Ancient Douglas fir trees populate Cathedral Grove, an old-growth forest.

temperature of 8°C (46°F). Family tours exploring Riverbend Cave take about an hour and a half, while other tours (just as family-friendly) take longer. Expect cable ladders, crossings over underground streams, and kids leading the charge through (optional) tiny crawl spaces.

ANIMAL ATTRACTION

Goats dot the grass-covered roof of the Old Country Market, a modern-day mercantile located in the nearby community of Coombs. Brimming with a potpourri of products that range from gourmet delicacies to art supplies to children's toys, families can easily spend more time than expected wandering through the jam-packed aisles. Step outside to view the goats—permanent tenants for the past thirty years—and stroll around the quaint market bustling with a variety of artisanal shops.

Tiger Lily Farm provides plenty of barnyard diversions to melt the hearts of animal lovers. Hug a bunny, milk a goat, bottle feed a kid goat, or opt for a pony ride. Horseback rides along scenic trails are also on offer.

Each spring, brant geese make the trek from Mexico all the way up to the Canadian Arctic. Parksville is an important stop in their journey and is noted by the annual Brant Wildlife Festival in March, when thousands of geese drop in along the east coast of Vancouver Island. The festival honours their return with wildlife tours, a bird counting competition, and an eagle release. If you can't make it for the festival, join the weekly bird walk that departs from the Parksville Community Park at 9 a.m. each Tuesday.

FROM WELLNESS TO WILDERNESS

With a mission to care for ill, injured, and orphaned wildlife, the North Island Wildlife Recovery Association (NIWRA) also educates the public on wildlife and environmental issues. Head here to view and learn about wildlife, and the problems they face, on guided or self-guided tours March through October. There are orphaned black bears, birds who've suffered wing injuries, and even ferrets who teach the responsibility of pet ownership.

KICKING AROUND TOWN

An annual summer sand sculpting competition draws in master sculptors from around the world during the Parksville Beach Festival. Suss out the masterpieces created from sand and water (and a lot of ingenuity) before hitting up Venture Land, a massive playground with more than twenty pieces of equipment, just off the boardwalk. In addition to a splash park and outdoor exercise equipment, kids can take to the zip line or ride the twelve-person teeter-totter.

There are two eighteen-hole mini-golf courses at Paradise Mini Golf and Fun Park. The features are pretty impressive, and you can cool off after hitting the links by getting sprayed and bashing into others on bumper boats. Got a need for speed? Fast Times Grand Prix is a go-kart track where you can race around a half-kilometre course at speeds of up to 31 miles (50 kilometres) an hour.

¶¶ TASTE

Pick up artisanal, handcrafted cheeses at **Little Qualicum Cheeseworks**. Their farm is open to the public, and you can even watch the 4 p.m. cow milking. Stroll through the trails on a self-guided tour, and make friends with cows, pigs, goats, sheep, bunnies, and even donkeys.

There are a variety of dining options to be found at the **Old Country Market** in Coombs. Hit up the cafeteria-cum-taqueria, or settle into Cuckoo, a trattoria and pizzeria that dishes out family-style platters of pasta, in addition to gluten-free meals.

At **French Creek Seafood**, a nearby dockside fish market, you can stock up on fresh crab and clams. In town, **Bread and Honey Food Company** focuses on fresh, local, and sustainable food.

⌂ NAP

While Parksville doesn't have enough hotel rooms to be considered a resort town, you'll feel like you're staying at one when spending the night at **The Beach Club Resort**. Floor-to-ceiling windows frame spectacular ocean views, but it's the fully furnished kitchens that make this hotel ideal for large broods. Families can take advantage of the pool, as well as complimentary bikes and skimboards, or opt to rent paddleboards and kayaks from the boardwalk.

Eager to please young travellers, **Tigh-Na-Mara** is a resort that doles out endless kid-friendly perks. Cradled within twenty-two forested acres, it boasts an indoor pool, an outdoor playground, and a wide stretch of sandy beach. During the school holidays, it operates one of the most robust resort recreation programs in all of Canada. Sessions range from a complimentary kids' club to teen tie-dyeing to family birdhouse building. While children under sixteen years of age aren't allowed into the cavernous mineral pool at Grotto Spa, they can enjoy milkshakes and partake in mini-spa experiences such as manicures. Rustic log cabins are kitted out with fireplaces and kitchen amenities, and there are laundry facilities for guest use.

The Parksville–Qualicum Beach area offers fourteen campsites ranging from oceanfront to riverside to forest campgrounds. Both **Surfside RV Resort** and **Park Sands Beach Resort** are family-friendly RV parks with enviable beachfront locations. Park Sands allows tents and has showers and laundry facilities, while Surfside offers a pool, hot tub, and clubhouse. The RV grounds at **Paradise Fun Park** are also well positioned, with easy access to the beach and a mini-golf course. For a tranquil experience, snag a spot at **Rathtrevor Beach Provincial Park**. Here all campsites are within a five-minute walk of the beach and are set under majestic Douglas fir trees.

⌖ GETTING AROUND

Parksville is a two-hour drive from Victoria or a twenty-minute drive from North Nanaimo. **BC Ferries** services both Nanaimo and Victoria (Sidney) via Vancouver. Or fly into the Qualicum Beach, Nanaimo, Comox, or Victoria airport.

⚙ FUN FACTS

- Douglas firs can live for over a thousand years, making them one of the oldest living tree species in North America.
- Vancouver Island is home to the highest concentration of caves in North America.
- Vancouver Island is the largest island off the west coast of North America. It's similar in size to Taiwan and the Netherlands.

✦ GET EXCITED ABOUT YOUR TRIP

- *Salmon Forest*, a book by David Suzuki and Sarah Ellis, is a powerful story that highlights the interconnectedness of all living species.
- Littles will enjoy watching the Youtube video of the song "Run Salmon Run" by Canadian children entertainers Bobs & LoLo.
- *Animal World with Northwest Coast Native Art* is a colourful preschool board book that showcases the many animals living in the Pacific Northwest.

The Aquabus ferry is a colourful and fun addition to False Creek.

Daisy, a resident harbour porpoise, was rescued and rehabilitated by the Vancouver Aquarium's Marine Mammal Rescue Centre.

Vancouver

Journey from Sea to Sky

If you only have time to visit one destination in Canada, you'll have your work cut out for you. It's rare to find a family with unlimited vacation time, though, so tough choices need to be made. Will you opt for a stimulating city break or a tranquil nature retreat? In Vancouver, you don't have to choose. Here, you can have it all.

What struck our family most was the juxtaposition of the Coast Mountains and the Pacific Ocean against such a slick modern metropolis. One hour we're strolling along the seawall, watching seals bob beside kayakers; the next we're deep in the heart of a coastal rainforest, gazing up at trees almost a thousand years old. And did I mention that we sweetened our adventures with a lavender latte and pistachio rosewater hot chocolate at one of the city's savviest brunch spots?

Throw in eclectic neighbourhoods, beautifully maintained parks, plus kid-approved attractions, and you'll find time spent in Vancouver rich and rewarding. Vancouver is repeatedly ranked as one of the best cities in the world to live in, and it's pretty obvious why once you get here.

STANLEY PARK

Draped with stately trees, you certainly won't feel like you're in the city when exploring this urban sanctuary. A combination of forest, beach, and dedicated paths for both walkers and cyclists hugs the sea wall rimming this oasis. There are several places to rent bikes in the city's West End, and you can circumnavigate Stanley Park within an hour.

You'll want to plan enough time, however, to stop at the little playgrounds that dot the park. In summer, bring your bathing suit, as there are plenty of opportunities to get wet. You'll find a splash pad (with full-body dryer!), and Second Beach Pool is heated with water slides and a sloped entry for little ones. Besides plenty of pebbly beach areas, there are long stretches of sand scattered with driftwood to scamper over. Keep your eyes peeled for seals along the coastline, and pay a visit to the intricately carved totem poles at the Brockton Point Visitor Centre.

VANCOUVER AQUARIUM

Home to over 50,000 aquatic creatures, Canada's first public aquarium is dedicated to the conservation of aquatic life. Every year its Marine Mammal Rescue Centre rescues, rehabilitates, and releases over 100 animals. For visitors, there's an impressive selection of international and local species—from the Arctic to the Amazon—to view and learn about. British Columbia is included as well, and it's fascinating to see what lies beneath the waves off Canada's west coast.

Children love watching eels poke their heads out of the sand, and are mesmerized by jellyfish, sharks, and even a pregnant male seahorse! Waddle over to see African penguins, Pacific white-sided dolphins, and a false killer whale (actually a dolphin) at outdoor exhibits. Next, dip your hands into the Discover Rays touch pool for encounters with two different types of stingrays.

Take a break at Clownfish Cove, an interactive area for kids. The little displays are kid-height, and children will delight in role playing at its animal rescue centre. With scales and other vet equipment, concerned kids gain experience treating marine mammal stuffies in a make-believe animal hospital before releasing them back into the wild.

FLYOVER CANADA

We all know how picturesque Canada is, but few of us have had a bird's-eye view of the country's most iconic landmarks. During this flight simulation ride, you'll soar above majestic icebergs, glide over

Epic views of the coastal rainforest are yours when crossing the Capilano Suspension Bridge.

vast open prairie, and peer into thunderous Niagara Falls. The 4D journey is enhanced by scent, sound, wind, and mist, making it an experience for all senses. This virtual ride operates out of Canada Place and is suitable for all ages, though there is a minimum height requirement of 40 inches (102 centimetres).

CAPILANO SUSPENSION BRIDGE PARK

You'll find more than a simple suspension bridge at this outdoorsy attraction situated within an ancient forest in North Vancouver. Take a wobbly first step on the 450-foot (137-metre) long suspension bridge, strung like a garland over the Capilano River, and keep on trekking; it's worth braving this crossing to encounter first-growth Douglas fir trees, many of which are between 400 to 800 years old.

Walking along this park's suspended bridges on the Treetops Adventure offers a view of the forest canopy from a unique

An eagle takes flight near Sunwolf Resort in Squamish.

Enjoy a treetop adventure at Capilano
Suspension Bridge Park.

Clownfish Cove offers an interactive children's
play area at the Vancouver Aquarium.

perspective. Take it in with all your senses—breathe in the clean, pungent scent of fir, hemlock, and red cedar, marvel at the curvy roots clinging to the side of cliffs, and listen to their branches creaking in the wind. If you're quiet, you'll hear the gushing of the river below and the twittering of birds high up in the treetops. Did you spot a squirrel? There are plenty of them around. But don't just look up: the forest floor is teeming with life. There are more species of beetles in this forest than there are species of mammals.

British Columbia is home to one quarter of the world's remaining coastal temperate rainforest, so kids are encouraged to take part in the Rainforest Explorers Program. This self-guided tour through the forest has them identify tree species and collect fun data, giving them a deeper understanding of this natural treasure. Parking is tight, so take advantage of the free shuttle service that operates from several downtown locations.

GRANVILLE ISLAND

Most kids aren't too keen on shopping, but when there's a market that caters to the under-twelve set, they're apt to change their minds—after all, what's not to love about discovering one toy store after the next inside the Kids Market on Granville Island? Inside these independent market-style shops are wonderful puppets, kites, and costumes, and an excellent selection of children's literature. There's even a multi-storey indoor play area, while outside features a life-size play boat on the banks of a duck pond. With plenty of green space to run around on, paved areas for scooters, and a large splash park (complete with waterslide), kids rack up plenty of outdoor time, while parents admire their purchases from the Public Market.

KICKING AROUND TOWN

No doubt you've seen Science World at TELUS World of Science—the white geodesic dome perched on the edge of False Creek so often captured in those iconic Canada Day fireworks photos.

It's just as dazzling inside, with live science demonstrations for family audiences several times each day. Kidspace is a gallery curated especially for children under six, while Eureka is a hands-on learning environment that focuses on light, sound, water, and motion. Known for housing the most extensive collection of works by Canadian painter Emily Carr, the Vancouver Art Gallery also deserves props for inspiring children to get their creative juices flowing. Accept a mission to explore the gallery every Sunday with Art Agents, or find out the many different ways you can look at a painting with Art Tracks. These child-oriented tours are led by dancers and musicians who offer a novel approach to thinking about art. Additionally, there are hands-on workshops and performances to draw inspiration from.

TAKE TO THE OPEN ROAD

One of North America's most scenic coastal routes lies between Vancouver and Whistler. Dubbed the Sea-to-Sky Highway, this epic road hugs the seaboard. From the sparkling waters of the Pacific to old-growth forests to waterfalls gushing out of the rock face of the Coast Mountains, the views are intense.

Peel off the highway once you hit Squamish, the self-proclaimed outdoor recreation capital of Canada. This authentic mountain town is often overlooked in favour of Whistler, its more glamorous neighbour, yet here you'll find a laid-back vibe and incredibly diverse experiences all in close proximity.

TAKE TO THE SKIES

To get a bird's-eye view of the Coast Mountains, take off on a scenic flightseeing tour. Think a flight tour is out of reach? Think again. Sea to Sky Air offers flights for under $100 per person, or flat rates for three passengers under $200. Expect to feel butterflies in your stomach as you sweep by the Tantalus Mountain Range and over the lush Squamish Valley. Spot fly fishermen in the rivers

Children can try their hand at mountaineering along the Via Ferrata course at the Sea to Sky Gondola in Squamish.

below, wave to the hikers on top of Stawamus Chief Mountain, and gaze into the deep blue waters of Howe Sound (technically North America's southernmost fjord and not a sound at all). On a clear day, it's even possible to see the Strait of Georgia and Vancouver Island, but nobody will believe you unless you bring your camera.

SEA TO SKY GONDOLA

Your ears will pop as you're whisked from sea level up into the heart of the Coast Mountain range. While taking in misty views of Howe Sound, you'll also want to keep your eyes peeled for eagles, as you ascend 2,903 feet (885 metres) above sea level. Once you arrive at the summit, an entire playground is at your disposal. Sway along the Sky Pilot Suspension Bridge to access the stroller-friendly Spirit Trail. The hiking is phenomenal up here, and there are many trails to explore, each affording breathtaking views.

In winter you can snowshoe or hit the tube park, and throughout the year kids over eight years of age can scramble along the Via Ferrata. During the ninety-minute assisted climbing adventure, intrepid families maneuver along a series of metal rungs drilled deep into the mountain face. You'll clip into a steel cable that runs alongside the course, with a guide accompanying you every thrilling step of the way. After your adventures, reward yourself with a meal inside Summit Lodge. There's a dedicated play corner filled with toys, puzzles, and board games should you wish to linger longer.

EAGLE EYES

Squamish has one of North America's largest congregations of wintering bald eagles. Its river valley is teeming with wild salmon, and from the end of November until early March, hundreds of bald eagles migrate here to feast on the spawning chum salmon. Volunteer interpreters are stationed every weekend at Eagle Run Park (a prime viewing spot) from December to February, and help families better view and understand both the eagle and salmon life cycle.

Kids as young as five years old and over 50 pounds (22.5 kilograms) can join their parents on a gentle eagle-viewing float trip with Sunwolf Rafting. Spot these birds of prey in their nests or soaring high above the treetops before swooping down to the river to snatch salmon with their talons. Tours end up at Sunwolf Resort, where you'll be treated to a roaring fire and hearty lunch.

Splashy fun continues from May to September with whitewater rafting trips down the Cheakamus and Elaho Rivers. In peak season, you'll bounce over Class II rapids while taking in spectacular views of the wildlife, old-growth forests, and the waterfalls that line the Paradise Valley.

GO UNDERGROUND

You wouldn't expect what was once the largest producing copper mine in the British Empire to morph into a family-friendly attraction with a strong environmental message, yet the Britannia Mine

Museum is just that. Don a hard hat, board a mini train, and rumble into the underground mine just as miners did almost a century ago. After the train tour, visitors can pan for real gold or dig deep inside the outdoor sandpit with dozens of toy dump trucks. Inside this national historic site, you can witness the transition from minerals to metals through hands-on exhibits, including a blasting box that makes a hearty kaboom once engaged.

TASTE

Don't be intimidated by the slew of awards garnered by **Hawksworth Restaurant**. Yes, this is one of Canada's top restaurants, but the posh eatery also offers an elegant children's menu (think steak frites, margherita pizza, and roast chicken).

For brunch, hit hipster **Café Medina** for Belgian waffles and creative riffs on hot beverages.

You won't feel like you're dining at a family-friendly restaurant at **Trattoria** in Vancouver's trendy Kitsilano neighbourhood. This bustling spot manages to sneak in high chairs without sacrificing style points.

No more fighting over which pizza to order. If you don't like your toppings at **Rocky Mountain Flatbread Co.**, it's your own fault. Situated close to Granville Island, families make their own pizzas every Sunday and Monday from 5 to 7 p.m. Shoo kids off to the pizza kitchen play area while you wait for your food.

Fergie's Café in Squamish might be tiny, but it dishes out big flavours. On grounds reminiscent of an English country pub, folks stretch out on picnic blankets they've brought in case tables are filled up. There's no dedicated kids' menu, but the chef can customize meals and portion sizes.

Squamish's **Howe Sound Inn & Brewing Company** is more than a rustic brewpub. Children are welcome in the pub until 9 p.m., and its restaurant offers a children's menu, high chairs, and change tables.

🔑 NAP

When staying at **Times Square Suites** in Vancouver's West End, steps away from Stanley Park, you'll feel like a local. Kitted out with all the comforts of home, furnished apartment-style suites offer full kitchen and laundry facilities. On the rooftop you'll find lounge chairs, picnic tables, and barbecues. Cribs and high chairs can be set up prior to your visit, and there's a grocery store right across the street.

Want to unplug? Head to the cozy cabins at **Sunwolf Resort**. Offering riverside cabins set under canopies of fragrant cedar and Douglas fir trees, it's rustic, but without the dust. Instead of watching TV, children roam freely around the 5-acre (2-hectare) property. This is just the spot to reconnect with nature; a stay here feels wild and remote, even though you're mere minutes from Squamish.

The campground at Alice Lake Provincial Park books up early, so make your reservations before it opens in the spring. Alice Lake sports a beach, non-motorized boat rentals, and a playground. **Four Lakes Trail** is a popular family hike you'll want to try, and there's a mountain bike park specifically designed for young children.

🗺 GETTING AROUND

The **Squamish Connector** provides daily shuttle service from different locations in Vancouver to the Sea to Sky Gondola, and in winter to Sunwolf Resort for eagle viewing.

Visit top Vancouver attractions via the **Aquabus**. This little rainbow-coloured ferry provides scheduled water taxi service along False Creek and is an adventure in itself.

Taking off from Vancouver to one of the nearby islands? **BC Ferries** gets you to Vancouver Island, the Southern and Northern Gulf Islands, and up the Sunshine Coast, while providing a host of amenities to make your journey more pleasant.

From **Vancouver International Airport**, the **SkyTrain** connects passengers to downtown Vancouver and the city of Richmond. Children under five ride free when accompanied by an adult.

FUN FACTS

- At over 1,001 glorious acres (405 hectares), **Stanley Park** is about ten percent larger than Central Park.
- **Kitsilano Pool**, Vancouver's only public saltwater swimming pool, is also the longest pool in Canada. It's nearly the size of three Olympic pools and is open mid-May to September.
- In 1994, **Squamish** held the world record count of 3,769 eagles.
- **The Western red cedar** is the provincial tree of British Columbia. The provincial flower is the **Pacific dogwood**, found on the southern coast near Vancouver and on Vancouver Island.

GET EXCITED ABOUT YOUR TRIP

- Written by Jeremy Moray, *Timmy the West Coast Tug* introduces children to life on BC's coast from the perspective of an adorable little tow boat.
- *My Vancouver Sketchbook,* by Robert Perry, explores Vancouver through the eyes of a young artist as she records her impressions of city attractions in her sketchbook.
- A dynamic story about the life cycle of salmon is found inside the illustrated pages of *Salmon Boy*, by Donna Joe.

Beach time awaits in Penticton at Lake Okanagan.

Kids can paddleboard with Penticton Paddle Surf.

From tots to teens, everyone has a good time at LocoLanding Adventure Park.

Penticton

Sparkling Lakes and Awesome Orchards

As I skim across the glassy water, I know I'm supposed to keep my eyes facing forward, but I can't help looking down to the sandy lake bottom, where rainbow trout dance beneath the quiet surface. Our family is paddleboarding on Lake Skaha, a tranquil experience that feels worlds away from the crowds on the beach. I stroke the water and inhale the fresh scent of pine, then stroke again and exhale my fears about applying too little sunscreen. Suddenly, my peaceful reverie is shattered: "Quit paddling so close to me!" admonishes my fiercely independent daughter. Whoops! How easy it is to morph from serene paddler to helicopter parent.

Penticton, sandwiched between Lake Okanagan and Lake Skaha, is one of the hottest summer destinations in Canada. Lush orchards and vineyards frame the town and provide the perfect backdrop for families keen to take a bite out of this sunny, semi-arid region known as Napa of the North. Those who've travelled with kids know how challenging it can be to find activities that appeal to all ages, but whether playing on land or water, or sampling the exquisite food and drink that Penticton has on offer, there's an abundance of options to satisfy each and every member of the family.

TAKE TO THE WATER

It gets deliciously hot here, so you'll want to spend time at one of the many local beaches. The City of Penticton maintains seven public beaches, Okanagan Lake Park Beach being the most obvious one, located on Lakeshore Drive. Splash about on the shores of the sandy lakes, or take advantage of the kiddie slides and rest rafts. If you've brought a pooch, Okanagan Lake Park Beach is where you can fetch an off-leash play.

We checked out Penticton Paddle Surf, a local company that rents paddleboards right on the shores of either Skaha or Okanagan Lake seven days a week. "Paddleboarding gives you that same pristine feeling surfers get when they're sitting in the ocean, waiting for the next break. It's just you, the water, and nature," says Susie Gay, co-owner of Penticton Paddle Surf.

When we expressed concern that our daughter (who at the time wasn't the most confident swimmer) would be too young, co-owner Bryan Gay assured me anyone can try it. "Kids as young as five years old can get out on their own board, and those younger can stand on the same board as their parents," he said. "Kids are so light and seem to have a natural balance on the board. She'll do fine." And he was absolutely right.

Hoodoo Adventures offers families custom kayaking tours with a wide variety of paddling options. Choose between bird watching, paddling out to a secluded beach for a picnic, or greeting the early morning with a sunrise glide and gourmet coffee. Local guides keep the tour safe and interesting by sharing tips on how to spot Ogopogo, the infamous local lake monster.

Those who prefer to have the paddling done for them can kick back on a Casabella Princess lake cruise. The forty-eight-passenger paddleboat provides narrated tours of Lake Okanagan. While they don't guarantee Ogopogo sightings, they do their best to track the infamous sea monster.

SAND AND LAND ACTIVITIES

Landlubbers should brake for LocoLanding Adventure Park. Boasting multiple attractions, this clean and compact park hits all the right buttons for visitors whether they're tots or teens. There's mini golf, bumper boats, and a bouncy castle for the younger set, while older kids can unleash on go-carts, the climbing wall, and a high-level ropes course.

Saturdays, from the end of April until late October, are always bustling at the Penticton Farmers' Market located at 100 Main Street. Not only is perusing the stalls an excellent activity for early risers, it also

Sun seekers line Lake Okanagan.

presents the opportunity to suss out the farm-to-table bounty of the region. As a bonus, you'll save money breakfasting on the treats found among the stalls; pick up provisions for your next al fresco adventure.

Hunkering down in one spot for the entire day is possible if you park yourself at Skaha Lake Park. The 21-acre (8.5-hectare) park features a long stretch of sandy beach—ideal for sandcastle building. Nearby, your crew is sure to enjoy the playground, basketball and volleyball courts, and a picnic area with fire pits and concession facilities. Parents who don't want to have to deal with the aftermath of sand in their camper or hotel room can direct children to the water park for a wet and wild time.

KETTLE VALLEY RAIL TRAIL

Proving there's more to the region than beaches and peaches, the KVR Trail is a must for cyclists (and tricyclists) of all stripes. This abandoned railway bed is a gentle and enlightening journey that winds its way between orchards and vineyards in the Okanagan boundary region of Southern BC. The best part is that it's gravity-assisted cycling, especially if you begin at Glen Fir and head towards Penticton, pedalling along the two-percent downhill grade. Along this easy cruise, you'll meander through tunnels forged out of the oldest rock in BC and past pictographs up to 1,200 years old.

KVR is part of the Trans Canada Trail, and the volunteer-maintained route offers rest stops, portable toilets, a water bottle refilling station, and even bike repair. Bring your own wheels and cycle the trail on your own, or saddle up with outfitters such as Monashee Adventure Tours, who provide bikes, helmets, and snacks.

KETTLE VALLEY STEAM RAILWAY

If cycling along a rail trail doesn't satisfy the train buffs in your brood, chug your way over to Summerland for a ride on a restored 1912 steam locomotive. You'll journey along on the last remaining section of the Kettle Valley Railway, said to be one of the most difficult railway passages ever built.

Riding in an open air carriage as the breeze ripples through the valley is a refreshing change from all the water activities, though you can book into an enclosed car if the weather isn't cooperating. Sashaying through the historic railway cars are banjo players, dancehall girls, and lawmen in period costumes entertaining the crowds with their stories and antics.

But this nostalgic, ninety-minute journey isn't all lush orchards and sparkling lake views—you're going to get robbed! This is the Old West after all, and just like in the olden days, train bandits on horseback will halt your train and shake you loose of all that spare change festering in your pockets. Never fear, the Garnet Valley Gang donate all their looting to charity. Be sure to check kettlevalleyrail.org in advance if you want to ride on a day this notorious gang is robbing.

TASTE

Noshing is easy in New Napa, with well-established restaurants hitting every price point. Near the marina try the **Bench Market**. Open for breakfast and lunch, it's pretty much always busy—but worth the wait, especially for their gourmet sandwiches, salads, and quality children's menu.

One of the region's best burgers can be found inside an old tire shop at **Burger 55**. Kids get a kick out of the mechanic theme, ticking off their selections from a clipboard.

Elite Restaurant is a retro diner that saw its last renovation in 1964. They don't pretend to be anything other than old-school, and with a slice of homemade flapper pie after a roast turkey dinner with all the trimmings, you're sure to agree that's just the way it should stay.

Families have been entertained for decades inside the whitewashed walls of **Theo's Greek Restaurant**. Theo's serves up classic dishes Greek dishes like souvlaki, but also lesser-known items such as sautéed amaranth greens that grow wild in both Greece and the Okanagan Valley.

Those suffering from wheat sensitivities can snap up a few loaves and luscious baked goods from **True Grain Bread**, an organic bakery that mills heritage grains by hand in nearby Summerland.

Since you're in the region, it would be almost criminal not to sample some liquid grapes from the award-winning wineries hugging the town. You can make it a family affair at **Elephant Island Orchard Wines**, where wee ones can picnic with teddy bears while parents swirl, sniff, and occasionally sip.

One of the best-kept secrets for a quick tasting is at **Upper Bench**, a delicious combo of creamery and winery, where handcrafted cheese and wine can be sampled together. If you like art, make a beeline for **Liquidity**. Art installations dot the vineyard grounds, its tasting room, and the delightful bistro.

NAP

There's a kitschy, nostalgic feel at the many motels bordering the beach along Lakeshore Drive. Two affordable choices are the **Golden Sands Resort**, with an outdoor pool and renovated suites, and the **Sandman Hotel**, which boasts an indoor pool, kitchenettes, and an onsite twenty-four-hour Denny's restaurant. The poshest accommodation in town is found at **Penticton Lakeside Resort**.

Set up camp on Skaha Lake at **Wright's Beach Camp**, where they offer a children's play area, outdoor swimming pool, and boat rentals. One block from the lake and across the street from the children's water park lies **Lake Skaha Tent & Trailer Park**. And it's a short stroll to downtown when camping at **Park Royal RV Park**.

GETTING AROUND

Fly into **Penticton Regional Airport** from Calgary or Vancouver, or into **Kelowna International Airport**, which services many more cities. Once you arrive, you'll probably want to rent a vehicle for the freedom of getting around, though many attractions in Penticton are within walking distance.

OK Wine Shuttle offers a hop-on, hop-off service to hotels, restaurants, and wineries within the Okanagan. It takes eight hours to drive to Penticton from Calgary and under five hours from Vancouver.

 FUN FACTS

- **Ogopogo** is a mythical creature rumoured to have been spotted in Lake Okanagan since the 19th century by First Nations peoples. They were most likely referring to a legendary water spirit, yet that hasn't hindered the active imaginations of visitors and retailers alike. Sightings of the humped sea serpent have been reported on and off for over a century, yet like Scotland's Loch Ness Monster, Ogopogo remains elusive and uncaptured.
- **Penticton** means "place to stay forever" in the language of the Syilx people, the original inhabitants of the Okanagan; the visitors who fell in love with the territory and made their permanent homes here are living proof. After a few days in this region, it's possible you might do the same.

GET EXCITED ABOUT YOUR TRIP

- *Ogopogo Odyssey*, by D.A. Hawes, helps children to understand the story of Ogopogo from a First Nations perspective.
- For older children, set them up with *The Creature in Ogopogo Lake*, a Boxcar Children Mystery.
- Teens will enjoy the Canadian classic film *My American Cousin*—as will parents who enjoyed the movie when they too were teens in the mid-eighties!

Dip your paddle into tranquil Lake Louise.

Throughout the year, Banff National Park is one massive outdoor playground.

Camping in Banff National Park is a rite of passage for many families.

Banff National Park

The Crown Jewel of Canada's Park System

Visiting Banff National Park in winter is like stepping inside a snow globe—glistening white, magical, and pure. Between events such as the Ice Magic Festival, a world-renowned ice carving competition, and Banff's charming alpine environment infused with public art installations, the enchanting atmosphere is immediately palpable, and lifts the spirit.

Yet most folks don't head to Canada's first national park for the art; they're here to get their Rocky Mountain high on. Inhaling the crisp mountain air, it's not hard to feel a rush at the possibilities, whether tackling the great outdoors or sitting serenely in a fragrant mountain meadow. Wilderness, wildflowers, and waterfalls are all on tap in one of the world's most phenomenal natural playgrounds. Families flock here for invigorating outdoor activities that range from hiking and biking in summer to skiing, skating, and snowshoeing in winter. Whatever way you chose to explore the crown jewel of Canada's park system, you and the troops are sure to glean many of the healing benefits spending time in nature guarantees.

SKIING

When skiing with kids, it's easy to convince yourself that your days of whisking down black diamonds are over. Not so at the resorts surrounding the town of Banff. At Lake Louise Ski Resort, green runs unfurl like ribbons from every single chairlift on the mountain. Their licensed daycare takes babes as young as three weeks old, and you have the option to set toddlers and older kids up with ski instructors.

Meanwhile, Sunshine Village has the only ski-in and ski-out accommodation in Banff National Park, allowing you to snag first tracks before anyone else is out of bed. This resort offers childcare services for kids nineteen months old and up, and hotel guests can take advantage of the family programming and a dedicated activity room. They also sport an on-site spa to soothe sore muscles after a heavy, leg-burner day on the slopes.

Closest to Banff, Mount Norquay is a popular hill for local families. Besides being the only ski resort to offer night skiing, its advantage is hourly passes that begin at the two-hour mark, allowing families an affordable option for trying out this pricey activity.

WINTER FUN FOR NON-SKIERS

Being one of the world's premier snow playgrounds means there's more to do during our famously frosty season than just swooshing down the ski hill. The great thing about the Canadian Rockies is that you don't have to be a skier or snowboarder to get that same adrenaline rush in the mountains.

Tubing

Want to feel the wind rushing through your hair as you barrel down a mountain without planks attached to your feet? Well, you're in luck! Both Mount Norquay and Lake Louise Ski Resort offer tube parks at their resorts. Tubing is a cheaper alternative to skiing and is a great option if some members of your family want to tackle the slopes while the others just wanna have fun.

Ice Skating

Life doesn't present many opportunities to twirl around an ice castle, so when you come upon the fairytale structure set on Lake Louise, you'll want to glide around it. This spectacular outdoor rink at the foot of Victoria Glacier is as romantic as it gets. Bonfires warm cold toesies, and there's often hot chocolate served up too. Skate rentals are available from the Chateau Mountain Sports rental shop, as are snowshoes and cross-country skis.

Take a twirl around Lake Louise.

Take a stroll along the Bow River and enjoy the beauty of Banff National Park.

Tourists have been soothing sore muscles in Banff Upper Hot Springs for over a century!

No gear? No problem! Bed down in an oTENTik at Two Jack Lake in Banff National Park.

Some of the best grizzly bear viewing in the Rockies is had from the Lake Louise Gondola.

Sleigh Ride

Dashing through the snow, in a one-horse open sleigh . . . make the classic "Jingle Bells" tune reality with an unforgettable horse-drawn sleigh ride from either Banff or Lake Louise. Don't underestimate the healing power of fragrant pine air, enjoyed while snuggled under a buffalo robe as you clip-clop your way through crystallized alpine meadows. Nap time will be a breeze after such an excursion.

EASY DAY HIKES AND BIKES

Lonely Planet ranked Sunshine Meadows the #1 hike in Canada. These meadows straddle the Continental Divide between Alberta and British Columbia, and the region is filled with one jaw-dropping view after the next. Come summer, a kaleidoscope of wildflowers is on display. Autumn brings out the golden hues of the larch tree, one of the rare coniferous trees that blaze with colour and then lose their needles each fall. Take a guided tour with White Mountain Adventures or hike on your own from late June until early October.

Tunnel Mountain Summit Trail is a popular hike for families, and you can't beat its proximity to town. Since it's only a 1.5-mile (2.5-kilometre) trek, this is a good option if you're not an experienced hiker, or if you're pressed for time. Still, kids get a rush from climbing a "real" mountain, and views of the townsite, Bow River, and Vermillion Lakes are pretty sweet.

Take it up a notch by tackling the trail to Consolation Lake near Lake Louise. It's only 1.8 miles (3 kilometres) from the Moraine Lake parking lot, and the elevation gain is minimal—about 295 feet (90 metres)—making it an easy jaunt for little ones. This trail requires a minimum of four hikers to walk together at a time, and bear spray is essential. While I've never seen a bear along this trail, bears and other potentially scary wildlife populate this entire national park. Don't assume one hike is safer than any other. Check with Parks staff and read online reports for wildlife sightings before embarking on any outdoor activity in the mountains.

Hiking in summer is generally preferable, but when you factor in unrelenting sun, bugs, and sharing the trail, it isn't always all it's cracked up to be. Winter hiking is an underrated and pleasant experience not to be overlooked. Almost any trail is fair game, and when you strap on snowshoes, it makes the excursion that much more enticing.

Johnston Canyon is a heavily trafficked trail in the summer, but in the winter it's much quieter and arguably more beautiful, as ribbons of frozen water twist themselves into surreal shapes. Bring some ice cleats for your boots, and you'll be able to follow the trail along the creek and over catwalks to the lower falls. If you're not keen to strike out on your own, a variety of tour operators offer easy snowshoeing excursions within the park.

LEGACY TRAIL

One of the most rewarding ways to experience the beauty of the Bow Valley is by biking the Legacy Trail. Stretching from the Canmore Visitor Information Centre into the town of Banff and beyond along the Bow Valley Parkway, this paved walking and biking route runs along the south side of the Trans-Canada Highway. The route weaves in and out through the woods, and the heady scent of fresh pine and wildflowers is easy to sniff out. The views are predictably impressive, and you'd be hard pressed to find a prettier dedicated trail anywhere in the world. Soak them up by stopping about half-way at the Valleyview Picnic Area. Here there are picnic tables and toilets, but no water refilling stations.

Bikes can be rented in Banff at Soul Ski and Bike or Backtrax, where children's bikes, Trail-a-Bikes, and Chariots are also on offer. If beginning your journey from the town of Canmore, Rebound Cycle or Gear Up is where you'll want to go for rentals.

TAKE TO THE WATER

Several tour operators offer rafting excursions that range from peaceful paddles to rip-roaring Class IV rapids. Some outfitters take tots as young as five years old, whereas eight and twelve years of age seem to be the magic numbers for others. Check before you book.

Those of any age can explore the striking glacier-fed lakes and rivers within the park. Kayaks and canoes can be rented from the Banff Canoe Club on the docks of the Bow River in Banff, at Lake Louise, and at Moraine Lake. Lake Minnewanka is the only spot in the park where motorized boats are allowed; rentals are available by the hour or half day. If you prefer to let others do the work for you, take an interpretive lake cruise with Brewster Travel Canada, where you'll learn about First Nations history, early explorers, and the region's fascinating geology (guides make this infinitely more interesting for kids than it sounds).

You can't visit a destination teeming with natural hot springs without taking a dip. Banff Upper Hot Springs is a historic spa and bathhouse that's been drawing tourists for over a century. Take to these waters and soak away any family tension while relieving sore muscles. The water temperature isn't too hot, allowing babes and toddlers to splash about in the shallow area. You can rent bathing suits and towels on-site, and there is a café in the building.

MORE VIEWS, LESS ACTION

If you're not up for hiking, hitch a ride to the top of Sulphur Mountain via the Banff Gondola. Visitors are privy to spectacular views of the Bow Valley Parkway, and there's a good chance a herd of bighorn sheep and marmots will be milling about. With six mountain ranges visible, this is a great spot to grab a family photo worthy of a Christmas card. The newly renovated facility offers a café and interactive displays in the interpretive area.

Dedicated to the arts, leadership, and mountain culture, the Banff Centre inspires creativity in numerous ways. That means affordable performances, from puppets to dance to live music running all year long. Check their calendar before your visit, and tote a swimsuit and runners to make use of the public pool and exercise facilities.

WILDLIFE VIEWING

The Canadian Rockies are most definitely where the wild things are, with forests heavily populated by elk, deer, and even moose and wolves. And it's not just skiers who love these alpine peaks and meadows: ski hill development creates wide-open spaces, which attracts grizzly bears and other animals during the summer months. As a result, one of the best spots to view grizzlies in their natural environment is at the Lake Louise Ski Resort.

From the Sightseeing Gondola, you'll be able to safely spot grizzlies foraging for food as it whisks you to the Wildlife Interpretive Centre at the top of the mountain. Once there, take advantage of complimentary programs led by interpretive guides. Afterwards, you can stroll around the summit on a variety of hiking trails, or opt for a guided walk if you're unsure about what to do in a bear encounter. Replenish lost calories with a meal at Lodge of the Ten Peaks, where children's meals are available.

For those keen for an animal encounter, but not sure where to hoof around to find one, wildlife safaris are the way to go. Several outfitters lead excursions to a range of habitats that best showcase currently active animals. Participating in a tour leaves visitors with a deeper understanding of the animals within the park and their relationship with it.

⚠ TASTE

Don't beat yourself up if you didn't get camping. **Park Distillery** recreates campfire cuisine with food cooked over open flames. Just because they craft their own spirits (this is the first distillery inside a national park) doesn't mean they're not kid-friendly. With its children's menu, all family members can get a taste of Canadian mountain cuisine.

An institution in Banff, the **Grizzly House** is an old-school fondue joint that's just as much about the experience as it is the food. Encourage the kids to make use of the retro phones at each table to call other diners and get suggestions. With so much dipping and dialling going on, it's unlikely other diners will notice any whining in this buzzy atmosphere.

The **Elk & Oarsman** is a gastropub, but until 10 p.m., families are welcome. Though they have a children's menu with the usual suspects, you may eschew it in favour of elk potato skins or a bison burger.

If pizza is what you're craving, thick and gooey pies are given the thumbs up at the **Bear Street Tavern**.

NAP

Perhaps the most iconic hotel in the Canadian Rockies, the **Fairmont Banff Springs Hotel** has graced many a postcard in its 100-year history. Modelled after a Scottish baronial castle, it's easy to see why it's nicknamed the Castle in the Rockies. Though rooms here occupy a smaller footprint, they don't scrimp on the family programming.

In winter, you can't get any closer to the slopes than staying at **Sunshine Mountain Lodge**. After your ski day, cozy up fireside and challenge your family to games in the activity room, or take a complimentary toboggan out for an epic ride.

If you suspect you'll be spending a fair amount of time in your hotel, consider **Douglas Fir Resort**. It can be challenging dragging kids off their indoor play set or the water slides, but free shuttles into Banff (the resort is located a five-minute drive away from downtown) are a good incentive. All units are equipped with kitchenettes, and you can opt for separate bedrooms.

For families who want to camp but don't have all the required gear, equipped campsites are available in Banff National Park at **Two Jack Main Campground**. Sites come with a six-person tent, picnic table, fire pit, and firewood. Once you're settled in, a Parks employee will visit your site and get you set up with a camp stove and lantern, and will offer tips on trails in the area. Families need to supply their own sleeping gear, food, water, and cooking utensils. In case of rain, tote a tarp and a rope to string it up with.

Have your own gear? **Tunnel Mountain** has three different campgrounds, one of which is more natural with its gravel patches on which to pitch tents (instead of pavement pads for campers at the other two sites). You'd never know Banff townsite is mere minutes away, and you can easily access the Tunnel Bench biking trails from this campground.

HI-Lake Louise Alpine Centre is a hostel that offers several private rooms. You'd be hard pressed to find more affordable accommodation in Lake Louise, especially when WiFi and parking are complimentary and towels and linens are provided. There's a kids' playroom, gorgeous vaulted-ceiling common areas, and two fully equipped, self-catering kitchens. Don't feel like cooking? Bill Peyto's Café, located on-site, dishes out affordable meals.

GETTING AROUND

The **Banff Airporter** bus offers a shuttle service between Banff, the **Calgary International Airport**, and Canmore. A regular shuttle between Banff, downtown Calgary, the Calgary International Airport, and other locations in the Rockies (Lake Louise, Jasper, Canmore, Kananaskis, and Stony Nakoda Lodge), with connections to Red Deer and Edmonton, is offered by the **Brewster Banff Airport Express**.

Get around in Banff with **Roam Public Transit**; it has routes to Tunnel and Sulphur Mountains, the Fairmont Banff Springs Hotel, Cave and Basin National Historic Site, and the town of Canmore.

 ## FUN FACTS

- Established in 1885, **Banff National Park** is Canada's first national park and the third oldest protected park in the world.
- There are more than 1,000 glaciers in Banff National Park.
- The mountains in Banff National Park date back 120 million years.
- The most endangered species in Banff National Park isn't the elusive wolverine or the grizzly bear—it's the Banff Springs snail! This freshwater snail that lives along Sulphur Mountain and at Cave and Basin National Historic Site is found nowhere else on earth.

- Banff is named after Banff, Scotland, the birthplace of two of the original Canadian Pacific Railway directors.
- **Lake Louise** was named after Queen Victoria's fourth daughter, Princess Louise Caroline Alberta.
- **The wild rose** is Alberta's provincial flower. It and other provincial symbols such as **Rocky Mountain bighorn sheep** and **lodgepole pine** are easily spotted in the Rockies.

✦ GET EXCITED ABOUT YOUR TRIP

- Read *Nuptse & Lhotse Go to the Rockies*, a wonderful illustrated story by Jocey Asnong.
- *In the Path of Great Bear*, by Carol McTavish and Lori Nunn, is also suitable for children.
- *Take a Hike with Your Children*, by Lynda Pianosi, features dozens of accessible hikes for families around Banff National Park.
- *Wayne Lynch's Canadian Rockies Wildlife for Kids* lets you know exactly what type of wildlife you may encounter on your visit.
- Explore Banff (and the rest of Canada's national parks) with Parka, Parks Canada's friendly beaver mascot. Visit pc.gc.ca/parka.

Extraordinary views of Calgary and the Rocky Mountains are yours from the top of the Calgary Tower.

Explore how the west was once at Heritage Park, a historical village.

Calgary
Cowboy Culture and the Spirit of the West

Stampede time is no time for horsing around. Dust off those cowboy boots and corral the kids to take in one of Canada's greatest festivals—the Calgary Stampede. What started as a tribute to the Old West over a century ago has morphed into "The Greatest Outdoor Show on Earth." For ten days every July, Calgary returns to its Western roots and celebrates the people, animals, and traditions that make up the unique spirit of the West.

The Calgary Stampede happens to be roped around a rodeo, but it's so much more than that. While there ain't no shortage of ways to experience this cowboy party, most parents prefer to take the wild out of the West. Fortunately, families have loads of options for horsing around at the Stampede. Here's how you and your little hayseeds can make the most of this iconic event. Giddy up!

STAMPEDE PARK

Most of the action takes place at Stampede Park, just south of downtown and conveniently accessible via the city's light rapid transit line (LRT). Of course, North America's largest mobile midway can offer plenty of thrills, but the Great Funtier (a kids' midway) is where you'll want to steer your little cowpokes. Here you'll find tamer rides, midway games, and even Mounties strolling about in their handsome red serge.

At its core, the Stampede is a cowboy festival, where cowboys and cowgirls throughout North America throw their hat in the ring during a tournament-style rodeo. The action kicks off each afternoon at 1:15 and includes events such as barrel racing, steer wrestling, and bull riding.

Though not part of the rodeo, the nightly chuckwagon races are what make the Stampede stand out. With hooves thundering down the track, dirt flying in the air, and thoroughbreds whizzing past, the GMC Rangeland Derby is the world's most engrossing and famous chuckwagon race. During these nightly heats, thirty-six drivers, supported by their outriders, race what's known as the "half mile of hell." If you're not into horse racing, you'll want to give this a miss, but if you're interested in a slice of Western Canadian culture most Canadians don't get to experience, this is a can't-miss event.

Standing Room Tickets go on sale each day of the Stampede at the Ticket Office starting at 11 a.m., and are a more affordable way to experience both the rodeo and the Chucks.

A section of Stampede Park is always reserved for Indian Village. Recreating life as it once was, the tribes of Treaty 7 set up their tipis on the park and camp out for the duration of the festival. The spot affords a unique opportunity to experience First Nations culture in a low-key setting. Families can peek into an actively used tipi or sample bannock, an Indigenous flatbread.

(In light of the growing awareness around Truth and Reconciliation, I want to assure readers that the Stampede has offered to change of the name of Indian Village to something more in tune with the times. As it turns out, First Nations elders are the ones who made the decision to let the name stand, to reflect their longstanding history with the Calgary Stampede.)

Entertainment abounds during the Stampede. In fact, the Stampede is one of Canada's largest music festivals, with more than 150 live acts. Families with young children will want to check out the Coca-Cola Stage to see their favourite TV characters perform. There are a number of other shows in both indoor and outdoor venues that are great for families to enjoy, all free with park admission.

The TransAlta Grandstand Show is the Stampede's version of the Superbowl halftime show. This nightly performance dazzles the

Colourful costumes with intricate beadwork adorn First Nations dancers at the Calgary Stampede.

Get up close and personal with wildlife from around the world at the Calgary Zoo.

First Nations have always played a prominent role in the Calgary Stampede. The tribes of Treaty 7 continue to participate in the Stampede Parade.

Stampede just ain't the same without sampling some mini donuts.

crowd with marching bands, performing artists, and Canada's most talented youngsters, the Young Canadians of the Calgary Stampede, before culminating in an explosion of fireworks. The show takes place after the chuckwagons, which might be too late for some children.

PARADE

The Calgary Stampede kicks off with a two-hour spectacle beginning at 8:55 a.m. sharp, always on the first Friday in July (unless that first Friday is Canada Day). This is one of the largest parades in North America at 2.5 miles (4 kilometres) in length, and features participants from around the world. Approximately 250,000 people attend the parade and even more watch it on TV. The extravaganza features over 700 horses, 20 bands, and 20 floats of all shapes and sizes. Head down early, as sidewalks along the 6th and 9th Avenue route get busy around 7:30 a.m. for the parade's prelude entertainment. Locals get up at the crack of dawn to snag a prime curbside seat along the downtown route, but you can guarantee yours by visiting parade.calgarystampede.com to pre-pay for a bleacher seat.

If the weather's too hot or rainy, snag a spot along the parade route on the Plus 15, a skywalk that connects buildings 49 feet (15 metres) above the ground. These glass-encased connecters are often less crowded than the streets, and you'll have access to indoor toilets. Portable toilets are set outdoors along the parade route too.

CRITTERS

The Agriculture Discovery Zone at Stampede Park is where you'll want to be if you have animal lovers travelling with you. Families can meander through the horse stalls and pet a variety of farm animals. There are loads of events going on, so grab a timetable to ensure you don't miss the heavy horse pull, cow milking demonstrations, or trick riding. And littles love participating in the mini-chucks, a race atop plush horses on wheels.

Strategic parents map out Weadickville, a serene green space where wee ones whoop it up on the grass or enjoy some shaded quiet time.

Spruce Meadows is a world-class show-jumping arena located on the southern edge of the city. The North American Tournament usually takes place around the same time as the Stampede, allowing families an opportunity to take in a different equestrian sport. Witness the best show-jumping horses on the continent, tour the stables, or horse around in the sizeable outdoor playground.

More animal adventures are found at Butterfield Acres, a hands-on farm and large petting zoo on the northern edge of the city. During the Stampede, many of the animals will be dispersed throughout Calgary at pancake breakfasts, so trot over here in the afternoon to roam freely with barnyard creatures, milk goats, or saddle up on a pony.

Visit the Calgary Zoo (Canada's second largest) for a chance to explore the animal kingdom beyond viewing its wild residents. Take a behind-the-scenes tour and feed your favourite species, or become a zookeeper for a day; these and many other opportunities are offered on a regular basis to educate guests on the conservation efforts for endangered species and ecosystems.

New visitors to Canada won't want to miss the zoo's Canadian Wilds exhibit complete with bears, wolves, and caribou, while lions, tigers, penguins, gorillas, hippos, and giraffes delight all. Outside of Destination Africa, there is a fantastic playground with equipment to occupy youngsters from two to twelve years of age, but there's also a toddler-specific playground, a wildlife carousel, and an electric train located in the Eurasia area.

For a real treat, time your visit to the Calgary Zoo during Safari Sunday Brunch. It has all the requisite stations, including a waffle bar and chocolate fountain. Reservations are essential.

PANCAKE BREAKFASTS

Back in 1923, chuckwagon driver Wildhorse Jack moseyed downtown with his cookstove and began serving pancakes hot off the griddle to a hungry crowd. The tradition continues to this day throughout the city, with over 200,000 flapjacks flipped at community breakfasts every day during Stampede.

It's worth saddling up to one of these easy-to-find breakfasts, as it's an affordable way to fuel the family while getting a slice of Stampede. At official Stampede breakfasts, you can meet chuckwagon drivers, eat pancakes, and watch marching bands without blowing your entertainment budget. Calgary's largest Stampede breakfast is held at the CF Chinook Centre, but there are smaller community events that are ideal for meeting locals. Use FlapjackFinder.com to get the deets on one closest to you.

COWBOY CULTURE WITHOUT THE CROWDS

Stampede is a city-wide event, and there are plenty of rootin' tootin' activities outside of Stampede Park to partake in. It's even possible to capture the essence of Stampede without stepping foot inside Stampede Park. "The whole city is ablaze with western themes and western dress, and it's impossible to try and escape it. Downtown there is just a buzz and feeling in the air," raves local mom Michaelle LeManne.

Your one-stop shop for marching bands, mini-parades, and even an old-fashioned gun fight is Fluor Rope Square, at Olympic Plaza. This downtown attraction dishes out free pancake breakfasts and a festival atmosphere in a much less crowded environment. From First Nations performances to square dancing to getting the opportunity to climb inside a chuckwagon, intriguing aspects of western culture are neatly packaged into a few hours each weekday during Stampede.

With so much non-stop action, you'll appreciate the chance to dial it down while stepping into the past at Heritage Park. Canada's largest living history museum is filled with good old-fashioned fun, including an antique midway with retro carnival games and rides to thrill everyone from tots to teens. Explore First Nations culture while taking part in hands-on activities based on centuries-old traditions. Learn to shoot a bow and arrow, help raise a tipi, or go voyageur at the Hudson's Bay Company Fur Trading Fort. You'd be hard pressed to find a more peaceful way to while away the day than by strolling through this historical village, but should you get pooped out, you can make your way via horse-drawn wagon or aboard the century-old steam train.

Tips

If you're looking for fewer crowds and only want to hit up the midway at the Stampede, mosey down to Stampede Park for Sneak-a-Peek from 5 p.m. to midnight the Thursday before Stampede begins. Admission is half price, and you'll find loads of specials and promotions.

Score a pancake breakfast and free admission by arriving before 9 a.m. on one of the two family days (typically held on the first Sunday and Wednesday of Stampede). Planning on riding the midway again and again? Snag a Midway Express Pass at North American Midway Entertainment (NAME) ticket booths. Additional discounts and passes can be picked up at Safeway, Sobey's, Costco, and Mac's retailers.

KICKING AROUND TOWN

Of course, there's much more to Calgary than the Stampede. Calaway Park, Western Canada's largest amusement park, lies on the western edge of the city and is a manageable size that's easy for families to navigate. This popular attraction is a wise choice during Stampede when you're keen to escape the crowds—and, what's more, they operate a campsite (with mountain views!) next to the park, allowing families to fall out of bed and be first on the rides.

The Glenbow Museum offers many different galleries that are intriguing for children. Treasures of the Mineral World is always a big hit, and families can learn more about Western Canadian and First Nations culture through the Blackfoot Gallery. Interactive displays reveal traditions and Niitsitapi history in a dynamic and colourful way.

TELUS Spark has got igniting a kid's sense of discovery down to a science. Its Creative Kids Museum has a tricked-out toddler and preschool area with a physics station and immersive tables for water play and magnetics. Popular exhibits for older kids are found in the Earth & Sky gallery or building toys in the Open Studio.

Outdoors, children can discover the science of play at The Brainasium. This outdoor park set on the grounds of the science centre boasts a tower leading to a 62-foot (19-metre) slide! There are a dozen different experiences within the 1-acre (0.4-hectare) space, all of them physically engaging and designed to combine brain and body adventures. This innovative park is open all year round—yes, even in winter!

🍴 TASTE

You can't go to the Stampede and not scarf down some of those mini donuts and good ol' Alberta beef, now can you? Dozens of new foods make their debut at the midway each year, but there are healthier options at **Stampede Park**, too. Look for beef and vegetable kebabs or corn on the cob to avoid getting "hangry." The best value, however, is found in the Ag area, where milk and cookies go for a few bucks.

Downtown you'll find **The Palomino**, a well-known honky-tonk joint, though it's lesser known for welcoming children until 4 p.m. (7 p.m. on certain weekdays). Here you'll find the city's biggest smoker, and families can feast on proper smokehouse cuisine such as beef brisket or ribs with a side of cheddar grits.

For tweens and teens who aren't easily impressed, gross them out with an order of deep-fried prairie oysters (bull testicles!). Find them at **Buzzards Restaurant & Bar** and **Bottlescrew Bill's Pub**, located next door to each other; the latter is licensed for minors until 9 p.m. That "ew" factor just might be the highlight of their trip—or at least what garners the most Facebook likes.

Sky 360 is the rotating restaurant at the top of the Calgary Tower. It's a two-in-one deal, where entrées include complimentary elevation to the viewing deck. They've got high chairs, a change table, and a children's menu, and those rotating views should prevent your tots from going too squirrelly.

Not only is Prince's Island Park a delightful oasis in the middle of the city, it's also home to **River Café**, one of Calgary's best restaurants. If their award-winning regional fare doesn't tempt wee ones, colouring pages, kid-friendly flatbread, and the children's brunch menu surely will.

NAP

Situated steps away from Stampede Park, **Hotel Arts** is a pet-friendly hotel that offers complimentary Brooklyn Cruiser city bikes. It's also one of the few hotels in Calgary that possesses an outdoor pool. True, the vibe is more Vegas than Disney, but that doesn't stop families from taking a dip. They don't offer a children's menu, but Yellow Door Bistro serves up one of the best breakfasts in the city and happily customizes meals for younger guests.

If the Stampede Parade is at the top of your hit list, it makes sense to book into a hotel located along its route. Both the **Calgary Marriott Downtown Hotel** and the **Fairmont Palliser** have indoor pools, children's menus, and private areas for guests to watch the parade.

GETTING AROUND

Calgary's Light Rail Transit (LRT) system can get you from Stampede Park to downtown attractions, as well as to the zoo, science centre, and several malls. To get to Butterfield Acres, Spruce Meadows, Heritage Park, or Calaway Park, you're best off renting a car.

From the **Calgary International Airport**, **Allied Airport Shuttle** departs every thirty minutes between 8 a.m. and midnight. It picks up from designated downtown locations on an hourly basis if there is a booking. Children under three years old ride for free.

FUN FACTS

- Each year more than one million folks attend the **Calgary Stampede**. The convoy of games, rides, and food trucks that service the Stampede is over 3.7 miles (6 kilometres) long.

- If you placed all the hot dogs eaten at the Stampede end to end, they'd stretch out over more than 11.8 miles (19 kilometres).

- Over 33,000 pounds (15,000 kilograms) of sugar, 2 million mini donuts, 50,000 candy apples, and 96,000 corn dogs are consumed within the ten-day Stampede. Practise moderation, folks, or be prepared for a cowboy-sized belly ache.

- With 162 miles (260 kilometres) of on-street bikeways, and 435 miles (700 kilometres) of pathways lining the **Bow** and **Elbow Rivers**, Calgary has the longest urban path system in North America.

GET EXCITED ABOUT YOUR TRIP

- Read *How the Calgary Stampede Began* by Ardith Trudzik.

- *C is for Calgary*, an alphabet book about a young boy exploring the Stampede through his grandfather's photo album, is written by Dave Kelly and illustrated by Mandy Stobo.

- Singer Jann Arden and indie pop duo Tegan and Sara hail from Calgary.

- If you're trying to get into the country and western spirit, tune into some Paul Brandt or Ian Tyson.

Survey the Badlands and hunt for fossils in Dinosaur Provincial Park.

Find dinosaur fossils at Dinosaur Provincial Park.

Apply a burlap cast to a dinosaur fossil at Dinosaur Provincial Park.

Dinosaur Provincial Park

Canada's Jurassic Park

What makes Dinosaur Provincial Park so appealing to all ages? This UNESCO World Heritage Site is one of the world's most significant fossil beds. "Very few places have this number of complete dinosaur skeletons and species," avows David Terrill, Alberta Parks Interpreter. Ideal for families, the park offers plenty of opportunities for encounters with T-Rex and his fierce friends. A visit here is a vacation 65 million years in the making.

"When we visited Dinosaur Provincial Park, my son was three," says Corrine McDermott, founder of the website Have Baby Will Travel. "He's now seven and he still talks about it. My kids were enthralled with the dinosaurs. I was blown away by the landscape. You have this idea in your head of what Alberta looks like, but I had never seen the Badlands before and had no idea this kind of landscape could be in Canada."

FOSSIL SAFARI

There are several options for families to peel back the layers of this desolate land. Self-guided tours allow kids to roam the grounds, just as these Jurassic giants once did. Strike out on foot and hunt for bits of teeth and vertebrae that litter the landscape. If you're keen to dig deeper into the prehistoric past, you can learn to identify dinosaur bones and explore the park's backcountry (including several excavated sites ripe with relics) on guided tours. Try your hand at fossil prospecting or traverse over rugged sandstone ridges to reach a bone bed chock-full of the remains of hundreds of horned dinosaurs on the Centrosaurus Quarry hike.

Families will love the Explorer's Bus, a hop-on, hop-off tour to several excavated sites. Your first order of business on this tour is learning how to identify dinosaur bones, a relatively easy process once you know what you're looking for. The trick is to spot what appear to be brownish-coloured rocks that have the texture of an Aero chocolate bar. "If you're not certain, go with the lick test," recommends Terrill. "A wet finger will stick a bit if it's a bone."

Our family dug in with the other kids, finding teeth, vertebrae, and bits of turtle shell. This spot holds one of the highest concentrations of dinosaur bones on the planet, and pretty much everywhere you look, you'll find fragments. Despite taking the tour on a hot summer day with too many toddlers to count, there were no meltdowns. I suspect it was because there were more than enough fossils to go around.

There's more hands-on learning besides picking through the fossils fields. Participants get a shot at using the field jack, a tripod that brings fossils out of the ground. Kids line up one behind the other and heave-ho on a rope to hoist up their bounty. Next, you'll learn how to apply a burlap plaster cast to a skeleton. This mummifying process is how fossils are safely transported from the field to museums around the world. Surprisingly, this process remains unchanged since paleontologists descended upon the site in droves in the early 20th century.

This region, riddled with the remains of the giant beasts, finally got on the map after John L. Wagner, a rancher from Drumheller, Alberta, went to the American Museum of Natural History in 1909. After his visit, paleontologists flocked to the region to collect specimens, and the period from 1910 to 1917 was known as the "Great Dinosaur Rush." Fortunately, the government put the brakes on plundering, and the park is now a dedicated natural preserve. This means you can hunt and admire the fossils, but you can't take them (or anything else) home with you. As much as science and protecting natural wonders has advanced in the past century, paleontology hasn't changed all that much. They're still using picks and shovels!

The valley of the Red Deer River makes for a pretty campground site at Dinosaur Provincial Park.

Some of the larger fossils found at Dinosaur Provincial Park.

The Canadian Badlands are filled with dinosaur fossils.

WORTHY SIDE TRIP

Most folks are surprised when they realize the Royal Tyrrell Museum isn't located within Dinosaur Provincial Park. This centre of paleontological research, noted for its collection of more than 130,000 fossil specimens, is located outside of the town Drumheller, about a two-hour drive from the park. Besides housing one of the world's largest collections of dinosaur skeletons, the museum offers programs—from fossil casting to junior dig experiences to raptor assembly—sure to pique your petite paleontologist's curiosity. How would you like to stand inside the jaws of the world's largest dinosaur? In Drumheller (known as the dinosaur capital of the world, by the way) you can! Climb up the 106 stairs to the top of this icon, stand behind her pearly whites, and take in views of the town and the surrounding Badlands. Want more dino action? With fossil digs, a play zone, and a climbing wall, Fossil World Dinosaur Discovery Centre is also a worthy stop for families, as is the Fossil Shop for those who'd like to take home a souvenir.

🌐 GOOD TO KNOW ─────────────────────────

Beware of "dinosaur snot"! When it rains heavily in the Badlands, the mudstones comprised of bentonite (a volcanic ash) turn green and become super slick. Watch your step to avoid slipping on this viscous material.

Interpretive tours in Dinosaur Provincial Park run mid-May until the end of September. Be sure to register prior to your visit, as these interactive programs book up fast. Visit albertaparks.ca/dinosaur.

🍴 TASTE ─────────────────────────────

No journey to the Canadian Badlands is complete until you've moseyed into the saloon at the **Patricia Hotel**. Located just a few miles from the park, the town of Patricia itself would appear to be almost extinct were it not for the bar's loyal patrons. Beloved by bikers, hunters, and families (who are welcome on Sundays), all walks of life converge to participate in the prairie tradition of grilling your own hunk of beef at the saloon's steak pit. For approximately $20, you can complement a New York strip, ribeye, or T-bone with soup, salad, and garlic toast, plus a baked potato with all the fixings.

In Drumheller, chow down at **Bernie & the Boys Bistro**, featured on Food Network Canada's *You Gotta Eat Here!* It's a cheery spot with large portions, extreme poutine, and a Mammoth Burger I dare you to polish off. For a real treat, nip into **Sublime**, where a Red Seal Chef will happily customize meals for you.

NAP

While it's possible to explore the park as a day trip from Calgary, it's best experienced over a few days. **Dinosaur Campground** at Dinosaur Provincial Park has a playground, and offers both serviced and unserviced campsites year-round. From mid-May until mid-October you'll find a food concession, convenience store, and laundry facilities, as well as showers and flush toilets.

If you're the sort who likes your creature comforts without the creatures, bed down in the park's **Comfort Camping** suites. These massive, safari-like tents are already set up and kitted out with a queen bed and a pull-out futon that sleeps two, plus bedding. It's wired, so you can cool off beside the electric fan or snuggle up in front of an electric fireplace, and, most importantly, recharge the iPad. Other amenities include cooking implements, mini-fridge, coffee pot, and toiletries. Firewood is provided, and a gas BBQ makes mealtimes a breeze if your fire-starting skills aren't up to snuff.

In Drumheller, both the **Ramada** and **Super 8** hotels have pools with a water-slide, complimentary breakfast, and WiFi.

GETTING AROUND

Dinosaur Provincial Park is a two-hour drive from Calgary, past golden wheat fields and snake crossing signs! It takes just under two hours to reach Drumheller from the park. Anticipate a ninety-minute drive from Drumheller to Calgary. Fly into **Calgary International Airport** and rent a car from there.

- The **Badlands** were so named by French voyageurs crossing the continent. They were expecting an easy hike across flat prairie, not a series of unforgiving hills. If you were carrying a canoe, you might also think this area was *les mauvais terrain* (translation: bad lands).
- Over 500 tipi rings have been found in **Dinosaur Provincial Park**, indicating the presence of a large First Nations community. Interestingly, the evidence of tipis was not found down in the Badlands, but on the prairie high above these craters. It's believed the First Nations chose that location out of respect, to not disturb what they considered to be a burial ground for these ancestors of the buffalo.

GET EXCITED ABOUT YOUR TRIP

- What do those dino skeletons get up to when everyone's asleep? You'll find out when reading *Drumheller Dinosaur Dance*, by Robert Heidbreder.
- For children ages eight to twelve, *Canadian Dinosaurs*, by Elin Kelsey, traces the discovery of dinosaurs across Canada.
- Watch *Great Canadian Parks: Dinosaur Provincial Park*, by Good Earth Productions.

Catch some waves inside West Edmonton Mall.

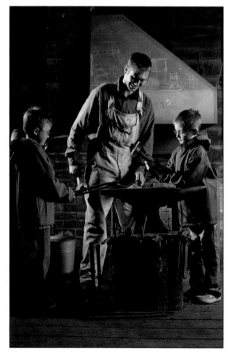

Learn the blacksmith trade at Ukrainian Heritage Cultural Village.

Find tufts of bison fur at Elk Island National Park.

Edmonton
City Filled with Festivals

A procession of drummers and nomadic performers, carrying glowing lanterns, weave their way through the wintery night. Children follow along as the convoy struts through the icy expanse of Hawrelak Park. Minutes before, festival-goers were encouraged to write down their fears and unhappy feelings, and place those thoughts into the lanterns.

The bombastic beats reach a crescendo when the parade arrives at the fire sculpture, and the sad thoughts written on wisps of paper are offered.

"Good people, tonight we burn our fears and grievances," says the leader of this procession, the self-proclaimed King of Winter. "Now, let's burn this thing!" And with that the sculpture is lit, a million sparks floating into the night sky. While it may sound like a pagan ritual, this spellbinding spectacle at the Silver Skate Festival is but one of the many clever ways Edmonton demonstrates its might as a world-class winter city.

FESTIVAL CITY

Edmonton is one of Canada's most festive festival cities. Hosting over sixty festivals a year, they celebrate everything from mid-autumn to ice to sand, even the gold rush. Of course, food, music, art, and culture rank up there, too, and most have a dynamic children's component. Not to miss for winter visitors is February's Silver Skate Festival.

Located at Hawrelak Park, this sporting event is as fun for families as it is for the athletes who compete in it. Along the festival site are dazzling ice sculptures, art dangling from trees, and plenty of demonstration equipment for folks who want to try speed skating, curling, or a multitude of other winter sports. Pre-formed blocks of snow are at the ready for families to transform into their own works of icy art. After you've carved out a snow sculpture, get lost in a snow maze before thawing out in a warming hut.

ICE IS NICE

It doesn't get much better than knocking off a few figure eights on the frozen expanse of Hawrelak Park's 12.4-acre (5-hectare) lake—unless, of course, you're taking in the majestic Alberta Legislature Building from their rink set underneath trees twinkling with tiny lights. There's also a public ice plaza at City Hall, and on Sunday's Swing 'n' Skate, live jazz music is performed. Skate on a Saturday and nip inside City Hall to warm up and browse the year-round farmers' market. Not to be missed along the river valley is the Victoria Pavilion, a wonderful building flanking the Victoria Park Oval, an outdoor speed skating track well loved by families. Rent skates at Hawrelak Park or Totem Outdoor Outfitters.

Edmonton may be hours away from the Rockies, but you can still swoosh down the slopes at local ski hills. Rabbit Hill Snow Resort is a 40-acre (16-hectare) hill with a terrain park, and green, blue, and black runs. Snow Valley Ski Club is another option off Whitemud Drive, with a terrain park. Sunridge Ski Area offers snow tubing in addition to snowboarding and skiing on the eastern edge of the city. Equipment can be rented on-site at each ski hill, and all three offer ski and snowboarding lessons.

What do you get when you take 25,000 tonnes of ice and 10,000 icicles (grown every day)? Why, an ice castle, of course! If you've got a *Frozen* fanatic on your hands, best schedule a trip to Edmonton between January and March when the Ice Castle is open. This hand-built castle is a true marvel. Wander through the palace made entirely of ice to uncover a waterfall, ice slide, and plenty of maze-like pathways. At night the castle shimmers with thousands of LED lights, transforming it into a breathtaking sight that will chill out those with a fiery demeanour.

Ice slides are one of the big draws at the Silver Skate Festival.

Teens enjoy a paddle down the North Saskatchewan River.

Help with chores at Ukrainian Heritage Cultural Village.

The magic of winter is revealed during the Silver Skate Festival.

CONQUER THE MALL

The largest shopping mall in North America, West Edmonton Mall welcomes over 30 million annual visitors. In a sense, West Ed (as locals refer to it) could be considered Alberta's third-largest city. Fortunately, this mall is so vast and bulging with so many attractions, it doesn't seem crowded.

Inspired by the traditional bazaars of ancient Persia, there are over 800 shops, plus dozens of dining and entertaining options seamlessly stitched together under one roof. You can swim, skate, surf, golf, ride a roller coaster, shake hands with a sea lion, and sleep in an igloo—all in one day! By the way, there's no provincial sales tax in Alberta, making this the place for large, guilt-free purchases.

Smack-dab in the middle of West Ed lies an NHL-sized rink (skate rentals available on-site). At one end of the mall lies what appears to be a pirate ship, but upon closer inspection you'll discover it's an exact replica of the Santa Maria. You know, that ship Christopher Columbus sailed across the Atlantic in 1492. Board it for a nominal fee and pretend to be early explorers about to reap the spoils of a successful shop. Nearby lies Sea Life Caverns, an underground aquarium housing over 100 species of aquatic life. Catch a performance at Sea Lions' Rock, or situate yourself on the other side of Deep Sea Adventure Lake to take it in for free.

You're not nearly finished! Hit the links at Dragon's Tale, a black-light mini-golf course, or wander through Crystal Labyrinth, a maze-like hallway of mirrors you have to find your way out of. Also housed inside the mall is Galaxyland, one of the world's largest indoor amusement parks. It's got a fantastic playpark for the under-ten set, filled with slides, chutes, and a ball pit. There are plenty of heart-in-your-throat rides to amuse the teens, too.

When winter is getting the best of you, escape to World Waterpark, a palm-tree-filled, manufactured paradise where it's a balmy 31°C (88°F) all year round. It's got everything under the sun, which you'll clearly spot through the glass-domed ceiling. (Edmonton boasts 325 days of bright sunshine a year!) Besides the wave pool, tricked-out kiddie pool, and water slides (all seventeen of them!), there's a FlowRider surf machine and an impressive Disney-esque 2-storey play structure. Make no mistake, children love directing the flow of water on that play feature, and will have a blast dousing unsuspecting friends.

MUTTART CONSERVATORY

A soothing respite from the hustle and bustle of family travel, Muttart Conservatory is an innovative botanical garden near the river's edge. Four glass pyramids enclose the flora of tropical, arid, and temperate climates. Revive flagging energy amid the greenery as you take in the perfumed scents while darting along the pathways to explore the biomes.

Pick up a laminated guide for a kid's scavenger hunt at the entry to each pyramid. It explains the scents, sights, and textures you will discover. Many plants change with the seasons, so each visit reveals something different. Free guided tours are available on weekends.

WHERE THE BUFFALO ROAM

Here's something that I bet has never happened to you while on vacation: getting caught in a bison traffic jam. Home to one of the highest densities of hoofed mammals in the world, Elk Island National Park—open year round—is a supreme spot for wildlife viewing.

A bit of background: in North America we went from 30 million bison to less than 1,000 in one human lifetime. In 1890 bison were almost extinct, and Elk Island National Park played a key role in bringing them back from the brink. Established in 1906, originally as an elk reserve, this fenced national park maintains herds of both plains and wood bison (who roamed with the mammoths during the last Ice Age). The park is also home to a staggering number of moose, elk, and deer, plus over 250 bird species.

There's plenty to do besides wildlife viewing, and the one-hour Bison Backstage Tour is well worth it. On your own, there are eleven different hiking trails of varying lengths to explore; you can also take advantage of the kayak, canoe, and paddleboard rentals from Lake Astotin. Pick up a discovery kit from the Astotin Theatre to delve further into this refuge with geocaching and pond-dipping kits. In the summer, your chances of spotting bison are best in the early morning or evening hours. (North America's largest land mammal likes to rest in the heat of the day.) Rainy days are a great time to visit, or drop by throughout the year when it's not too hot outside. Dramatic bison behaviour is on display in August when the bulls begin fighting each other, showing off for the ladies they hope to mate with. Head here in May or June to see the adorable baby bison taking their first tentative steps on the prairie. The park is part of Beaver Hills Dark Sky Preserve, a UNESCO-designated biosphere, and throughout the year you can catch spectacular light shows in the night sky.

A word about viewing bison: Maintain your distance. Bison have different personal space needs than humans. You'll want to be at least three bus lengths away from all wild animals if you're on foot. A raised bison tail means they're not happy to see you!

SUMMER FUN

Nestled against the North Saskatchewan River, Fort Edmonton Park gives families an educated sense for how earlier generations lived. Set along 158 acres (64 hectares) of wooded parkland, the site dives into four distinct eras in Edmonton's past, focusing on the fur trade and pioneering years. Highlights include the 1920s-style midway, which offers a glimpse of life as a North-West Mounted Police officer, and the Jasper House Bakery, where you can nip in for a home-baked treat.

Ukrainian Cultural Heritage Village is an open-air museum that depicts the experience of thousands of Ukrainian pioneers who settled in east-central Alberta from the late 1800s until the 1930s. Open from the May long weekend until Labour Day, over thirty-five historical buildings and costumed role-players portray real pioneers, giving children an immersive and authentic peek into the past. Time your visit so you arrive hungry—this is the spot to tuck into traditional homemade Ukrainian foods such as *pyrohy* (perogies), *holubsti* (cabbage rolls), *kovbasa* (garlic sausage), and *borscht* (beet soup).

Families can visit with a shopkeeper organizing his ward, stop by a pioneer kitchen for tips on baking bread, and learn how to make shoes for horses in the blacksmith shop. Kids who like to push the envelope can try to get into trouble inside the one-room schoolhouse, but they just might find themselves standing in the corner. Better to encourage them to help the pioneers with chores. Tasks range from gathering eggs from the chicken coop to carrying firewood into the home to moving milk cans at the train station. This is pioneer life, and everyone pitches in! For a more hands-on experience, roll up your sleeves and sign up for an experiential tour. Learn the art of writing *pysanky* (delicate egg decorating), get down and dirty in the garden, or try to find that needle in the haystack with programs inspired by *Amazing Race* and scavenger hunts.

KICKING AROUND TOWN

There are plenty of parks and green spaces in Edmonton. Flanking the North Saskatchewan River, Edmonton's River Valley is a trove of over 99 miles (160 kilometres) of trails that wind their way through the city from the southwest to northeast corners. In fact, the River Valley is the longest stretch of urban parkland in North America, and is twenty-two times larger than New York's Central Park! Reconnect with nature and explore by foot, ski, bike, snowshoe, or even Segway. Look to River Valley Adventure Co. for Segway tours and bike rentals. Revolution Cycle also offers bicycle rentals.

TELUS World of Science captures children's imaginations with interactive displays that foster their sense of discovery. The Discoveryland gallery focuses on creative learning through play at water and role-playing exhibits. The Tot Galaxy encourages sensory exploration for toddlers and infants, while the Science Garage lets the older set tinker and test their way through wind tunnels, a climbing wall, and a magnetic ball wall. Angular momentum, kinetic energy, friction, and gravity—it's all taught here in a much more interesting way than in a school science class.

Take advantage of the many exploratory activities that help families connect with the art featured at the Alberta Art Gallery. BMO All Day Sundays take place one a month, and Tours for Tots is a weekly drop-in program filled with gallery adventures for pre-school-aged children. The Royal Alberta Museum will be the largest museum in Western Canada when it reopens in late 2017 or early 2018. Head here for a dedicated Children's Gallery and Bug Room to keep your entourage entertained.

🌐 GOOD TO KNOW

The Edmonton area is known for being a prime vantage point to catch the Aurora Borealis (Northern Lights). Cruise to AuroraWatch.ca to receive real-time reports of the night sky. Sign up for their email alert service so you don't miss the Northern Lights dancing during your trip.

🍴 TASTE

Just off trendy Whyte Avenue, **MEAT** is an excellent choice for hungry carnivores and their families. Tuck into BBQ ribs, some apple-glazed smoked chicken, or a pound of pulled pork. You'll be able to sample it all—the meat is served up on one big platter, family style. Worthy sides range from massive pickles, decadent mac and cheese, and slices of homemade cornbread to mop up the juices.

Tres Carnales is a traditional Mexican taqueria, where you order first and then snag a table. There's no dedicated children's menu, but all meats are served up taco, quesadilla, or torta (sandwich) style. Quesadillas are most popular with kids, and the chips and guacamole are as good as you'll find anywhere north of the border.

Modelled after a Parisian tea salon, **Duchess Bake Shop** is elegantly outfitted with dozens of handcrafted temptations. With high chairs and an upholstered bench in the women's washroom (in case you'd like some breastfeeding privacy), it welcomes families who appreciate classic French pastries and from-scratch lunch items. Quality is the name of the game in this delectable spot, so don't feel guilty about packing home a few baking provisions. (I returned three times in twenty-four hours!)

Set inside an atmospheric 1903 home, **Little Brick Café** is a café and general store in the Riverdale community, flanking the river near downtown. Thoughtful touches for the young'uns, such as reduced heat for hot drinks, smaller serving sizes, and lower prices, as well as high chairs and baby change stations, make this a charming spot for breakfast, lunch, or a snack. Little Brick also sports a mighty big back yard for littles to run about in.

The **Old Strathcona Farmers' Market** has been an Edmonton favourite since the early '80s. Vendors abide by a strict code to either make it, bake it, or grow it. Pick up a wide range of produce, wild game, and—if you're lucky— ready-made perogies and green onion cakes, both Edmonton specialties.

NAP

Sleep in a mall? You bet! It's every shopaholic's fantasy come to life, and with over 100 themed rooms, kiddies love staying at **Fantasyland Hotel** inside West Edmonton Mall just as much as their sleep-deprived parents. Sleep like royalty in a princess- or Roman-themed room. Put the kids in the driver's seat in a truck-themed room, or hibernate inside an igloo. Just don't reserve a Hollywood room—unless you want to explain what a pole is doing on its own platform.

A haven for both four-legged and two-legged creatures, **Elk Island National Park** is great for camping from mid-May until mid-October. There are over seventy unserviced sites (with flush toilets, showers, and food storage lockers in a common area) that can be reserved from January on. Don't have all the gear? Reserve an equipped campsite and avoid the hassle. Bring your own food and bedding, and they'll provide the rest. Backcountry camping is also available.

GETTING AROUND

Edmonton International Airport is a thirty-minute drive south of the city, give or take. **Skyshuttle** departs the airport hourly to several locations throughout the city. **Edmonton's Light Rail Transit** (LRT) can get you around downtown and to the University of Alberta campus. Public bus services whisk visitors to West Edmonton Mall, but tourists will find renting a vehicle from the airport to be the most convenient way to get around the city.

FUN FACTS

- Edmonton is the northernmost city in North America with a metropolitan population over 1 million.
- Edmonton is named after an English estate owned by a Hudson's Bay Company deputy governor. The name Edmonton is a Latinized version of a Saxon word meaning "happy hamlet."
- The **Alberta Legislature** sits on quicksand! Patches of quicksand were discovered during the 1908 construction. Fortunately, concrete piles were driven in before the footings were set into the ground.
- Constructed in Edmonton, the **Al Rashid Mosque** was the first Muslim mosque in North America. It's now located at Fort Edmonton Park.

GET EXCITED ABOUT YOUR TRIP

- Read *Why I love Alberta*, illustrated by Daniel Howarth.
- Author Marion Mutala's illustrated books *Baba's Babushka: A Magical Ukrainian Christmas* and *Baba's Babushka: A Magical Ukrainian Easter* teach children about Ukrainian traditions
- While the movie *Snow Day* takes place in Syracuse, New York, Edmonton was one of its filming locations.

Old-fashioned fun is had at Government House.

Saskatchewan Roughrider fans at Mosaic Stadium.

Regina

City of Unexpected (and Affordable) Adventures

Heralded by a lone bugle call answered by the beat of a snare drum, drill staff step up and put cadets through their paces. "Eyes right and dress!" they shout. Instantly the recruits stand shoulder-to-shoulder, crisp in their lines before marching in formation. After standing at ease, at attention, participating in roll call, and passing inspection, the band strikes up again as the cadets march out.

Such is the scene at the Sergeant Major's Parade, at the RCMP Depot Division in Regina, Saskatchewan. Who would've thought that a parade with neither floats nor candy would capture the attention of children? That's the draw of the Mounties in the Royal Canadian Mounted Police. A pillar of Canada's cultural and historical landscape since 1873, Mounties with their red serge are part of the Canadian identity.

RCMP HERITAGE CENTRE

To become an RCMP officer, cadets must go through a rigorous six-month training program that takes place at the RCMP Academy Depot Division in Regina. From May to September, visitors can take guided walking or driving tours to understand what it really takes to become a Mountie.

While cruising past cadet dormitories, the officer's mess, and horse stables, you'll feel like you're inspecting a military outpost. It also makes you question what year it is, with pieces of our history layered into RCMP traditions. The highlight of the tour is the Sergeant Major's Parade, originally used to mark attendance during the Great March West in 1874. The tradition continues promptly at 12:45 p.m. on weekdays throughout the year. And yes, there is a real, honest-to-goodness sergeant major bellowing orders at the cadets throughout the thirty-minute spectacle. From July until mid-August, the Sunset Retreat Ceremony is also worth scheduling in.

After touring the Depot, take a stroll through the Heritage Centre, where the story of the RCMP, and its role in protecting and forming our country, is brought to life. During self-guided tours, the history of one of Canada's most esteemed institutions is told from the time when the force was first created in 1873 through to the end of the 20th century. There are snazzy red serge jackets to try on, Louis Riel's handcuffs to admire, and a host of shiny metals and police weaponry to pique interest.

Not to be missed is Crack the Case gallery, where clues are presented and real forensic work must be done. To solve the crime, all suspects must be carefully considered. Fingers are put into an optical reader to determine which of the five categories your fingerprint is in (just so everyone is ruled out, you know). Rest assured, after DNA examinations are complete, you'll determine who the real culprit is.

While at the RCMP Heritage Centre, make sure you go just to the right of Guest Services. You'll find activities for children, such as "I Spy" and scavenger hunts, to get them interacting even more with the exhibits.

GOVERNMENT HOUSE

This former home of the Lieutenant Governor offers a glimpse into high prairie society at the turn of the 20th century. You'd think such a spot would be a snoozer for children, but they've gone out of their way to ensure it's not. Case in point: kids can tour this museum and interpretive centre with a loaner backpack filled with games and props to enhance either indoor or outdoor play. In the basement lies Once Upon a Time, a permanent playroom loaded with a playhouse, dress-up clothes, toys, and books. Complimentary geocaching and scavenger hunts customized by age group invite children outside to explore the 7.5 acres (3 hectares) of Edwardian gardens.

The bubble station is a big draw at the Saskatchewan Science Centre.

Who says there are no beaches on the prairie? Check out Regina Beach Recreation Site.

Meet Queenie at Candy Cane Park in Wascana Centre.

Salute the RCMP at the RCMP Heritage Centre.

Tots taste fruit at Over the Hill Orchards.

SASKATCHEWAN SCIENCE CENTRE

Don't be surprised when the water fountain begins talking to you at this well-developed, interactive museum. Thank the water fountain for letting you know how much you drank (and how much your body needs per day to function properly) before moving onto exhibits that range from space to farming. A John Deere tractor kitted out with a farming simulator game is a hit for city slickers curious about country life, and you can step inside a giant hamster wheel to see how many watts you create while walking, and what devices could be charged with that energy.

Test your weight on Mars or Ganymede (Jupiter's largest moon) by hoisting yourself up in the space chairs. There is also a Gyro Gym developed by NASA, which visitors strap into to experience the sense of weightlessness in space. All ages are mesmerized by the bubble zone, especially when you encase yourself in one ginormous bubble. Unbeknownst to children, they're experiencing light and refraction firsthand—but don't burst their bubble by pointing out that they're actually learning during play.

There's an indoor play area for toddlers and preschoolers, and a separate enclosed soft play area for the very young. At the outdoor playground there are massive musical instruments to play upon, and lots of experiments to be done, like clapping your hands in front of the echo tube and telling secrets to the whisper dishes.

From the Science Centre, continue along Wascana Drive to find the Candy Cane Park playground. This all-ages play area is crammed with equipment, including climbing structures and rock climbing walls for all heights.

ROYAL SASKATCHEWAN MUSEUM

Get a taste for the province's natural, cultural, and environmental legacy at the Royal Saskatchewan Museum. Saskatchewan is rich with geological and mineral resources, not to mention giant reptiles and other extinct creatures (like their favourite dinosaurs) that walked upon this land in the past 2 billion years. Admire the impressive skulls and skeletons of prehistoric creatures in the Earth Sciences Gallery; there are living fossils such as spotted gar (a primitive fish) to investigate, too.

The First Nations Gallery showcases the traditions and history of Aboriginal peoples and their relationship to the local land. Migration is thoughtfully explained in a way that kids enjoy, especially when they can light up displays showing the routes of long-distance birds and butterflies in the Life Sciences Gallery. More natural wonders are revealed as littles peer deep inside a hibernaculum—after all, who isn't interested in learning what goes down in a snake den? If attention begins to fade, break for the Paleo Pit, open daily during summer and on weekends the rest of the year. This fun, dino-inspired play area is best suited for children under eight.

RIDER NATION

Are great sporting cities made from the quantity or quality of their teams? When it comes to Regina, a city with only one professional sports team, it's all about quality—of the fans, that is. While the Saskatchewan Roughriders are a respectable team in the Canadian Football League, their fans are in a league of their own. More than a league, actually. In fact, they're a "nation": Rider Nation.

What does it mean to be a part of Rider Nation? What drives fans to buy every single watermelon in the city and fashion them into hats? For this I turned to Twitter:

> Marcy Stickle @Maplegirl66: Wherever you go, if you wear that green shirt, you are part of something bigger. It's a family.

> Rod Broughton @roddy_broughton: It means that in a corporate sports world, you are a part of a community that is bigger than the competition.

You'd be hard pressed to find another city in Canada with such unwavering support for their team (who unfortunately have only won four Grey Cups). Even if you've yet to bleed green, try to time your visit during a home game, so you can experience the phenomenon firsthand.

WORTHY SIDE TRIPS

The Prairies don't produce optimal growing conditions for tree fruit, but that hasn't stopped Dean Kreutzer of Over the Hill Orchards from growing thirteen different kinds of fruit in the lush Qu'Appelle Valley near the town of Lumsden. Stop by for a tour of the orchard (weekend afternoons during summer months), and get your hands dirty. Plant your own strawberry, hear the bird calls that scare animals away, and get up in the grill of insects that keeps the plants alive. Afterwards, taste this local fruit inside their on-site tea house. The dessert bar is completely gluten- and nut-free, and they're open from Mother's Day to Canadian Thanksgiving.

HIT THE BEACH

Believe it or not, the landscape around Regina is not flat-as-a-pancake prairie. Outside the city are rolling green hills and lovely lakes to romp around in. The town of Regina Beach makes for an excellent day trip. Locals hit the sandy shore of Long Lake, fish off the pier, and snack on fish and chips from the Blue Bird Café. The beach is well treed with plenty of shade, and there's a beach volleyball net as well as a playground. Forget hauling all your beach gear—pretty much everything you need (besides towels) can be rented.

TUNNELS OF MOOSE JAW

You learned all about cops at the RCMP Depot, but what about robbers? In Moose Jaw, a quick forty-minute drive from Regina, families can literally go underground and explore subjects polite society would rather keep secret. The city is famed for its tunnels originally used by steam engineers to make it easier and safer for them to get from boiler room to boiler room, avoiding the harsh prairie winter when sopping wet. Tunnels of Moose Jaw is an attraction that takes history underground on guided theatrical tours.

The journey along the Passage to Fortune tour begins in 1907, when Chinese labourers were taken advantage of and rarely saw the light of day working for Burrows and Sons Laundry. Weaving your way through the underground maze, you'll discover that the discomfort started with the living quarters: cement floors, grubby stone walls, and sleeping three to a bed in a narrow bunk. It's hard to believe there was a hefty head tax for the pleasure of living and working in such a hostile environment. Chinese immigrants paid $50 to enter Canada in 1885, but by 1903 the head tax was $500!

But there's no time for thinking, not when you're treated as cheap labour and being led by a gruff period character through secret passageways. Our country's treatment of these immigrants as slaves is a blight on our history, but history is often repeated unless it's confronted, which is what makes this tour so important and intriguing for families.

The tunnels don't stop there—they're associated with 1920s-era Chicago, a city then rife with corruption and gangsters. The Chicago Connection tour reveals how Moose Jaw served as a safe haven for the richest man in America and public enemy number one: Al Capone. What was this famous American gangster and bootlegger doing in Moose Jaw? To find out, slide into Miss Fanny's Club and morph from well-meaning tourist into thirsty bootlegger.

After getting the lay of the land inside Miss Fanny's speakeasy, you'll make like a bootlegger on the run, hiding out in secret rooms and escaping through the tunnels. While guns, gangsters, and liquor aren't topics most parents are keen to introduce their children to, what child hasn't played cops and robbers? In Moose Jaw these fantasies come to life and show that what lies beneath the surface is often more fascinating than what's above ground.

MORE IN MOOSE JAW

This traditional prairie town on the Trans-Canada Highway is less than an hour's drive from Regina. The tunnels are the big draw, but you'll want to wander through downtown, where pretty murals decorate the sides of buildings and tell different stories of the city's history. While here, stop in at Burrowing Owl Interpretive Centre, Western Development Museum, and Temple Gardens Mineral Spa, where you don't have to be a guest to swim in their therapeutic pools.

TASTE

A Regina institution, **Milky Way** is an old-fashioned dairy bar and takeaway joint that makes their own soft ice cream, plus dozens of other frozen treats at affordable prices.

Start your weekend off on the right foot with the waffle extravaganza at **Fresh and Sweet**. They sport a robust children's menu, plenty of high chairs, and homemade cinnamon buns that are hard to resist.

Near Wascana Park, **Tangerine** offers picnic platters and anything on the menu can be packaged to go.

In Moose Jaw, the **Gallery Café** is tops for lunch. There's no specific children's menu, but from-scratch biscuits, homemade soup, and peanut-butter-and-Saskatoon-berry-jam sandwiches fill tiny tummies. If you're a fan of iced tea, you must try their Saskatoon berry version. With wingback chairs, a loveseat, and a fireplace, the ladies' room is an ideal place to nurse or take a time out.

⌂ NAP

Those who appreciate the finer things in life will love the Old World charm at **Hotel Saskatchewan**. Located across the street from Victoria Park, there's no pool, but you'll find enough distractions with a hot tub and downtown amenities.

A perennial favourite, **Travelodge Regina** is famed for its Soaked! Waterpark. With two waterslides, a swimming pool, a hot tub, a spray pad, and a toddler area, don't think you're getting out of here in less than two hours. Guest rooms come with a mini-fridge, plus there's a fitness facility, complimentary parking, and WiFi.

In Moose Jaw, **Temple Gardens Mineral Spa** is located a few blocks off the tunnels and within walking distance of Main Street. A soak in the therapeutic geo-thermal mineral waters in their indoor and outdoor pool ensures a quick and easy bedtime for all.

⧉ GETTING AROUND

The attractions around Regina are spread out, so you're going to want to rent a vehicle. The good news: no arguments over stopping for directions as the city is well laid out in a grid-like fashion. Moose Jaw is approximately forty-five minutes away by car, Over the Hill Orchards is a twenty-minute drive, and Regina Beach takes half an hour to reach from the city centre.

◌ FUN FACTS

- The RCMP was originally known as the North-West Mounted Police. Women weren't allowed to be regular members until 1974. There is only one place in Canada to train to become an RCMP officer, and that's in Regina.
- Regina is known as the **Queen City**, named in 1882 after Queen Victoria, the reigning monarch at the time. The original name given by early settlers was Pile of Bones.
- Once a barren grassland with no trees and little water, 350,000 trees were hand-planted in Regina. The city is now lush and green, and filled with plenty of parkland.

- Regina is home to one of North America's largest urban parks. Wascana Centre is a 2,300-acre (9.3-square-kilometre) park surrounding Wascana Lake.
- The **prairie lily** is the provincial flower of Saskatchewan, while the **paper birch tree**, used to make canoes, baskets, and utensils by First Nations communities, is the provincial tree.

✦ GET EXCITED ABOUT YOUR TRIP

- *The Always Team*, by Holly Preston, is an illustrated storybook about Rider Nation with a message of perseverance and sportsman-like behaviour.
- *If You're Not from the Prairie*, by David Bouchard, *Owls in the Family*, by Farley Mowat, and *Who Has Seen the Wind*, by W.O. Mitchell, are classic Canadian reads.
- The older set will also enjoy reading *Strange Saskatchewan*, by Carson Demmans, and *Tunnels of Treachery*, by Mary Harelkin Bishop.

One of Canada's best outdoor playgrounds lies at the Forks National Historic Site.

Polar bears swim overhead at the Journey to Churchill exhibit inside the Assiniboine Park Zoo.

Winnipeg

Historic Meeting Place and Tributes to Winnie the Pooh

Set smack-dab in the middle of Canada, Winnipeg might not be the first Canadian metropolis that comes to mind when thinking "family holiday." Make no mistake: this is a city on the rise. The Red, Assiniboine, La Salle, and Seine rivers all wind through Winnipeg like gleaming ribbons, and there has always been a vibrant Aboriginal and Métis population. Yet for too many years, Winnipeg wasn't on the map. Minds starting shifting in 2010 when Winnipeg was named the Cultural Capital of Canada by the Department of Canadian Heritage.

The accolades and enhanced visitor experiences have been steadily coming ever since. (Hooray for the return of the NHL Winnipeg Jets!) With a recently remodelled international airport, an emerging food scene, and easily accessible attractions, Winnipeg has quietly undergone a cultural metamorphosis and is one of the most family-friendly cities in Canada. When hankering for an affordable city break, you'll want to consider this provincial capital.

THE FORKS

A historic site, green space, and cultural hub, The Forks is an ideal place to begin exploring the city. Often referred to as a giant pop-up book come to life, it's situated downtown, at the confluence of the Assiniboine and Red Rivers, a location that's served as a meeting place for thousands of years. Early Indigenous peoples traded here, as did European fur traders, pioneers, and thousands of immigrants. There are endless attractions and excursions that begin from here, including one of the world's longest naturally frozen skating trails.

Bringing the region's 6,000-year history to life, Variety Heritage Adventure Park is perhaps of most interest to the elementary-aged set. There are seven themed zones representing Winnipeg's history, including a fur trading post playset, a climbing wall, and a settler's boat where kids can pretend to navigate. Families can cool off from the hot prairie sun by romping around at the splash park.

CHILDREN'S MUSEUM

Located inside The Forks and housed in the oldest surviving train repair facility in Manitoba, this hands-on museum is fun with a capital F, with twelve permanent galleries to spark creative learning. Begin your journey by hopping aboard the 1952 diesel locomotive, or enjoy some quiet time reading in comfy seats inside the 1910 Pullman passenger coach. (Yes, there are real, full-size trains inside the museum!)

Do your children play with their food? At Lasagna Lookout, the food plays with them. Kids charge through string cheese, squeeze through the rigatoni roller, and chill on ravioli pillows in this indoor play structure. Meanwhile, perceptions are tested in the Illusion Tunnel before kids go whizzing down the psychedelic slide. There's also a super-duper craft area crammed with all the supplies you could wish for.

Each gallery is tactile and interactive, appealing to children of all abilities under ten years of age. For the tiny set, there's a Tot Spot loaded with cushy toys and seating for caregivers. Preschoolers will want to soak themselves when performing water experiments in the Splash Lab, and more than one Bob the Builder fan will try to work some magic on the levers of the mini-CAT digger.

CANADIAN MUSEUM FOR HUMAN RIGHTS (CMHR)

As the first national museum in Canada built outside the National Capital Region, the CMHR is a big deal. Besides its impressive architecture, this is also the world's first museum solely dedicated to human rights. Now, if your first thought is that it must be snooze-worthy or not appropriate for children, think again. CMHR is not your typical museum. There's not an overabundance of traditional artifacts on display; instead you'll uncover hundreds of stories told through art, objects, and interactive digital elements that engage and educate.

Meet muskox and other Arctic creatures at the Journey to Churchill exhibit at Assiniboine Park Zoo.

The Canadian Museum for Human Rights is an iconic structure that inspires visitors to become good citizens.

Burn off energy at the Nature Playground inside Assiniboine Park.

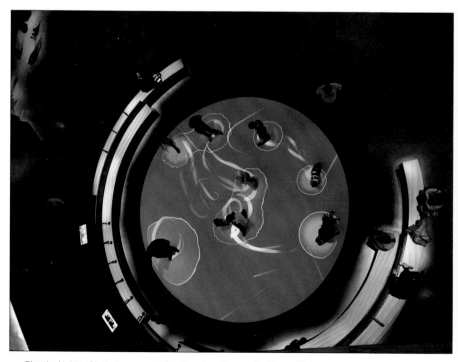

Play the Lights of Inclusion game at the Canadian Museum for Human Rights.

It's not a collection of the worst behaviour ever recorded, nor is it a little shop of horrors. It is, however, an inspiring spot that fosters discussion and inspires change. "The goal wasn't to become a catalogue of human rights stories from around the world, but to illuminate the concept of human rights and provide a motivational space to assist children in becoming good citizens," says Maureen Fitzhenry of the Canadian Museum for Human Rights.

True, some exhibits (such as the one that depicts the Holocaust) contain heavier subject matter, but several were designed with youngsters in mind—in particular, the Lights of Inclusion floor game found in the Canadian Journeys Gallery. In this motion-sensor light game, children step into a circle while a colourful projected light follows them around the space. When players interact, their spheres of light merge and grow bigger, symbolizing the power of inclusion. It's pretty cool to witness kids clue in to how their movements affect the lights. There are also crafts, scavenger hunts, a story time, and learning activities about human rights throughout the museum.

The building itself is part of the experience. The towering structure of glass, stone, concrete, and steel is built on a historic meeting place— on Treaty One territory near the site of the Métis rebellion under Louis Riel. Designed by Antoine Predock, every architectural component of the museum is a physical expression of human rights ideals, from the Tower of Hope, to the Glass Cloud, to the CMHR's exterior that mimics the folded wings of a dove, to interior ramps guiding visitors on a journey from darkness to increasing light. These illuminated ramps that take you from floor to floor do not go along a straight path. But, as you're about to find out, human rights don't follow a direct course, either.

With eleven permanent galleries and 24,000 square metres (258,333 square feet) of floor space, you likely won't be able to hit up the entire museum in one go, so be sure to take in the final galleries to bring the concept of human rights home. Digital displays in the Rights Today gallery prompt children to consider how everyday objects affect their rights. It's easy to leave here feeling hopeful and part of something bigger than yourself, especially if you finish off your visit by taking in the panoramic views from the Israel Asper Tower of Hope. To make CMHR visits more fun:

- Check the website for family days to see what special activities (like scavenger hunts) are happening before you visit.
- Stock up on souvenirs at the boutique, where only fair trade and ethically sourced products are sold. You'll find quality toys, games, jewelry, and art as well as a wonderful selection of books about First Nations and Canada's North.
- Spread out your visit by lunching at the museum's ERA Bistro. The locally sourced menu offers enticing options on the children's menu.

ASSINIBOINE PARK

One of North America's great parks, this vast green space is ranked among the best urban parks in the world. In fact, Frederick Todd, the landscape architect who designed the park over a century ago, studied under and worked for Frederick Olmsted, the man who designed Central Park in New York and Mount Royal Park in Montreal. Set on a massive area encompassing over 400 acres (162 hectares), Assiniboine Park is a fifteen-minute drive from downtown, give or take. Fortunately, you needn't worry about tuckering out the troops when winding your way through this woodland area. All summer long, a complimentary hop-on, hop-off shuttle bus ferries families past acres of trees, gently rolling hills, and beautiful gardens to all the main attractions.

There are gardens galore, where you'll get your dose of green, but you'll likely spend most of your time at the Streuber Family Children's Garden inside the Nature Playground. Inspired by the classic childhood board game Snakes and Ladders, and designed with youngsters in mind, adults will have to duck under the frame of the child-sized door in order to gain entry. With slithering serpent slides, crow's nest ropes, willow tree tunnels, and a water and sand play area, children's imaginations run wild as they explore this enchanting space. Next to the playground, many friendly fowl can be found at the expanded Riley Family Duck Pond.

Cool off at the Forks National Historic Site.

After your play, amble over to the Assiniboine Park Zoo to interact with more than 150 species of animals from across the globe. Exotic animals include snow leopards, red kangaroos, and Amur tigers. It's certainly worth checking out the animals of the Grasslands and Boreal Forest, especially since Canada's boreal region is one of the few great forests left in the world. Another popular spot is Journey to Churchill, the world's most comprehensive northern species exhibit of its kind. Head here for encounters with caribou, Arctic foxes, wolves, musk oxen, and, yes, polar bears, along with many other species that call Canada home.

Crawling through the Polar Playground is likely to be a highlight, as is having polar bears and seals gracefully float over top of you in the underwater viewing tunnel. It's an enriching and surreal experience, and you'll lose track of time while mesmerized by these Arctic creatures. To make your visit more educational, check out the Interpretive Centre inside the Leatherdale International Polar Bear Conservation Centre. Here you'll learn more about the Arctic ecosystem, climate change, and ways to reduce your ecological footprint.

And here's an added bonus that the whole family will enjoy: A tram makes regular stops along the zoo route, carrying you through the 80 acres (32 hectares) of exhibits.

KICKING AROUND TOWN

Fantasizing about how efficient your home could be while traipsing through the aisles of IKEA likely isn't at the top of your vacation bucket list. But, then again, this location has one of the largest Småland play areas in Canada (not to mention affordable meals and delightful items you can't possibly live without).

Discover how coins are made for up to seventy-five countries around the world at the Royal Canadian Mint. Take your family on a guided tour to learn how the Mint makes up to 15 million coins in one day. Visit the boutique where you can strike you own medallion and hold a real gold bar.

WORTHY SIDE TRIP

Wildlife lovers will want to spread their wings at Oak Hammock Marsh, a reclaimed wetland area and conservation centre, located outside the city. This is one of North America's birding hotspots, with over 300 species of birds having been spotted here—that's over half the total number of species in Canada! But you don't have to be a birder to feel an immense jolt of joy when holding a tiny wren in the palm of your hand before it flutters away to freedom. Families can assist on-site naturalists in important research by helping to band and release the birds back into nature. During bird-banding activities, you'll also learn why this wetland is such an important stop on the migratory path.

This refuge isn't just for the birds: over ten different species of frogs and toads jump all over the place. Would you believe wetlands rival rainforests for species diversity? They do! Wetlands are one of the most productive ecosystems on earth. Visitors can investigate nature's marvels by critter-dipping along the docks, scooping up the bugs, fish, and amphibians that live in the marsh. To get even more up close and personal with waterfowl, canoes are available for a gentle paddle. Guides teach voyageur songs and show you the best way to sample cattails, a marsh delicacy. If dry land is more your thing, stride along the trails that lace their way through the site. To visit some of the less-observed parts, go on a guided hike with an interpreter. Inside the interpretive centre, there are interactive exhibits to wander through, and a café with a bird's-eye view of the marsh.

¶¶ TASTE

The Forks Market allows you to dine around the world without having to step foot on an airplane. There are many gems to hit up, but don't miss the freshly baked goods from the **Tall Grass Prairie Bread Company**. This market is an opportunity to load up on snacks, and you'll find it all here—from pizza to perogies to Sri Lankan cuisine to fish and chips.

Situated in The Peg's trendy Exchange District, **Across the Board Game Café** is a haven for families looking for a little fun. For a nominal cover charge, gamers are granted access to over 900 games and can play for as long as they like. There's a children's menu and diverse offerings for adults inside this licensed restaurant.

🛏 NAP

Snag a poolside room or a kid-themed suite at the **Victoria Inn** and you'll be the most popular parents in town. The hotel is located right next to the airport, but it's a quick drive into the main sites. Dino Beach Water Park is what lures most families here with its 160-foot (48-metre) corkscrew waterslide, plus two waterspouts for little swimmers. The hotel also offers coin-operated washers and dryers, plus an in-room mini-fridge.

Another popular hotel with a water park is the **Clarion Hotel**, with a 2-storey waterslide, a kiddie pool, and a hot tub. A spa and twenty-four-hour fitness centre make it an enticing location for Mom and Dad, too! The pet-friendly property is located near the airport, and offers a mini-fridge and microwave in all guest rooms.

With several locations throughout the city, **Canad Inns** are the way to go when kids desperately need a break from their parents. Who can blame them for wanting a bit of space when specialty kids' rooms are kitted out with bunk beds, themed décor, and an XBox or PlayStation? They have waterslides and kiddie pools too, plus an Adventure Kid's Club to help pass the time.

🗺 GETTING AROUND

After flying into the recently expanded **Winnipeg James Armstrong Richardson International Airport**, your best bet for getting around is by car. Public transportation is available in Winnipeg, but with the exception of attractions in The Forks, many touristy hot spots are spread out across the city.

💡 FUN FACTS

- **Winnie the Pooh** is not just a beloved storybook character created by A.A. Milne. This very real black bear has ties to Winnipeg. During WWI, the female bear was sold by a trapper to Lieutenant Harry Colebourn, while the soldier was travelling across Canada en route to England. The cub was named Winnipeg after Colebourn's hometown and became a pet amongst the soldiers. Before Colebourn was shipped to France he arranged for the London Zoo to care for "Winnie" until his return. So gentle was she, children would ride on her back or feed her directly.

- In 1871 Winnipeg's population was 271. That grew to 7,985 in ten short years. By 1891 there were 25,642 people living here; today, a century later, over 793,400 people call Winnipeg home.
- Held in Winnipeg each summer, **Folklorama** is the world's largest and longest running multicultural festival.
- "Winnipeg" is the Cree word for "muddy waters."
- The **great grey owl** is the provincial bird, while the **plains bison** is the province's symbolic animal. Look for the **prairie crocus** and **white spruce**, the provincial flower and tree, respectively.

✦ GET EXCITED ABOUT YOUR TRIP

- Of course little ones must be read *Winnie-the-Pooh*, by A.A. Milne.
- *Finding Winnie: The True Story of the World's Most Famous Bear*, by Lindsay Mattick, is a must read for fans.
- *Finding Winnipeg*, by Darlyne Bautista, and *Wild and Wonderful (in Winnipeg)*, by D.J. Solvason, are both good introductions to the city.
- Teenagers should read *The Stone Angel*, a CanLit classic by Margaret Laurence, to get a taste of rural Manitoba. It was also made into a movie that was shot in Manitoba.
- Listen to "Prairie Town," a song written about Winnipeg, by Randy Bachman (guitarist with The Guess Who and Bachman Turner Overdrive).
- "Red River Valley" is a famous cowboy folk song that's been recorded by numerous artists over the decades.
- Children's entertainer Fred Penner hails from Winnipeg. Be sure to download some of his songs for the preschool set.
- Both *A Bear Named Winnie* and *Beethoven's Christmas Adventure* were filmed in Winnipeg. Watch them and see if you can spot city landmarks.

A polar bear and her cubs are spotted outside Churchill.

Be prepared to meet some friendly beluga whales in Churchill.

Churchill

Go on an Arctic Safari

Zipping along in a Zodiac somewhere between Button Bay and Eskimo Point, we spot our first polar bears. A mother and her cub are sauntering the shoreline, when suddenly, baby cub clambers onto the rocks and belly flops into the icy bay. Mama bear joins him, and they have a grand time frolicking in the waves. Just when I think it can't get any more Nat Geo than this, an iridescent beluga juts its head out of the water, a mere 100 feet (30 metres) in front of the frisky bears.

Welcome to Churchill, Manitoba, land of Arctic creatures and intrepid outdoor experiences. The polar bear capital of the world is one of the few human settlements where visitors can observe these bears in the wild. This northern town was built on the migrational path of polar bears, and every autumn, hundreds of these confident mammals meander their way through town on their way to the ice floes. Even if you visit during the summer months, you'll still find plenty of polar bears about. They're resting around town, waiting until the river freezes (faster than the saltwater of Hudson Bay), and once that ice forms, they're off like a shot on the hunt for seals.

Let me tell you, happiness is seeing the joy in a child's eyes when they witness polar bears or belugas in their natural environment. Churchill is wild, remote, and ruggedly beautiful. Authentic experiences that blend wildlife with local cultures are yours to be had when travelling here. This is a spot to experience the spirit of Canada's national anthem firsthand—the True North is indeed strong and free.

POLAR BEAR WATCHING ON THE TUNDRA

There are a variety of ways to get out of town and start hunting polar bears—with your camera, of course! Best is with an expert guide at the wheel of a custom-made monster tundra vehicle sporting 15 feet (4.5 metres) of wheels. Heading out on the sub-Arctic terrain in this monolithic vehicle, we cruise through what appear to be mini lakes, getting tossed and turned as the buggy ambles over the rough land in search of northern creatures.

"When you're looking for nature, the best thing is to look for something that doesn't belong or seem to fit. It's an energy thing. Relax and they'll come to you," advises our guide, Jim Baldwin. Jim reckons he's had a fifty percent success rate during his summer tours, and has experienced only four unsuccessful days without polar bear sightings during ten-plus years of guiding during the prime autumn season.

We think luck is upon us, spotting an unkindness of ravens, tundra swans, and a sandhill crane, but after three hours of plodding along the tundra taiga, there are no polar bears to be found. We begin to lose hope, but then Jim parks us at the aptly named Polar Bear Point, whips out his binoculars, and spots a white rock about 328 feet (100 metres) away. But as it turns out, it's not a rock, despite what our untrained eyes tell us. After a few minutes the bear leisurely shifts to all fours. He sniffs the air and ever so slowly waddles in our direction, taunting those of us without zoom lenses. The bear stops halfway, takes a seat, then resumes his stone-like, stoic behaviour, lying on his back. We use the opportunity to tuck into soup, sandwiches, and "tundra-cino"—a mix of hot chocolate and coffee provided by our tour operator.

There are few places in the world where you can find yourself in a reverse zoo. If the bears want to come up and investigate the primates in the mobile cage, they will. Since polar bears are just as fast as racehorses and hit their full speed in two strides, there is no getting off the bus, but you can take advantage of the outdoor viewing platform.

As we head back to base, we're rewarded with more animal kingdom moments. A family of Arctic foxes rush out of their den. Three adorable cubs play leapfrog over each other, while Mom or Dad cautiously watches our vehicle before taking off to hunt for dinner.

View polar bears and other Arctic wildlife on Tundra Buggy tours with Frontiers North.

After spotting so many creatures upon our Arctic safari, the adults become just as giddy as the kids. When a preschooler begins belting out "What Does the Fox Say?" we all join in.

KAYAK WITH WHALES

The adventures in Churchill keep on rolling, especially if visiting within the summer months, when approximately 3,000 beluga whales make their way from the bay into the warmer waters of the Churchill River to give birth and feed. This is perhaps the only place in the world where your kayak will be beluga powered. "Whales love to play with the rudder of your kayak. They may even bump you a bit, and it's pretty fun!" says our kayaking guide, Alex de Vries.

Fun is an understatement. Shouts of "I just got blow-holed!" and "How close was that!" echo across the river within minutes of dipping our oars in the water. There are dozens upon dozens of smooth white backs gliding in and out of the water.

You'll hear these belugas before you see them (their breathing sounding not dissimilar to Darth Vader), and when you do, brace yourself; these naturally curious creatures want to play. Belugas dart among the kayaks, giving you a nudge from behind and playing bumper cars with your rudder. Getting beluga bumped is a rush like no other.

If you plan to photograph your adventure, bring only waterproof cameras. Otherwise, hand your non-waterproof camera over to the safety boat following your group.

SNORKEL WITH BELUGAS

Hankering for more beluga action? Go belly-to-belly with these intelligent mammals on a snorkelling excursion. You'd think it would take a lot to get a dog-paddling mother to swim in the 5°C (41°F) waters of Hudson Bay, but the belugas are so plentiful, there's no stopping me from belly flopping out of the cozy confines of our boat. Yes, it's utterly cold for about ten seconds, but it warms up quickly thanks to ultra-thick 0.3-inch (7-millimetre) wetsuits.

Once in the water, it's all about waiting to see if these curious creatures want to pay you a visit. Some snorkellers report being so close they could see the scratches etched from the ice on the belugas' backs. Our day was murky, but we were still able to make out their outline, kind of like a ghost whooshing by. Even if you can't distinctly make them out, you'll know they're close when you feel their air bubbles against your face or hear their heart-melting underwater squeals and buzzes. Snorkelling is available for children twelve years of age and older. Be sure to check out the river's live beluga cam at explore.org.

PRINCE OF WALES FORT

Built by the Hudson's Bay Company between 1732 and 1782 to protect their vital trade of beaver pelts with the First Nations, this fort is tops for families to explore. Arrive via the *Sea North II*, a custom-built Arctic boat; you'll likely come across pods of belugas en route.

A Parks Canada guide bearing arms will escort you from the dock to the fort, as this stretch of land is frequented by those carnivorous locals who blend in with the white rocks. Roughly forty of the original hand-cast cannons are still placed around the premises, and children are given free reign to climb over them and perform reenactments. In the summer months, you'll often find researchers excavating the site, and they're more than happy to show off their finds, such as quills and bits of pottery, with you.

TOWN CENTRE COMPLEX

Can you imagine what life in a town of 700 inhabitants must be like during dark winter months? Fortunately, the Town Centre Complex offers a respite from cabin fever. Open to tourists and well loved by locals, this massive building gives an insider's glimpse into life in the North. Housed under the same roof you'll find the school, library, movie theatre, bowling lane, swimming pool, gym, hospital, and community centre. Best for families is the abundance of indoor playground equipment, including dozens of plasma cars. Not every northern community is this lucky. It's the only facility of its kind in Canada.

ITSANITAQ MUSEUM

Formerly known as the Eskimo Museum, this must-see attraction for understanding life in the North is a treasure trove of some of the oldest and best preserved Inuit carvings and artifacts in the world. See just how massive a grey wolf truly is, and check out the 1,500-pound (680-kilogram) walrus, 800-pound (363-kilogram) polar bear, and 1,200-pound (544-kilogram) muskox. The museum is also one of the best spots in town to purchase books on Canada's North and soapstone carvings.

🌐 GOOD TO KNOW ───────────────────

Pack lots of layers and waterproof gear. Even during the summer months, you'll wish you had a warm hat and gloves if the sun sneaks behind the clouds.

Beluga activities in Churchill are dependent on weather conditions, and scheduling is dictated by tides. Not to worry: tour operators are in close contact with one another and the hotels where their guests stay. They'll do their best to rejig your schedule so you can pack it all in. The season runs from mid-June until late August.

 TASTE ────────────────────────────────

Treat yourself to amazing baked goods at **Gypsies**, one of the most popular restaurants in town (and the only bakery). The atmosphere in this Portuguese, family-run deli is jovial, and their famous fritters can't be missed.

If you're looking for wild game and northern dishes, consider this your hint to dine at the **Tundra Inn Dining Room**. You'll find hearty entrées such as venison, elk, caribou, and bison, but their tasty veggie Borealis Burger has been known to convert many a meat eater.

A pleasant dining experience can also be had at **Lazy Bear Lodge**, an aesthetically pleasing, hand-built, log-cabin-style lodge and restaurant. Tuck into sirloin muskox roulade, or caribou pepper steak.

Bear in mind that because you're in the North, prices for importing food are steep. With no road south, all products arrive by rail or air. Many hotel rooms offer full kitchens, and you'll save money toting your favourite snacks in your suitcase and supplementing with a trip to the grocery store.

NAP ────────────────────────────────

You'll feel right at home at **Polar Inn and Suites**. The rooms aren't fancy (they know you'll be trudging in with muddy gear), but they are comfortable. Owner Louise Allen is like a second mother, making sure you're bundled up appropriately and foisting her freshly baked muffins on you. Rooms are kitted out with full kitchens, and a continental breakfast is included.

GETTING AROUND

Flights to Churchill can be pricey—this is one destination worth cashing in your Air Miles points for.

Many families like the option of taking the train to Churchill on **VIA Rail**. While it's a lovely journey, be sure to expect train delays, and budget that extra time (perhaps days) into your schedule. You can use Air Miles for VIA Rail tickets, too.

 FUN FACTS

- **Belugas** are known as sea canaries because of their strange, high-pitched whistles, clicking, chirping, and other underwater vocalizations. You can listen in on their conversation thanks to the hydrophones carried by most water excursion operators.
- Rumour has it that it's illegal to lock car and building doors in Churchill, so everyone has an escape route should they encounter a polar bear in town. While it's actually not illegal, it is a code most residents abide by.
- An estimated 900 to 1,000 polar bears populate the Western Hudson Bay, as do approximately 3,000 beluga whales.
- Churchill was not named after the famous British prime minister Winston Churchill. The town was named after John Churchill, the third governor of the Hudson's Bay Company and the Duke of Marlborough. It so happens that Winston Churchill was a direct descendent of John Churchill.
- **Fort Churchill** was once the largest joint Canadian/American military base. Until it closed in 1979, the fort was used for cold weather testing of weapons and equipment.

GET EXCITED ABOUT YOUR TRIP

- Read *Polar Bear Dreams* and other wildlife children's books by Daniel D'Auria.
- *Winston of Churchill* is a cute storybook by Jean Davies Okimoto, for children aged three to eight years.
- Watch the PG-rated movie *The Journey Home*, about a teenage boy willing to risk his life to save a polar bear cub.

Meet animatronic prehistoric creatures at Dinosaurs Alive inside Canada's Wonderland.

Chelsea Beach at Centre Island boasts a blue flag rating.

Toronto

Multicultural World-Class City

Touring Canada's largest city can be a big hit with both younger and older children—if you choose your attractions wisely and don't plan on covering too much ground in one day. Toronto is internationally recognized as one of the world's most multicultural cities. Over 140 languages are spoken in this teeming metropolis, allowing families a rare opportunity to explore several different cultures within a few blocks. Each neighbourhood has a pulse of its own, and there's always something stimulating going on. Whether you're looking for the cultural escapades a big city affords, a chilled-out day at the lake, a spine-tingling theme park ride, or a major sporting event, you're sure to find what you're looking for in Hogtown.

RIPLEY'S AQUARIUM OF CANADA

If you've ever wondered what lurks beneath the surface of Canada's Great Lakes and the oceans surrounding our country, then consider this your cue to dive into this underwater world. Canada's largest indoor aquarium has seventeen curated habitats that highlight the diversity of the world's oceans and lakes. Journey along a moving walkway beneath the all-glass Dangerous Lagoon, where stingrays float above you and sand tiger sharks show off their menacing teeth. Highlights also include a touch tank, indoor play set, and crawling through a glass tunnel as sharks swim around you. If you're on social media, you'll want to share the slow, methodical dance of the ethereal sea jellies performed inside their beautifully illuminated tank.

When planning to go to the aquarium, remember that it can get quite busy during school holidays; you may want to consider making this an after-dinner activity since they're open late.

TORONTO ZOO

There aren't many animals you won't see on a trip to the Toronto Zoo. Wandering through regions that span from one edge of the globe to the other, you'll spot penguins, pandas, and even a polar bear. Or how about a gorilla, lion, or lynx? They're all here, plus 5,000 other animals from more than 460 species, inside this 710-acre (287-hectare) park. When you need a break (and you will), trot over to the Discovery Zone. Here you'll find a children's zoo, animal demonstrations, and Splash Island, a delightful spray park with mini water slides and animal figures spouting water—be sure to pack a bathing suit and towel for wee ones.

ART GALLERY OF ONTARIO

Chock-full of over 80,000 works of art spanning from 100 AD to the present, not only is the AGO one of North America's largest art museums—it was revitalized and expanded by legendary architect Frank Gehry. To make your visit more engaging, be sure to download their Time Tremors app before you arrive. The app encourages children ages seven and up to explore the galleries on an interactive treasure hunt.

Inside the Kids' Gallery, children encounter paintings, sculptures, and photographs within specially curated exhibits that rotate throughout the year. There's a dress-up station that allows children to become living works of art while posing behind a super-big frame, and there are colourful storybooks and materials on hand to help them unleash their creativity. Hungry? Families can nosh on seasonal fare made with all-natural ingredients at caféAGO, where tots five years and younger eat for free (though this offer is only available with an AGO membership).

ROYAL ONTARIO MUSEUM

From a massive T-Rex to a bat cave to a 100-million-year-old amethyst, ROM is another museum that opens minds and invites conversation. Hands-on displays give children a chance to investigate

You'll be surrounded by sharks as they swim inside the Dangerous Lagoon at Ripley's Aquarium of Canada.

Prepare to get very wet at Splash Works inside Canada's Wonderland.

It's one thrilling ride after the next at Canada's Wonderland.

Dive bomb into the pool at the Chelsea Hotel or barrel down their waterslide.

It's rare to find a kids' club at a city hotel, but there's one at the Chelsea Hotel.

treasures from around the globe, and artifacts in the Roman and Egyptian galleries are sure to wow, especially the partially decomposed mummy circa 600 BC. There are even animal mummies, in addition to richly decorated tombs and elaborate mummy masks.

The Discovery Zone is set up just for kids. Dress Henry VIII in his armour (or try some on yourself), play in a tipi, or guess by touch which meteorites are oldest. Preschoolers will have a blast gently sweeping away sand (and a lot of glitter) with a paint brush to uncover fossils, just like real archeologists. Those with very young children will appreciate the enclosed toddler play area with seating for caregivers.

Something to keep in mind: if you're looking for the perfect souvenir or gift, museum gift shops have many creative and unique offerings, so check out the ROM Boutique.

CN TOWER

The city's most iconic structure, the CN Tower, was once the tallest freestanding structure in the world. It isn't any longer, but the views are still spectacular—unless it's foggy, which is often the case being mere blocks from Lake Ontario. If you've got the nerve, stand on the terrifying glass floor and peer 1,122 feet (342 metres) straight down. These views aren't cheap, though, so if it's not a clear day, you might want to give this a miss and save some cash.

THEME PARKS

If your brood needs to burn off some energy, a visit to Canada's Wonderland, a 300-acre (121-hectare) adventure park, could be just the ticket. Both wet and dry experiences are available (for the price of one), so plan to spend an entire day here. Big kids will want to battle Leviathan, Canada's longest wooden coaster, while the younger set can enjoy milder thrills inside KidZville. At the water park, there are tube rides, carpet rides, a lazy river, and a wave pool. Wee ones can plunge into the kiddie pool, splash pad, and gentle water slides inside Splash Island. As with most theme parks, the food options aren't overly healthy or cheap. There are Dairy Queen and Tim Hortons kiosks within the park, but many families pack a cooler and picnic on the grassy area beside the parking lot. Remember to get your re-entry stamp before exiting.

It's nowhere near the size of other LEGOLANDs, but if your child is a major fan, it's worth visiting LEGOLAND Discovery Centre Toronto. This indoor play space is situated inside Vaughan Mills Mall, and is best suited for children aged three to ten years. Besides impressive model displays and a quick factory tour, there's a LEGO Racers build-and-test zone, plus loads of opportunities to create and build. The 4D Cinema plays several mini-movies each hour, allowing everyone a rest.

Neshama Playground is Canada's first accessible playground designed for all children to enjoy, and is specifically inclusive for those with special needs. Situated in Oriole Park, this playground offers a wide variety of equipment, including Braille panels, sensory toys for children with autism, and swings for kids in wheelchairs. A splash pad is open in the summer months and, for safety's sake, many features are enclosed.

TORONTO ISLANDS

A refreshing respite from the hustle and bustle of the big city, the Toronto Islands are an archipelago of fifteen islands in Lake Ontario, located just 1 mile (1.6 kilometres) south of the downtown core. Lush with both rugged and groomed green space, the islands are a sweet sanctuary with miles of park land, sandy beaches, and arguably the best views of Toronto's jagged skyline.

If you're travelling with kids under eight years old, check out Centreville, a 14-acre (6-hectare) amusement park designed to look like a turn-of-the-century Ontario village. (If your child is still into bouncy castles, they'll love it; if they've outgrown that stage, they might find it too babyish.) With over thirty rides and attractions, you can bet wee ones won't want to leave this perfectly proportioned park. What's great about this midway is that it suits the ability levels of even the smallest guests. There's a "light" roller coaster, and one of those log flume water rides that splashes everyone at the end, but with a drop that isn't terrifyingly steep. Break out the hand sanitizer—there's also a petting farm with over forty different species of farmyard animals and exotic birds.

Got a buccaneer in your brood? If so, take your scallywag to Pirate Life, an interactive family theatre and adventure cruise. Mates of all ages get decked out à la Captain Jack Sparrow and sail aboard a pirate ship in search of sunken treasure.

Step away from the action by renting bikes and cruising along the little trails that weave their way across Centre Island. There are playgrounds to stop at, art installations to suss out, and several restaurants to try (though most are quite touristy, so either pack a picnic or hit up Rectory Café for a delightful meal). If you brought your frisbee, you're in luck! There's even a disc golf course.

While there are a few beaches to choose from, Chelsea Beach is tops for kids. This is a lifeguard-patrolled beach with several picnic tables and a swing set. Large boulders make a natural boundary to keep your swimmers in view. What's most notable, however, is its blue flag rating, an international eco-label awarded to beaches for excellence in water quality. Heads up: there's also a clothing-optional beach, but it's tucked away on the west end of Centre Island, so there's little chance you'll run into a show.

When planning your visit to the Toronto Islands, keep in mind that they can get crowded, especially in summertime. Plan to visit early, and pack lots of provisions (food, bathing suits, frisbee) so you're able to make the most of your visit.

🍴 TASTE

Explore the city's diverse culture by taking your stomach on a tour. Do as locals do: pick a direction, choose a cuisine, and go on an adventure. **Chinatown** is an affordable, vibrant experience with exotic smells. Picture menus are plastered on many restaurant windows to help you decode what's on offer. **Gerrard India Bazaar**, **Kensington Market**, and **St. Lawrence Market** are vibrant food destinations that make it easy to sample a variety of the cuisines that make up Canada's diverse multicultural mosaic. The quintessential Toronto treat is a peameal bacon sammy (try one at the St. Lawrence Market's **Carousel Bakery**), and you ought to sample an ooey-gooey butter tart, too.

NAP

Aloft Vaughan Mills is conveniently located across the street from LEGOLAND Discovery Centre Toronto and is within walking distance of Canada's Wonderland. Though sleek and contemporary, there's enough room for a family of four to sling suitcases around an average-sized guest room. There are grab-and-go options in the lobby (and mini-fridges in each room), and the Vaughan Mills Mall food court is across the street. Complimentary parking, bottled water, and WiFi make it easy on the wallet.

Situated downtown, **Chelsea Hotel** caters to families just as much as they do their corporate clients. The experience begins at check-in when children receive an age-specific welcome gift after saddling up to their own check-in counter. Every Friday and Saturday in summer, and all through March break, there's a carnival atmosphere, with free popcorn, a movie, and tiny tot chairs set up just off the lobby. Action heroes, buskers, and even a robot chat up guests during check-in.

The indoor pool has a 130-foot (40-metre) corkscrew water slide, plus there's a Family Fun Zone that's home to two bunnies! Older kids can play old-school video games in the Teen Lounge, and babysitting services are available for children aged two to twelve. In the women's pool change room you'll find coin-operated washers and dryers. Their Market Garden has several different food stations serving up everything from grilled entrées to salads to kids' favourites. Portions are large, and children six years and younger eat for free off the children's menu, while kids aged seven to twelve years eat off the regular menu for half price.

GETTING AROUND

Get your bearings and have some fun by taking a ride on one of those red double-decker sightseeing buses. Yes, it sounds cheesy and looks super touristy, but **City Sightseeing Toronto** stops at all the major attractions, allowing you to hop on and off to your heart's content (plus kids totally dig the double-decker thing). The ticket is valid for three days and includes a Toronto Islands cruise.

This is one city where you don't need to avoid the subway. The **TTC** is fast, efficient, and free for children under twelve. **Go Transit** trains serve the Greater Toronto and Hamilton area and can even get you to Niagara Falls on summer weekends. From the airport, trains depart every fifteen minutes on the **Union Pearson Express**. This air-rail link whisks you from **Toronto Pearson International Airport** to **Union Station** within twenty-five minutes. Children twelve years and younger ride for free.

 FUN FACTS ─────────────────────────────

- Toronto is Canada's largest city. Greater Toronto has a population of over 6 million.
- More than thirty percent of Toronto residents speak a language other than English or French at home.
- According to the *Guinness Book of World Records*, **Yonge Street** is the longest street in the world, stretching 1,178 miles (1,896 kilometres).
- **Toronto Island** lies on top of a 900-acre (364-hectare) floating sandbag!
- A 31-storey office building can fit inside **Rogers Centre** (home of the Toronto Blue Jays baseball team) when the roof is closed.

GET EXCITED ABOUT YOUR TRIP ─────────────────────

- Read *A Big City ABC*, by Allan Moak, and *Good Night Toronto*, by Adam Gamble.
- Many movies have been filmed in Toronto, including *A Christmas Story*, *X-Men*, and *Cheaper by the Dozen 2*.
- Listen to Drake, Blue Rodeo, Gordon Lightfoot, Barenaked Ladies, and The Weeknd—all famous music artists from the Toronto area.

Nighttime fireworks take place several times a week directly over the falls.

It's selfie time during Voyage to the Falls with Hornblower Niagara Cruises.

Niagara Falls

Dramatic Nature

It's hard to describe the thunder and wonder of Niagara Falls. How can one be anything other than awestruck when realizing that twenty percent of the world's freshwater cascades into the Niagara Gorge? Yet there's more to the falls than the immensity of their size and the roar of the water: there's also the whisper of the water's crystalline spray. I was a full two blocks away, not even within view, when I thought I was being pelted by rain droplets. At first I was confused; it was, after all, a cloudless, sunny day. When I realized what it actually was, it dawned on me just how magnificent and powerful this waterfall is. And then, of course, there's the rumble that only increases in volume the closer you get. Well before you lay eyes on the falls, you'll feel their mighty presence in the mist and in the deep vibration of sound.

ACCESSIBILITY VERSUS AFFORDABILITY

A visit to Niagara Falls is an easy day trip from Toronto, and, even better, it's pretty much free. Sure, there are plenty of excursions you can pony up for, and many of them allow you to experience the falls in a variety of different ways. But the great thing is that without paying admission, anybody can walk right up to (and I mean *frighteningly* close to) the railing that separates visitors from the brink and the beauty of the falls.

Though the falls are indeed spectacular, the surrounding environment might begin to bug. If you don't love Boxing Day shopping and get frustrated navigating crowds, it's best to stay away during summer weekends. This is Canada's top tourist attraction, receiving over 10 million visitors a year, with the majority visiting in July and August. From steep parking rates to tacky souvenir shops to pricey chain restaurants, it can be hard for budget-conscious families to find their way in this touristy town—challenging, yet not impossible.

Despite the crowds, viewing one of the seven natural wonders of the world is definitely worthwhile. Yes, the town is loud and often overrun with tourists, but if you know what you're in for, it takes the sting out of it. If you're the sort of family that likes to pack a lot in, you're sure to find value in the Niagara Falls Wonder Pass or Adventure Pass; both provide opportunities to experience the falls from a variety of unique angles.

HORNBLOWER NIAGARA CRUISES

If you're going to splurge on one thing when visiting Niagara Falls, this is it. Venturing into the heart of the Niagara Great Gorge is pretty incredible, and you'll likely kick yourself if you don't step aboard one of these two purpose-built catamaran boats aptly named *Niagara Wonder* and *Niagara Thunder*. Operated by Hornblower Cruises, the 700-seat tour boats take you as close as possible into the basin. Sailing past American Falls, Bridal Veil Falls, and into the heart of the infamous Horseshoe Falls gives you the opportunity to get up close and personal with the famed waterfalls in a way that wasn't feasible until these boats came into existence. The rhythmic pounding of the water as it gushes into the basin, the corresponding spray that drenches you—it's all utterly thrilling, and the kids will talk about it for ages. Wear waterproof mascara, moms!

NIAGARA'S FURY

Prepare to get wet in this sensory experience that tells the story of the falls' creation from the last Ice Age. Visitors step into a chamber encircled by a 360-degree screen and begin the journey, complete with temperature drops, a simulated blizzard, and, yes, plenty of water to douse you. Fortunately rain ponchos are handed out before the show begins, but wearing them is up to you. Kids are kept engaged by an animated beaver narrating this natural history phenomenon, and with all the bells and whistles, they won't even notice that they're getting an educational experience.

You'll get soaked by the spray if you don't wear your complimentary rain slicker at Journey Behind the Falls.

Escape the hustle and bustle of the touristy areas with a peaceful jaunt along the White Water Walk.

Thousands of tropical butterflies float freely inside the Niagara Parks Butterfly Conservatory.

It's easy to see why Niagara Falls is one of the most visited tourist attractions in Canada.

JOURNEY BEHIND THE FALLS

Of all the ways families can take in the falls, Journey Behind the Falls (located in the Table Rock Welcome Centre) was our favourite. At first glance, this adventure doesn't seem like much, but don't underestimate what's in store: Let the elevator whisk you 150 feet (45 metres) down a shaft carved through bedrock over a century ago. Once the elevator deposits you at the foot of several tunnels that lead one-third of the way behind the mighty Horseshoe Falls, you'll know that you're in for an adventure.

The waterfall begins 13 storeys above where you now stand, and there are viewing platforms along which you can take in these massive sheets of water as they tumble down over 2,138 square feet (2,800 cubic metres) every second, travelling 40 miles (65 kilometres) per hour! How did the Niagara Parks Commission cut into this rock? What was it like to take a tour with a lantern-carrying guide in the late 1880s? Were those families as awestruck then as we are today? Many questions percolated in my mind as we ventured farther behind the falls. Soon, my curiosity was satisfied: the history of how this attraction came into being is displayed on exhibits that line the cavernous walls.

FLOWER POWER

The falls aren't the only impressive bit of nature found in this lush pocket of Ontario. The region is also considered the daffodil capital of North America. Each year Niagara Parks plants over 30,000 daffodils. As the bulbs have naturalized, it's estimated that there are now millions of sunny blooms—best viewed in spring—throughout the park.

If you've chosen to wade through the amusements along Clifton Hill's World Famous Street of Fun, refresh your senses by surrounding yourself with the cornucopia of stunning flowers, shrubs, and trees found at Niagara Parks Botanical Gardens. Families can explore this serene setting comprised of beautifully maintained gardens, brick walkways, and ponds set over 99 acres (40 hectares).

If the kids are hyped up, make a beeline for the Butterfly Conservatory. Here, they're sure to calm down within a matter of minutes as they meander through the rainforest-like setting. Hundreds of colourful butterflies dance in the air, and are apt to take a fancy to one of your lot, landing right on their shirt, hands, or hair. Along the self-guided walking tour, you'll come across over 2,000 butterflies, made up of forty-five different species, floating freely in this enchanting space. Exotic, tropical greenery and flowers line the paths that wind past a pond and waterfall. Be sure to hand the kids a camera to record their experience.

WHITE WATER WALK

This refreshing walk is the perfect change of pace on a sweltering summer's day. At 1,000 feet or a ¼ mile (305 metres), the boardwalk that runs along the rapids isn't long, and is suitable for grandparents, toddlers, and strollers. The path leads to two observation areas at the edge of the river and is strewn with lots of interesting factoids along the way. It's incredible to witness how fast the water surges through the Whirlpool Rapids. The Class 6 rapids combined with the cool breezes that float off the water will rejuvenate all who take this walk.

WORTHY SIDE TRIP

Considered one of Canada's prettiest towns, Niagara-on-the-Lake is as historic as it is charming. A haven for British loyalists fleeing the United States during the American Revolution, the town was named the first capital of Upper Canada (now the province of Ontario), and was razed to the ground during the War of 1812 by American forces.

The Olde Angel Inn is steeped in history and welcomes families in both their English-style pub and the dining room. The pub is atmospheric, with low ceilings and exposed hand-hewn beams reclaimed from the fire of 1812. Plenty of paranormal activity has been reported here, and if you're into ghost stories, book into one of the five guest rooms. At a minimum, you're sure to soak up some history and interesting vibes if you drop in for a bite. Children who aren't easily spooked can get a spine-tingling taste of the town while on a ghost walk that traipses through the old town.

Across the street from the Olde Angel Inn, the Old Niagara Bookshop on Regent Street is a worthy stop, and you'll want to take a stroll down Queen Street, stopping into the many boutiques, heritage buildings, and outdoor patios. Pause for an ice cream or pick up traditional English treats like Eccles cakes, sausage rolls, and a vast selection of butter tarts at Niagara Home Bakery. Take your provisions to one of the many leafy green parks in town. Simcoe Park is within walking distance of the old town and has a wading pool. Queen's Royal Park juts up against Lake Ontario, and you can spend considerable time here skipping stones or wading in.

🍴 TASTE

Niagara Falls is chock-a-block with chain restaurants. If you're looking for a light bite, there's a **Tim Hortons** across the street from Horseshoe Falls. For a memorable meal, avoid the chains and set yourself up with a view over the falls at **Elements on the Falls**. Given its sublime location, this could very well be a hyper-touristy restaurant, but surprisingly it's not. Certified by Feast On (a criteria-based culinary program where restaurants are required to procure Ontario food and drink whenever possible), this restaurant offers not only the best views but also fresh and local tastes, even on the children's menu.

Many of the parking lots near the falls are flanked by vast green spaces, making picnics a wonderful option. You'll spot many families hauling out their coolers and settling down for a few hours, while the kids run laps or watch impromptu cricket games on the green. If you make it to Niagara-on-the-Lake, be sure to pick up fresh produce at one of the many farm fruit stands dotted along the roads.

🛏 NAP

Niagara Falls makes for a great day trip from Toronto. Sure, your day will be long, but if it means saving $500 on food and lodging it may be worth the bleary eyes. Depending on what time of year you visit, hotels could be out of range for the average family. Those that are within budget might be populated by young adults keen to blow off steam. (There were no less than three stag parties being hosted at the motel we stayed at one summer weekend.)

One exception to this is the **Americana Hotel**. It boasts an indoor water park, organized family activities, and some of the best room rates in town.

If you're keen to stay within walking distance of the falls, consider splurging on one of the three hotels connected to the Fallsview Indoor Waterpark: **Sheraton on the Falls**, **Crowne Plaza Niagara Falls**, or **Skyline Hotel & Waterpark**. Naturally, the tricked-out water park will tire out the kiddies, but if you're lucky enough to score a room facing the falls, the nighttime illumination is the perfect prelude to dreamland.

A short drive away from the falls, **Great Wolf Lodge** was built with families in mind. The all-suite property offers a variety of room styles—many of which are themed, with a miniature log cabin nook built right into the room. Kitted out with bunk beds and a TV just for kids, it's the ultimate sleepover space. Dining options range from sit down to buffet to grab and go. This is a place where you won't want for high chairs or any other baby and toddler accessories. To keep the kids entertained there's a game room, an ice cream–themed spa designed for little divas, plus supervised children's activities. Your biggest challenge could very well be deciding what to hit first: the massive indoor water park or the child-friendly bowling alley? For Mom and Dad, there's a twenty-four-hour fitness centre and a spa, but you may be too tuckered out to partake in any "me" time.

GETTING AROUND

Niagara Falls is an easy day trip from Toronto, especially if visiting during the summer months. **VIA Rail** offers several departures each day, as do **GO Transit** train and bus services from several city locations. **WEGO** is a year-round bus transportation system that connects Niagara Parks attractions to your hotel and other tourist areas in Niagara Falls. Two days of hop-on, hop-off WEGO transportation is included with every Niagara Falls Wonder Pass and Adventure Pass.

Zoom Leisure Bike Rentals has three locations in the Niagara region, and offers a variety of bikes to rent (including children's bikes, tandems, baby trailers, and trail-a-bikes). Strike out on your own or opt for a customized bike tour of the area.

FUN FACTS

- There isn't just one Niagara Falls waterfall. Three separate waterfalls make up Niagara Falls: **Canadian Horseshoe Falls**, **American Falls**, and **Bridal Veil Falls**.
- Niagara Falls is one of the most well-known waterfalls on the planet, though it isn't the tallest or the widest waterfall in the world. The Canadian Horseshoe Falls, however, is the most powerful waterfall by volume in North America.
- The falls are the site of many daredevil activities. Many people have died as a result of attempting to go over the falls. In 1859, the first tight-rope walker successfully crossed Niagara Falls. More recently, in 2012, **Nik Wallenda** was the first person in 116 years to cross the falls. He was required to carry his passport and presented it upon entry to the Canadian side of the waterfall.
- Niagara Falls has been known as the "Honeymoon Capital of the World" since the 1800s. The daughter of Aaron Burr, the third vice president of the United States, spent her honeymoon here in 1801. Three years later, Napoleon's brother Jérôme Bonaparte did the same with his new bride. Others keen to emulate the rich and famous quickly followed suit.
- Approximately 50,000 couples continue to honeymoon here each year, and if your family's up for some tackiness, it's not difficult to find a hotel that offers heart-shaped Jacuzzi tub suites.

GET EXCITED ABOUT YOUR TRIP

- Illustrated history books *ABACA Flows Over Niagara Falls*, by Timothy Butcher, and *Barreling Over Niagara Falls*, by Nancy Kelly Allen, make young children even more eager to visit.
- *The Niagara Falls Mystery* is a Boxcar Children classic suitable for young readers.
- *I Am Canada: A Call to Battle*, by Gillian Chan, transports readers ages ten to fourteen back to the War of 1812, and tells the story from the perspective of a thirteen-year-old.

Take in sweeping views of the Niagara Escarpment from the open-air gondola at Blue Mountain Resort.

After a day of outdoor adventure, the pool at the Westin Trillium House, Blue Mountain is waiting for you.

Blue Mountain

Accessible Outdoor Playground

From my vantage point atop the platform, the Blue Mountain Apex Bagjump doesn't seem so bad. Spread out in front of me is a delicate meadow flanked by a rich tapestry of trees. Yet looking down fills me with dread. A humungous air bag lays in wait, but I can't seem to garner the gumption required to free fall into it. Children as young as eight years old are diving off the deck, and I'm unable to take that leap of faith. "Wow! I think you're the only person who's failed three times in a row," declares my well-meaning husband, after I shamefully creep back down the stairs. Ah, the joys of family travel!

The Blue Mountains, a stunning section of the Niagara Escarpment, offer a four-season playground. Rising 1,000 feet (300 metres) above the ground and overlooking Georgian Bay, the region is a natural hub for nature-loving families. Only a two-hour drive north from Toronto, many city slickers flock to Blue Mountain in winter to blast the cold-weather blahs on Ontario's premier ski hill. It's easy to understand the draw, yet there is much for families to discover once the frost subsides. From soaring above the tree line to delving deep below the surface, the resort delivers plenty of possibilities for relaxation and outdoor adventures all year round.

BLUE MOUNTAIN VILLAGE

Begin your getaway meandering through the adorable village. It hits all the right buttons with a mix of family-friendly restaurants and shops dispensing toys, candy, and ice cream. After exploring the plaza, work those large motor skills at the outdoor playground, or opt for a leisurely kayak or paddleboat ride on Mill Pond.

You don't have to spend money to have fun here. There's an outdoor fountain that doubles as a spray park, and life-size games of chess and checkers are constantly in use. A few nights a week during the summer months, family movies are shown in the Village Plaza at dusk and there's frequently live music on the Village Stage. Since you're probably an early riser now that you're a parent, you might as well take advantage of the open-air yoga classes on the Mill Pond docks and give yourself a chance to get grounded before the day begins in earnest.

Though there are miles of sandy beaches and most resorts have their own pool, it's worth diving into Plunge! Aquatic Centre. This indoor water playground has slides and chutes set at just the right height for littles, an awesome rope swing, plus indoor and outdoor pools.

Despite so many options for being ridiculously active, Blue Mountain is also ideal for not doing much at all. Curl up and read a story on the massive Muskoka chair set on the edge of the pond, or let your gaze wander and see if you can spot a great blue heron. You'll have to watch your step along the boardwalk encircling the pond, though: tiny leopard frogs hippity hop themselves across the trail, and the kids will have a hoot trying to catch them. There are even more critters in the pond, best discovered by bringing a net to dip and collect marsh specimens.

BLUE MOUNTAIN RESORT BASE CAMP

A dizzying array of activities just beyond the village ensures families will be plum tuckered out by day's end. Besides the Apex Bagjump, which is more challenging than it appears, there's a climbing wall suitable for all ages, a low ropes course, and zip lines for children aged ten and older. A bit higher up, you'll come across a high ropes course and Mountaintop Segway Tours that thread through the wooded terrain.

The big draw, however, is the Ridge Runner Mountain Coaster. To avoid lineups, it's best to hit this first, even making your way over before it rolls out each morning. Barrelling down the long course

Treetop canopy walking and ziplining are available on the Eco Adventure Tour at Scenic Caves Nature Adventures.

Hop aboard Rocky the Train and view the lifesize wooden carvings at Scenic Caves Nature Adventures.

Mine for gemstones at the man-made tower at Scenic Caves Nature Adventures.

Explore the caverns and crevasses at Scenic Caves Nature Adventures.

You control the speed on the Ridge Runner Mountain Coaster.

under canopies of trees as the wind whips your hair proves not all adrenaline-inducing activities take place here in winter. Riders can control their own speed, making this coaster more palatable to the younger or nervous set.

For a natural high, hike the troops up the mountain itself. There are four different trails to choose from, each ranging in difficulty, yet all with sweeping views of the Niagara Escarpment. Budget approximately forty minutes along a beautifully manicured trail to get to the top. After admiring the views, reward yourself with a complimentary open-air gondola ride back down. If you're new to hiking, take advantage of the complimentary daily guided hikes offered by Columbia Sports in the Village Plaza.

Ontario's largest bike park is found at Blue Mountain. Mountain bikers have sixteen downhill runs to choose from, with challenging features for all skill levels. There are double-black runs, but it's a particularly good spot for beginners and those who've never tried the sport before.

If your kids like mini golf, they'll love Cascade Putting Course, an 18-hole, par-67 putting course complete with water hazards and bunkers. It's just like a full-size course, but on a smaller scale, making little hackers feel grown up. Adults don't mind it either, as the course is landscaped to take advantage of the region's natural surroundings with a limestone backdrop and panoramic views.

SCENIC CAVES NATURE ADVENTURES

A series of caves and lookout points formerly used by the First Nations has become an eco-attraction allowing families to uncover just what makes the Niagara Escarpment a UNESCO Biosphere Reserve. Located mere minutes away from Blue Mountain Resort, the Scenic Caves are part of a 450-million-year-old story, carved during the Ice Age. You'll even find the remnants of ancient seas and coral beds.

On self-guided tours, families can explore this labyrinth of caves and crevices—up to 70 feet (21 metres) deep—once inhabited by

Paleo-Indian hunters, First Nations peoples, explorer Samuel de Champlain, and the Jesuits. The first cave is a natural refrigerator thanks to the steady flow of cold air that keeps it at a constant temperature of 4°C (39 °F) in the summer months. Next, you'll descend into the ice cave—a crevasse so deep and cold that snow and ice often remain here through early summer.

From there, you'll meander along the trail to a series of lookouts with magnificent views of the picturesque countryside. Most fun for kids is watching their parents squeeze through Fat Man's Misery, a crevice that's only 14 inches (36 centimetres) wide in one section. Don't worry, folks, you can also go over the top. From there, it opens up into Fern Cavern, where exotic vegetation such as the unexpected maidenhair fern pokes through ancient slabs of limestone.

Step to the edge of these limestone cliffs to take in panoramic views of the valley, from the shimmering waters of Georgian Bay to Lake Huron to a cathedral of 200-year-old hardwoods. These red oak, sugar maple, birch, and white cedar specimens are some of the oldest trees east of the Rockies, with thick roots jutting out of the ground for children to scramble over. Keep your eyes peeled for birds' nests and bear hibernation caves, too.

After your trek, children can pan for mineral treasures. Children sift through gem bags with panning trays along a wooden sluiceway, experiencing firsthand what it's like to pan for gold. There's a major strike inside each bag, plus an ID card so they can identify the minerals discovered.

The attraction also features an electric train ride, an adventure playground, mini golf, and a pond where children can feed (but not fish) rainbow and speckled brook trout. For more spectacular views, stroll across one of Ontario's longest suspension bridges. Those over 70 pounds (32 kilograms) can tackle the aerial treetop walking course and zip lines. Head here in winter for cross-country skiing and peaceful snowshoeing.

Tips

- There's a concession stand and plenty of picnic tables onsite.
- Closed-toe shoes must be worn at all times.
- Strollers are only permitted in the playground and picnic area. Baby carriers are recommended when hiking in the caves, and can be borrowed at no charge.

BRILLIANT BEACHES

The first provincial park in Canada to be awarded blue flag designation, Wasaga Beach is a comfortable spot where families can shift gears and laze the day away. It's a thirty-minute drive from Blue Mountain Village. The water is clear and surprisingly warm, and a wide expanse of sand makes it a supreme spot for sandcastle building.

Stretching along the South Georgian Bay coast for 8.7 miles (14 kilometres), it's the longest freshwater beach in the world. A member of Ontario Provincial Parks, Wasaga Beach is part of a natural area that protects the natural wildlife habitat. If you're something of a birder, keep your eyes peeled for nesting shorebirds like the endangered piping plover, in addition to 200 other bird species. The beach is a day-use park that's been divided into eight areas, each with parking. Playgrounds are located at beaches 4 and 5, while a pet area is on beach 1.

Guests staying at any of the Blue Mountain resorts receive complimentary access to a private beach. Located a ten-minute drive along the shores of Georgian Bay, you'll find all the necessary services, from change rooms to complimentary children's sand toys to beach volleyball and croquet equipment. Find a shady spot and relax on a lounge chair, or get on the water with a rented kayak or stand up paddleboard. Courtesy shuttles run every hour from the village to the private beach.

WINTER FUN

For skiers, the vertical feet total at Blue Mountain isn't huge, but there are over forty trails ranging from beginner to double black diamond.

The ski resort offers a snow school, a tube park, and the Badlands Terrain Park—a popular spot with good features for freestylers.

Skating is delightful on Mill Pond, one of the largest outdoor rinks in the region. Rent snowshoes and explore picturesque trails, or go on a guided tour with Columbia Sports, offered during winter weekends. Sleigh rides and snowmobile tours are also on tap.

¶¶ TASTE

The Niagara Escarpment is the cornerstone of Ontario's greenbelt. The region is very much farm-to-fork, with a focus on sourcing from local producers. It's also one of Canada's largest apple-growing regions and home to the Red Prince, Canada's winter apple. Harvested in fall and cellared until January to let its sugars develop, this varietal is best eaten from January until mid-summer. An **Apple Pie Trail** guides visitors to over forty tasty stops that best showcase the scrumptious fruit. Pick up an Apple Pie Trail brochure, so you can plot your meals accordingly.

Worth sniffing out for its Chelsea buns and ribbon-worthy pies is **Thornbury Bakery Café**. Sit down for breakfast and lunch or take away. If anyone in your crew has food sensitivities, they are sure to find something to enjoy among Thornbury's selection of gluten-free, dairy-free, and egg-free products.

Locals like to lunch at **Ravenna Country Market**, a charming mercantile less than a twenty-minute drive away from Blue Mountain Resort. Kids can customize their own flatbread sandwiches, and foodies will love the abundance of gourmet toppings. Like many spots in the region, they're pretty proud of their homemade butter tarts. If you've never tasted theirs, be sure to let them know and your first one is on the house.

⬚¶ NAP

Westin Trillium House, Blue Mountain is the perfect bolthole for families. Kitchenettes or full kitchens are found in all of the rooms on the pet-friendly property. There's a heated outdoor pool as well as hot tubs, and the hotel has an indoor connection to Plunge!, the indoor water park.

An unsupervised toddler area is loaded with toddler and preschool toys, while the arcade games inside the games room tempt the older set. Private babysitting services for children of all ages can be arranged through the Kids at Blue Childcare Facility.

Set on the southern shores of Georgian Bay, **Craigleith Provincial Park** offers a variety of camping spots, some with laundry and shower facilities. There's a mix of electrical and non-electrical sites for tents and trailers. Area C is ideal for families, as it features a playground, a large playing field, horseshoe pits, and a volleyball court.

GETTING AROUND

It's approximately a two-hour drive from Toronto to Blue Mountain Village. **AUC** runs shuttle buses on a daily basis during the ski season from Toronto and Scarborough to Blue Mountain. **Greyhound** also buses to the resort.

FUN FACTS

- **The Chippewas of Rama First Nation** believed a thunderbird who controlled the weather lived in his nest on Blue Mountain.
- Before the 17th century, thousands of First Nations lived in villages along the Niagara Escarpment. One of the villages, known as **Ekarenniondi**, was located on the very site of Scenic Caves Nature Adventures.
- Ontario's provincial bird is the **common loon**; the **white trillium** is its symbolic flower, and the **eastern white pine** its tree.

GET EXCITED ABOUT YOUR TRIP

- *Lake Huron*, by Anne Ylvisaker, provides information for the K–Grade 3 set on early people, how the lake was formed, and how it's used today.
- Teenagers may enjoy the book *Bruce Trail: An Adventure Along the Niagara Escarpment*, by Rich and Sue Freeman.
- Watch *Great Canadian Parks: Bruce Peninsula National Park* or *Georgian Bay Islands National Park*, by Good Earth Productions. Short clips are free to view online, or you can purchase the full films through goodearthproductions.com.

Take in the Parliament Buildings along the Rideau Canal.

You'll be amazed how interesting kids find learning about Parliament to be—especially when stepping inside the Senate.

Ottawa
Charismatic Canadian Capital

Cruising around the capital feels oh-so patriotic. As if by cue, we glimpse the iconic Canadian Parliament Buildings the exact moment City Hall bells begin pealing, heralding the top of the hour (and, as we'd like to think, our arrival). But that's not all we timed just right: our visit is in spring, a full-blown sensory experience when hundreds of flowering trees are in blossom. We're here for the tulips, though, and like dutiful children, they're out to greet us, too.

Things have changed in the nation's capital since your junior high school field trip. While Ottawa's museums and green spaces alone are worth the trip, there's more to this city than government headquarters and cultural institutions. This is a city for water lovers, with options ranging from rip-roaring paddles to peaceful floats along the historic Rideau Canal.

Of course, when you're the pulse of the country's political scene, you have your fair share of events and attractions—especially in 2017, the 150th anniversary of Confederation. If you've never visited Canada's capital city, now is the time. And even if you've visited before, you'll want to get back for this momentous celebration.

MONUMENTAL MUSEUMS

As you'd expect from a national capital, the museums in Ottawa showcase the very best of Canadian art, culture, and natural resources. "Even if your kids say they hate museums, the ones in Ottawa are great for families," avows Laura Byrne Paquet, editor of OttawaRoadTrips.com.

Laura's right. Most museums in the capital region have exhibits and activities specifically designed for children, which makes soaking up snippets of history and culture infinitely more interesting. There's no dearth of options for culture vultures. If you think you'll be visiting three or more museums, save money by purchasing Canada's Capital Museums Passport. Pick it up at any of the participating museums (some are described below) or at the Capital Information Kiosk, located at 90 Wellington Street.

CANADIAN MUSEUM OF NATURE

Families can explore the entire country from one location with a visit to the Canadian Museum of Nature. As you journey into the world of Canadian flora and fauna, you'll come face-to-face with dinosaur fossils, mammals in recreated habitats, and a dazzling display of rocks and minerals from some of the oldest land formations on the planet. Head to the fossil gallery to learn more about the largest predator to ever have walked on the earth, or feel the fur of the polar bear, seal, and muskox inside the Mammal Gallery.

For size, check out the skeleton of a blue whale. For sound, discover just how noisy the ocean is by listening to recordings of marine mammals inside the Water Gallery. For tactile types, it's all hands on deck when children play inside the research ship, pretending to be captain and steering the vessel where she needs to go. Every weekend there are events geared towards families, and the museum operates a nice café, plus a dedicated nursing room.

CANADIAN MUSEUM OF HISTORY

With 1 million annual visitors, the Canadian Museum of History is the most popular museum in Canada, and for good reason: inside this architectural masterpiece lies the Canadian Children's Museum, brimming with colourful exhibits to encourage cross-cultural understanding. While it may be on the other side of the Ottawa River (and technically in Gatineau, Québec), it's so close to Parliament you'll want to include it on your Ottawa itinerary as it's a cinch to get to.

Begin your visit by wandering through the magnificent Grand Hall. Next, grab a passport book at the entry to the Children's

Meet *Maman* and other intriguing works of art at the National Gallery of Canada.

Who can say no to a game of hide-and-seek amid the totem poles at the Grand Hall in the Canadian Museum of History?

You don't need skates to enjoy the Rideau Canal National Historic Site in winter, but having them does make the experience a lot more fun.

Kids transform into queens and other theatrical roles inside the Canadian Children's Museum at the Canadian Museum of History.

Museum and stamp your way through the fun exhibits. Natural performers won't be able to resist giving impromptu performances in the mini theatre; the backstage dressing room overflows with costumes to enhance the entertainment.

Parents can take a rest inside a Bedouin tent while children play inside the nearby pyramid. There's a dedicated area for toddlers to enjoy a safe play that's filled with toys and games. Perhaps your crew would like to try their hand at dockyard work, using a crane to lift packages from the ship in the Port of Entry area. In the market place, children can try on Dutch clogs, arrange wooden toy tulips, and work a market. Need some quiet activities? Put on a shadow puppet show or sit on a Japanese tatami mat and fold origami.

NATIONAL GALLERY OF CANADA

When you're welcomed into any art space by a giant spider, you know it's going to be good. At the National Gallery of Canada, *Maman*, a ginormous spider sculpture, introduces children to the concept of contemporary art. After bidding Maman *bonjour*, head on in to view one of the largest collections of Canadian art in the world. The visually appealing paintings, unique in their splashes of colour and lumpy paint textures, by the Canadian Group of Seven is one collection not to miss. Also worth investigating is the Indigenous art, in particular the fantastic Inuit carvings made of stone, antler, whalebone, and sinew.

For families, the gallery is best visited whenever school is out (weekends, holidays, summer), because that's when Artissimo is running. This family program encourages art appreciation through scavenger hunts and art buddy tours with dolls that replicate figures found in paintings. In the Great Hall, there are crafts and costumes to dress up in on Artissimo days. Ask if you can complement your visit with one of their feely boxes, which allows children to match what they feel inside the box with the art they're viewing in the gallery.

VISIT PARLIAMENT

Do you feel it's your patriotic duty to tour Parliament when visiting the capital? Parliament Hill is the superstar of Ottawa's already impressive cityscape. Sitting atop the Hill and perched over the Ottawa River, our Parliament Buildings are spectacular gothic structures definitely worth sussing out. Visitors can roam the grounds (bring a frisbee), and sculptures of notable Canadians are peppered throughout the property.

Complimentary guided tours of Centre Block (home to the Senate, House of Commons, and Library of Parliament) take place daily. While this tour isn't specifically geared towards children (at least not those under twelve years old), it's something they'll remember for years to come.

During Centre Block tours, you'll learn who sits where in the House of Commons, plus what the role of the Speaker is. You can even contact your MP in advance to score free tickets to Question Period. Get a feel for history as you saunter by the official portraits of former prime ministers and Canadian monarchs in the cavernous Senate foyer. The Library of Parliament is interesting because it's one of the few structures that survived the 1916 fire, plus it houses over 600,000 books, which, if stacked up, would be twice as tall as Mount Everest!

A better bet for younger children is taking one of the self-guided tours. If you visit during the summer months, don't miss the Changing of the Guard ceremony that takes place each morning on the grounds. Also in summer, a light show set to words and music is projected onto the Parliament Buildings every evening. Both events are complimentary.

Tip

Centre Block tours are said to take between twenty to fifty minutes, depending on parliamentary activity. That estimated time doesn't factor in going through robust security, taking in views from Peace Tower, or visiting the Memorial Chamber and gift shop. If you want to do it all, budget a minimum of ninety minutes at Parliament.

TAKE TO THE WATER

The Rideau Canal is so much more than a fabulous surface to skate upon. Linking together lakes, rivers, and canals all the way from Kingston to Ottawa, it provides one of the most visible links to the past. Planned after the War of 1812 as a military supply and communications route, the canal has evolved from strategic to recreational use. This World Heritage Site (the only one in Ontario) can be explored by families keen to stroll, bike, or in-line skate along its wide, paved paths. Sneak in some history by paddling your way along the canal via the Voyageur Canoe Tour, which is run by Parks Canada from the Ottawa Locks.

Each winter the historic canal transforms into a 5-mile (7.8-kilometre) skating rink snaking its way from downtown to Dows Lake. According to Guinness World Records, the Rideau Canal Skateway is the world's largest naturally frozen skating rink. There are few things more quintessentially Canadian than gliding your way past iconic Canadian structures along this historic waterway.

A thirty-minute drive from the city is Calypso, the country's largest themed water park. Here you'll find 35 water slides, 100 water games, and a 52,000-square-foot (4,831-square-metre) wave pool. The Zoo Lagoon is where you'll want to take wee ones, while thrill seekers can plummet down the tallest freestanding water slide tower in North America. And don't miss Jungle Run, the floating river and water obstacle course. On-site are several restaurants and cabana suites to rent for the day.

Looking for a more natural way to ride the rapids? Adventurous families can challenge the swells and eddies of the Ottawa River on whitewater rafting day trips. Besides floating down the river, children can bodysurf the waves, go swimming, and get plenty wet when the foaming water curls up against the side of the boat. Several tour operators offer family paddles, though children must weigh a minimum of 50 pounds (23 kilograms).

WINTERLUDE

During the first three weekends in February, this celebration of all things snow and ice makes winter visits equally alluring. On the Gatineau side of the Ottawa River, Jacques-Cartier Park transforms into Snowflake Kingdom, reputed to be the largest snow playground in the world. Families can pedal go-carts on snow, barrel down an ice slide, and participate in a flurry of exhilarating icy activities. Downtown, Confederation Park morphs into Crystal Garden with dozens of dynamic ice sculptures made more dazzling thanks to special lighting. Naturally, the Rideau Canal is another hot spot with skate rentals available on-site and welcoming, cozy chalets to rest up in.

GREEN SPACES

To commemorate the 150th anniversary of Confederation, the City of Ottawa partnered with Sinking Ship Entertainment to build Canada's largest playground. Each of the country's provinces and territories will be represented with a unique play space inside the Canada-shaped playground at Mooney's Bay Park. Let's hope it breaks the record for the world's longest set of continuous monkey bars!

Take a time out and stroll around the stately grounds of Rideau Hall, the official residence of the Governor General. This tranquil environment is flush with sugar maples, red oaks, and ceremonial trees planted by visiting foreign dignitaries. See if you can spot those planted by John F. Kennedy, Nelson Mandela, or Queen Elizabeth II. There's also a play structure, and the Ceremonial Guard provides colourful entertainment during Relief of the Sentries, an hourly march performed in summertime. On weekend afternoons from January to March, families can skate on a historic rink and feel a million miles away from city life.

Tip

On Friday and Saturday afternoons in summer, Rideau Hall hosts Storytime in collaboration with Frontier College, a Canadian non-profit that promotes literacy. Families are invited into the reading tent to delve into dozens upon dozens of titles and participate in fun literacy activities. If you're lucky, your hosts might even be the Governor General and their partner.

Tiptoe through the tulips—all 1 million of them! There are over 100 flowerbeds providing a vibrant dose of colour throughout the capital region. Head to Commissioners Park by Dows Lake for the largest flowerbed, where a whopping 250,000 tulips of sixty different varieties bloom in springtime.

Why are there so many tulips in Ottawa? During WWII, Dutch princess Juliana of the Netherlands and her daughters lived in exile here. In 1945, the Netherlands sent 100,000 tulip bulbs as a postwar gift for the safekeeping of the royal family and to thank the Canadian soldiers who liberated their country. When Juliana became queen in 1948, she continued to send gifts of tulip bulbs by the thousands each year during her reign.

During the Canadian Tulip Festival, events are held throughout the city, and it's worth a wander through indoor Aberdeen Tulip Pavilion at Lansdowne Park. With loads of rope structures, climbing is the name of the game at the park's large playground. There are also huge blackboards for kids to scribble on and a small skateboard park for the elementary and preschool set.

A mere fifteen-minute drive north of the downtown core, Gatineau Park is laced with lakes, lookouts, and heritage features. Families can cruise along 20 miles (32.5 kilometres) of scenic parkways or hit the trails for biking, hiking, snowshoeing, or cross-country skiing. Flip to the Outaouais, Québec, chapter to find out more about this National Capital Region park.

The city's first park, Major's Hill Park, is an oasis amid the hustle and bustle of the capital's core. Map it out to take a breather between museums and the ByWard Market district. With winding pathways, plus a prime position overlooking the Ottawa River and the Parliament Buildings, it's the perfect spot for a stroll and family photos. From here, if you happen to walk along MacKenzie Avenue from the Fairmont Château Laurier, keep your eyes open for the Connaught Building. This impressive Tudor-Gothic pile is home to the Canada Revenue Agency. While kids may not see the irony of Canada's tax man residing in a castle-like building, you can bet your bottom dollar parents do.

FRIGHTFUL FUN

Tweens and teens who aren't easily spooked enjoy an eerie evening on a Haunted Walk of Ottawa tour. Led by lantern light, you'll weave your way in and out of the downtown core, where to this very day skeletons are still being dug up during construction works. Spooky locations include the Bytown Museum, a haunted high school, and spots along the Rideau Canal. Other options for the older set are the Ghosts and the Gallows walk or the Crime and Punishment Jail Tour, both of which run year round. During your chilling encounters, you'll uncover what living conditions were like at the old Carleton County Gaol—and what the consequences were if the wrong man was hanged.

BYWARD MARKET DISTRICT

One of the city's most historic neighbourhoods also happens to be one of its hippest. Laid out in 1826 by Royal Engineer Lieutenant-Colonel John By, the ByWard Market boasts wide streets populated by specialty food shops, restaurants, and boutiques. Inside the ByWard Market building are more shops and food stalls. Need Canadian-made souvenirs? Pick up jams, mustards, and other condiments from Canada in a Basket. After touring around, sneak into one of the ByWard's leafy courtyards and enjoy the quiet, as the market bustles beyond the stone walls.

The outdoor farmers' market runs year round, and with over 1,100 farms within Ottawa city limits, you're sure to find produce freshly picked within hours of your visit (May to October). While you shop, pay attention to the vendor signs. Green signifies a farmer/producer, yellow means they produce sixty percent of what they sell, and red denotes a reseller booth. One stall not to miss is Maple Country Sugar Bush, where you can buy affordable maple syrup and candy tapped from their maple farm.

🍴 TASTE

In the ByWard Market, **Zak's Diner** is famous for their milkshakes and all-day breakfasts, and the kids' menu caters to the under-ten set. At nearby **Tucker's Marketplace,** the line begins to form well before they open for dinner service at 5 p.m. The all-you-can-eat buffet has an attractive price point, especially when you factor in that children eight to twelve years old eat for half price, and those under eight years old pay a dollar for each year of their age. **The Grand** is a casual pizzeria also in the ByWard, where a kids' menu, high chairs, and half-price happy-hour pizzas tempt families during the week.

For a treat, take afternoon tea at **Zoe's** inside the Fairmont Château Laurier. Offered every day of the week, the Prince and Princess Tea is a sure winner with the option of tea or hot chocolate, plus scones, mini sandwiches, and cupcakes. Still need to satisfy a sweet tooth? **BeaverTails** originated in Ottawa in 1978. Shaped like the wide flat tail of a beaver, the fried pastry is topped with a myriad of sugary options such as maple syrup.

🛏 NAP

Built in the style of a 16th-century French château, **Fairmont Château Laurier** is all about location, location, location. It is just steps from Parliament, the Rideau Canal, the National Gallery, and the ByWard Market, so you won't need a car to get to most attractions. As you'd expect from a luxury landmark hotel, it's very grand, but families are welcome and have the option of connected rooms. Cribs are available upon request. Best is the large art-deco style pool, which children love parading down to in their child-sized bathrobes.

The **Ottawa Marriott** lures little ones with popcorn and candy stations in their lobby on weekends, plus a welcome gift for children. In addition to a pool, the hotel has a teen room with foosball and gaming devices, plus a Kids' Zone Playroom for younger kids.

GETTING AROUND

The **Aqua-Taxi** ferries families from the Ottawa dock to the Canadian Museum of History. This water taxi shuttle service is a refreshing way to get from A to B, while taking in the sights along the river. The service runs from mid-May to mid-October and is cash only.

Ottawa is a cyclist's dream. There are over 109 miles (175 kilometres) of paved paths crisscrossing the capital. During Sunday Bikedays (which run from mid-May until early September), Colonel By Drive along the Rideau Canal and other scenic roadways are closed to traffic. Score a rental near Parliament with **Rent-a-Bike** offering hybrids, city bikes, tandems, trail-a-bikes, and carriers, plus helmets and locks.

Get your bearings and save yourself the hassle of parking by taking a hop-on, hop-off **Gray Line Bus Tour**. The cheery red double-decker weaves its way past notable embassies and crosses the river into Québec, before driving along Sussex Drive. You'll spot the prime minister's residence and pass by other official residences in the posh neighbourhood of Rockcliffe. The tour makes pit stops at several museums, Rideau Hall, and the RCMP Musical Ride training grounds.

FUN FACTS

- Ottawa was chosen as the **capital of Canada** by Queen Victoria in 1857.
- 12 miles (19 kilometres) of the 126-mile (202-kilometre) **Rideau Canal** are man-made and were dug out by hand.
- Ottawa has more agricultural land within its city limits than any other city in Canada. Over 1,100 farms are located within its borders.
- **A new tulip** has been developed to commemorate the 150th anniversary of Confederation. Christened Canada 150, this elegant bloom with white petals and a red flame bears a striking resemblance to the Canadian flag. Bulbs can be purchased at Home Hardware, the exclusive retailer.

- *Who Runs This Country, Anyway? A Guide to Canadian Government*, by Joanne Stanbridge, takes a humorous approach when guiding readers through Canada's electoral and governing processes.
- *Love Is All Around Ottawa*, by Wendi Silvano and Joanna Czernichowska, is a heartwarming children's picture book that encourages families to tune into their surroundings.
- Fall visitors will want to snap up *A Halloween Scare in Ottawa*, by Eric James.

Test the ropes course at Arbraska Laflèche Park.

Outaouais

Invigorating Outdoor Adventures

O uta-what? Expect many friends to ask this after you disclose you're keen to visit this Québec region. "Ou-ta-way," you'll reply, smug that you know how to properly pronounce a *oui* bit of français. Hard to pronounce but easy to love, Outaouais is nestled against eastern Ontario, yet this region is much more than Gatineau. Invigorating Outaouais is bursting with robust outdoor activities, and because it's so close to the nation's capital, it enjoys big city pleasures, too. But that's likely not why you'll visit. This is a place to get comfortably close with some amazing North American animals and to reenergize in a tranquil, natural setting.

GATINEAU PARK

It's rare to have such close proximity to the great outdoors from a major metropolis. The National Capital Region's Conservation Park is a wide green belt that covers 140 square miles (361 square kilometres), stretching from where the Canadian Shield meets both the St. Lawrence Lowlands and the Ottawa River. It's only a fifteen-minute drive from Parliament Hill, and the park has many points of interest and diversions for families all year round.

One of the largest networks of winter trails in North America can be found here, and four of the starting points to over fifty trails can be accessed by public transport. Snowshoes can be rented from the Visitor Center in Chelsea. If you want to rent cross-country skis, simply stop into Greg Christie's Ski and Cycle Work in Chelsea.

Come summertime, you'll find lake beaches at both Philippe and Meech Lakes. Boating is a popular Canadian pastime, but there's no need to shell out for a vessel of your own, not when rentals are available at Philippe Lake and La Pêche Lake. King Mountain Trail affords stunning views of the Ottawa River Valley, and the just-under-1.2-mile (2-kilometre) trek is lined with lookouts and interpretation panels. Lusk Cave is another easy hike that's super interesting for kids. This one is a bit longer, but the 6-mile (10-kilometre) round trip to the marble cave should take you less than four hours to complete.

On summer Sundays, Gatineau, Champlain, and Fortune Lake parkways are closed to motor vehicles from 6 a.m. to 11 a.m., allowing families over 18 miles (30 kilometres) of streets to roam on bicycle. In particular, the section north of Chemin du Lac-Meech is tops for young cycling families, and bikes can be rented at Philippe Lake.

CANADIAN MUSEUM OF HISTORY

The most visited museum in the country documents over 20,000 years of human history. Don't worry, nobody's going to get bored here, not when admission grants you access to both the Canadian Children's Museum and a free IMAX Theatre show. With its impressive collection of totem poles, the Grand Hall is one of Canada's most spectacular indoor public spaces, with stunning views of Parliament Hill. Make sure to pay a visit to the First Peoples Hall to take in its impressive collection of artifacts showcasing the resourcefulness of Canada's First Nations, Métis, and Inuit peoples.

CANADIAN CHILDREN'S MUSEUM

Housed inside the Canadian Museum of History, this delightful treasury was designed to enhance children's understanding of arts, culture, and history. Going on an adventure is the name of the game as youngsters travel the world through interactive exhibits, stamping their passports along the way. Step inside a pyramid or board a richly decorated Pakistani bus; children will enthusiastically dive into these inquiry-based learning experiences.

Enjoy a dose of greenery inside Gatineau Park.

Visitors to Parc Oméga are allowed to feed carrots to the wildlife.

SO MUSH FUN

The pièce de résistance in Canadian outdoor adventure just might be found at Chiens Traîneaux Petite-Nation, where you can drive your own team of five huskies across the hilly Outaouais countryside. If you're looking for a gentle, flat ride inside a cozy sled, you're in the wrong place. (OK, OK, you have the option of sitting back and enjoying a comfy, scenic cruise, but where's the fun in that?) Driving the sled is mostly dependent upon weight, but usually children ten to twelve years of age are able to do so, while the younger set must ride seated.

Upon hearing *"on avant!"* (the French equivalent of "mush!"), dogs leap into action. Then it's up to you to navigate groomed snowmobile trails through unfamiliar woods at breakneck speed. As I pinned around tight corners, the words of my guide, Bruno, echoed through my head: "Whatever you do," he advised, "don't let go of the sled. Unless, of course, you're being dragged along by it."

I probably could've used a bit more advice, but this nugget of wisdom came in handy when the sled toppled over and I found myself being yanked on my belly through the backcountry. The dogs eventually broke free of the branches (and their driver), leaving me stranded. I found them a few minutes later waiting patiently and looking mockingly at their amateur driver. Should you face a similar fate, don't feel embarrassed about the number of times you fall and lose your team. Go ahead and give it another try, because as the expression goes, you always want to get right back up on that dog sled.

Visiting in summer? Training doesn't stop when the snow melts. Mushers exercise their team all year round. Learn how to harness and hook up a team of sled dogs with Timberland Tours Dog Sled Adventures before participating in dry land sprints inside a custom-made rig.

MONTEBELLO

Families looking for a restful rural retreat without sacrificing big-city pleasures would do well to consider Montebello. Situated halfway between Ottawa and Montreal, this charming village houses gourmet shops and glamping options. It's a good town to use as your base camp, as both Parc Oméga and Arbraska Laflèche Park are close by.

If you arrive hungry, the Fromagerie Montebello is an ideal place to stock up on snacks. Sampling cheeses like the creamy tête à Papineau will leave you wanting more, or maybe you'll prefer the cheese curds that are so fresh they squeak as you bite into them. Across the street, ChocoMotive is now located in Montebello's historic train station. Equal parts workshop, storefront, and museum, this economuseum and artisanal chocolatier welcomes chocoholics from around the world. When it comes to organic, fair-trade chocolates from high-quality Peruvian cocoa, pretty much everything is worth the calories, especially the local favourite, the Marie-Gourmande, which is filled with house-made caramel and hazelnut cream.

ARBRASKA LAFLÈCHE PARK

"Before we get started, I need to know if anyone here has a problem going into a contaminated cave," asked Marc-André Dorval, our charismatic guide at Arbraska Laflèche Park. Children's eyes light up while the adults laugh nervously, too afraid to speak up, lest we miss out on the opportunity to tour the largest natural cave in the Canadian Shield.

Fortunately, Dorval doesn't wait for an answer before explaining that the cave is home to little brown bats that have been infected with white-nose syndrome, a disease that's taken the lives of over 1 million bats. "Not to fear," assures Dorval, "the cave is perfectly safe. White-nose doesn't affect humans. We just don't want anyone spreading this disease from their boots to other caves." Somewhat relieved, we don helmets with headlights and trek underground to explore the crevices and frozen ice formations that permeate this historic cavern.

At Laflèche, you can have invigorating experiences that take you from the tops of trees to deep underground. Open year round, the cave is accessible to anyone over the age of five and isn't too daunting. In fact, local Boy Scout troops sleep here overnight. In the caving world it's still relatively undiscovered, and speleologists continue to uncover new passages. After clambering up the chimney (that's caving lingo for a steep, narrow climb) and crouching through low passageways, you'll marvel at the frozen stalactites and stalagmites, and can view firsthand those infamous hibernating bats.

Come springtime, touch the sky by scrambling over fifty-five suspended bridges and flying along zip lines, the shortest of which is 551 feet (168 metres) long. Children over the age of five can challenge themselves along the Children's Course. It takes about two hours for kids to maneuver their way along suspension bridges, ropes, ladders, and zip lines in this treetop adventure. Whether they tackle this miniature obstacle course or harness their powers of observation finding lost animals on the GPS Rally, they're sure to feel satisfaction after reaching their goals.

PARC OMÉGA

Close encounters of the fur kind are found at Parc Oméga, a vast wildlife refuge minutes away from Montebello. Animals such as elk, bison, wild turkey, wild boar, and several types of deer roam freely throughout the 2,200-acre (890-hectare) park of varied terrain. Visitors can drive along a 10-mile (17-kilometre) trail, past prairies, woods, and meadows, observing and even feeding some of the animals.

You'll want to bring or buy bags of carrots to feed the friendlier critters. Provisions can be picked up at Park House, and while you're there, ask if the Park Nursery has welcomed any new baby animals. Occasionally they take in baby foxes, deer, or raccoons whose lives are in danger, and guests have the opportunity to witness their progress.

As you cruise along the trail in your vehicle, animals with homing radars rush out to greet you. They know where their next meal is coming from! These cute creatures will flatter passengers with their attention; they're after—and usually get—your carrots. Be careful, though! They'll brazenly snatch treats from little hands, which is why Parc Oméga advises visitors to keep vehicle windows half closed.

Ditch the car and explore even more of the park on foot. Rest assured, the walking paths are protected, and only non-aggressive animals are in the area. With picnic tables and washroom facilities, it's a lovely spot for lunch. Just don't make your snack too appealing or more than ants will be after it.

From the end of June until Labour Day, you can walk the 1.8-mile (3-kilometre) trail to the Old Farm. This restored historical barn and farmhouse serves as a living history museum. Kids can interact with their favourite barnyard animals and peek inside the farmhouse for a view of historic rural life.

ADVENTURE ON THE BAYOU
It may not be the alligator-infested swampland one associates with the marshy outlets of the Southern US, but that matters not to families keen to explore the Ottawa River. Hour-long airboat adventures are offered by Bayou Outaouais, and give passengers an up-close-and-personal look at the distinct flora and fauna that inhabit these wetlands. Watch beavers at work and great blue herons swooping down for a snack as you whiz along the waterway in an air-propelled vessel.

SNOW DAYS
Edelweiss ski resort offers 160 acres (65 hectares) of skiable terrain with a vertical drop of 656 feet (200 metres). Night skiing is available every night of the week, and well over half the trails are lit. Take a break from skiing or snowboarding and zoom down the snowy hills of the tube park for a change of pace. As far as ski resorts go, this one is affordably priced, including their snow school rates.

TASTE

In Chelsea, **Les Fougères** offers a wonderful selection of pies, soups, and other pre-made meals. After a day spent outdoors, the home-style comfort food served at **Chelsea Pub** really hits the spot. From lunchtime until about 7 p.m., the family ambiance is in full swing amid a rustic interior.

Over the past two decades, Gatineau's **La Station** has attracted a loyal following. This family-friendly diner serves up three squares a day, plus affordable children's menu options.

NAP

There are three campgrounds located within **Gatineau Park** that offer over 300 semi-rustic campsites, as well as ten ready-to-camp units. Rest your head in the great outdoors—even in winter!—with a stay in either a four-season tent, yurt, or cabin; alternatively, you can opt for winter campsites if you have your own gear.

At **Parc Oméga**, you could sleep in a treehouse, yurt, or small log cabin from May to October. Bring your sleeping bags, pillows, and portable cots, and wake up with the animals.

Fairmont Le Château Montebello is a splurge-worthy stay for an authentic lodge experience. Not only does it have the largest indoor pool of any hotel complex in Canada, it also offers ice fishing and an indoor curling rink.

Kenauk Nature is more of a glamping destination than luxury hotel. Located on the largest private reserve in North America, this is the type of place where you can rent a cabin on private lake. All sixty-seven lakes on the 66,000-acre (26,700-hectare) property are stocked with bass and trout. With neither electricity nor WiFi, this is a place to visit only if you're serious about unwinding. Thanks to gas, you'll have full kitchen amenities and heat. Guests receive complimentary access to the amenities at Chateau Montebello, though once ensconced at Kenauk, you probably won't want to leave.

GETTING AROUND

If you fly into **Ottawa International Airport**, it's best to rent a vehicle from there. Gatineau, the main city of the Outaouais region, lies directly across the Ottawa River from Ottawa's Rockliffe Park. It's an hour's drive to Montebello from Ottawa, and it takes an hour and a half to reach Montebello from Montreal.

FUN FACTS

- **Félix-Gabriel-Marchand Bridge** is one of the longest covered bridges in Québec. Drive across this marvel in the Pontiac Region of Outaouais.
- **Fairmont Le Château Montebello** is considered to be the world's largest log building.
- Many people live in **Gatineau, Quebec**, the largest city in the Outaouais region, and go to work in another province. Ottawa, Ontario, lies just across the river from Gatineau, and the two are connected via the **Royal Alexandra Interprovincial Bridge**. In celebration of Canada's 150th, an interprovincial picnic will take place on the bridge on July 2, 2017.
- Quebec's provincial symbols are the **snowy owl**, the **blue flag iris**, the **yellow birch tree**, and of course, the **fleur-de-lis**.

GET EXCITED ABOUT YOUR TRIP

- *The Hockey Sweater*, by Roch Carrier, is a classic Canadian short story.
- Check out *The Sweater* on YouTube, narrated by Carrier.
- Watch *Great Canadian Rivers: Ottawa River*, by Good Earth Productions. Short clips are free to view online or you can purchase the full film through goodearthproductions.com.

Meet Bonhomme at the Québec Winter Carnival.

The Plains of Abraham is not only historical, but also a wonderful green space for families to recharge their batteries.

Québec City
A Historic City That Knows How to Celebrate Winter

"Would you like to play the baby foot game?" Julie Moffet asks. "It will warm you up," she promises, noticing my hesitation. I'm a bit chilly after being outside all day taking in the Québec Winter Carnival, so I put my trust in this local, whom I've just met.

It turns out to be a lost-in-translation moment, where "baby foot" equals "life-size human foosball." Still, it's as good a translation as any. Strapping ourselves to poles, we let the local kids show us how it's done. Trying to outwit the fancy footwork of preschoolers definitely warms the feet—and the heart.

The Québec Winter Carnival is one of the big draws to Québec City, but it's far from the only attraction. Founded in 1608, Québec City is the only walled city north of Mexico, and is a unique blend of First Nations, French, and British influences. The city has evolved to successfully capitalize on their assets, mainly winter and the great outdoors. A visit here packs a one-two punch as you'll net both a city and a nature break, and this party makes the most of it all.

QUÉBEC WINTER CARNIVAL

Held in the dead of winter to encourage people to gather together, the Québec Winter Carnival, or *Carnaval* in French, has snowballed into a major tourist event since its inception in 1962, now welcoming over 400,000 visitors a year. Lasting over three weekends, typically starting at the end of January, the seventeen-day festival embraces Canada's famously frosty season. "In Québec City, we don't just celebrate Christmas, we celebrate winter," says Steeve Gaudreault, local and guide. Shops and citizens keep their dazzling light displays up until after this festival, and everybody on the streets seems happy—joyous, even, if the number of revellers tooting red trumpets is any indication.

Everything you could want to experience in winter is concentrated in one place: the Plains of Abraham. This historic site morphs into a crystallized playground, where attendees dive mitt-first into a wide range of winter activities, from dog sledding to skiing and snowboarding. Inside the designated children's zone there are life-size marionettes, winterized play structures, and ice slides. You can join in a game of street hockey, meet animals at the petting zoo, and ride the ferris wheel.

Bonhomme, the ginormous 7-foot (2-metre) snowman, is the most visible aspect of this festival. For Québec children, Bonhomme is a bigger deal than Santa Claus. "Children here know there are many impersonating Santa, but there is only one Bonhomme," explains local mom Paule Bergeron. Only seen during Carnaval or when he's on official business promoting Carnaval around the globe, Bonhomme lives in the North Pole for most of the year, but returns to his ice palace in Québec City during Carnaval after receiving keys to the city from the mayor.

The Ice Palace itself is a marvel. Composed of 2,000 blocks of ice, it takes three weeks to build the frame and another week to fashion the furnishings. The theme is different each year, but you can be sure there'll be a snowman cave complete with an (ice) pool table and couches to entertain guests. Should you have the opportunity to become enveloped in the most marshmallowy of hugs, you must take it. A chat and a snuggle with the charismatic and bilingual King of Winter is something you'll never forget.

The best thing about Carnaval is that it hasn't morphed into one of those corporate sponsorship events. It's still firmly rooted in community and local traditions. Families don't need much money to take full advantage of all this festival affords. Tickets are under $20 and last the entire seventeen days. Impressively, all festival attractions are free with admission.

Long after Christmas has passed, Québec City still looks like a fairytale village.

Skating at Place d'Youville.

Zip down green, blue, and black runs at Village Vacance Valcartier.

On certain days, children are welcome at Sibéria Station Spa.

SOAK UP SOME HISTORY

In the only fortified city in North America, 2.8 miles (4.6 kilometres) of walls and gates surrounding the old town are yours to explore. A path allows you to wander along this defence system built by the French in the 17th and 18th centuries. The Citadel, the largest British military fortification in North America, is still garrisoned by regular troops. Guided tours are available all year long, and in summer you can watch the Changing of the Guard.

The Plains of Abraham is where Generals Wolfe (British) and Montcalm (French) faced off in their epic 1759 battle. It's since become one of the world's first urban parks, a vast green space encircled by cannons and towering elms. Outdoor concerts are held here during the summer months, and Québec's national holiday, St. Jean Baptiste Day, is celebrated at this spot on June 24. It's an epic site for a stroll or a picnic, but don't be dismayed if you visit in winter. When the snow's on the ground you can skate, snowshoe, or cross-country ski by taking advantage of on-site rentals.

STROLL AND SHOP

Sipping a sinfully rich hot chocolate at an outdoor café in Quartier Petit Champlain will make you feel as if you've stepped back in time to 17th-century New France. Cobble-stoned streets are lined with period buildings, whose windows are festooned with greenery, berries, and bows in the winter months. The setting couldn't be more enchanting, and children are rewarded with an abundance of shops selling sweet treats and touristy items amid the galleries and restaurants. Play old-fashioned games in the square while roving characters perform historical reenactments during Carnaval and summer's New France Festival.

Walking down to Place-Royale is one thing; getting back up is quite another. When it's too taxing for little legs to make the return journey, step aboard the Funiculaire. You'll be able to take in epic views of the St. Lawrence River, plus the historic area that cradles this mighty river, while rising above the crowds as you're transported to the upper entrance at Dufferin Terrace. The lower station entrance is inside Maison Louis-Jolliet, along rue du Petit-Champlain in the Place-Royale district.

Reward wee ones for dutifully checking out all the sights with a trip to Benjo, one of the country's best independent toy shops. Located in the Saint-Roch district, on St. Joseph Street, a tiny child-sized door transports children into a place of magic and creativity. This enchanting store has several departments that range from books and baby gear to toys, plus a candy shop and café.

GLIDE AND SLIDE

Who says history has to be boring? Make like residents two centuries ago and zoom down the Dufferin Terrace on a toboggan. One of the oldest attractions in town, Toboggan Slide Au 1884 has three lanes to ride down on wooden sleds that can reach speeds of up to 44 miles (70 kilometres) an hour. It's an incredible rush made even more magnificent while taking in views of the St. Lawrence, Île d'Orléans, Fairmont Le Château Frontenac, and Old Port.

You'd be hard pressed to find a more atmospheric outdoor ice rink than the one at Place D'Youville. Rent some skates and soak up the atmosphere of Old Québec as you glide by Saint Jean Gate and the Capitole de Québec, a beaux arts–style theatre. Warm up afterwards with a cup of cocoa at Café-boulangerie Paillard.

A larger skating area is found at the Louise Basin inner harbour. The 0.6-mile (1-kilometre) ice path is magical at night, but during the day you'll be able to browse the nearby Old Port Market. Then there's the oval loop on the Plains of Abraham. Snacks and rentals are available inside the heated skater's chalet.

EXPLORE AN ICE HOTEL

You don't have to bed down on a sheet of ice to get a glimpse inside Canada's famed ice hotel. Made entirely out of ice and snow (500 tonnes of ice and 30,000 tonnes of snow, to be exact), Hôtel de Glace is a marvel worth seeing. Modelled after the original ice hotel in

Sweden, this impressive structure is built from scratch each December, and is open to the public from January until mid-March.

The doors are fur covered, the walls are three times stronger than concrete, and everywhere you look there are brilliant ice sculptures. Even the furniture is made entirely of ice and snow. Talented artists work a different theme each year, and the attention to detail in 3D murals is jaw dropping—well, that and the awesome ice slide you can barrel down as many times as you wish.

Families are welcome to stay overnight on a conventional mattress and inside a sleeping bag designed for -15°C to -30°C (5°F to -22°F). If you choose not to overnight, there are day passes that let you wander through the property, and you can rent snowshoes to access their 3 miles (5 kilometres) of trails. Guided tours are also available.

TUBE TIME

Going down identical tube runs at a ski hill is one thing. Bombing down more than forty specially-crafted lanes sitting on a rubber tube is quite another. Half an hour outside Québec City lies Village Vacances Valcartier, North America's largest winter playground. Thrill seekers can swoosh down Everest, the highest tube (and waterslide) run in North America, and reach speeds of up to 50 miles (80 kilometres) an hour! If you're not up for that, consider stepping aboard the Tornado, a round inflatable vessel designed on the same principles as white-water rafts. In this turbo-charged teacup, riders face each other and whip around as though they're being swept up inside a tornado. It's a crazy spinning rush, and one best experienced before, not after, eating lunch.

Because a tube park of this nature is pretty new to most Canadians, the park offers amenities much like those found at a ski resort. You're towed up the hill by ropes, and runs are categorized by their difficulty level with green, blue, and black diamond markings. There are runs for all ages and abilities, which means family members don't have to make many compromises. Let the adrenaline junkies loose on the black diamonds and take the tots to the mini ice slides inside the children's playground. Remember to pack ski goggles or sunglasses as there can be quite a bit of glare when hurtling down the slopes.

There are several on-site restaurants and an indoor arcade, and mascot otters mill about. An ice skating path winds its way through the park, and, yes, there's on-site skate rental here, too. In summer, Village Vacances Valcartier morphs into the second-largest water park in Canada with thirty-five heated waterslides and two themed rivers.

GET PAMPERED IN NATURE

Most nature spas have a strict adults-only policy, but Sibéria Station Spa makes it easy for families to unwind together by granting potty-trained children access every Sunday morning and during the mornings of school vacations (spring break, summer, and Christmas). Children are treated just as well as any adult spa-goer, with kid-sized bathrobes and a children's menu at their café. They even offer discounted massages for youngsters!

While it may be too hot in the steam bath for little ones, the infrared and dry saunas could possibly be tolerated for a few minutes at a time. In winter, families are invigorated by rolling in the snow before slipping into an outdoor hot tub. A river cradles the property, and guests are encouraged to take a dip in it, too! Relaxation rooms range from yurts to igloo-shaped tents, and are filled with wood-burning fires and pod-like hammocks. See if you can curl up like a bat and catch a few winks.

Tips

- Towels are provided, but you need to bring your own bathing suit and flip-flops.
- Check with your doctor before visiting with children or if you're pregnant. The extreme temperature fluctuations between hot and cold are not suited for everybody.

KICKING AROUND TOWN

Close to 10,000 species reside inside the Aquarium du Québec. The site is vast with indoor and outdoor areas to explore. Catch polar bears, walruses, and seals at play, or look for opportunities to observe their feeding times. Don't leave without traipsing along the tree-to-tree pathway, designed especially for children.

Inspired by the Boston Children's Museum, the Museum of Civilization is a site for human adventure. Head to the Youth Zone for the most kid-friendly galleries. Earth's Unveiled offers tactile exhibits and answers kids' questions, such as, "What causes tornadoes?" Feel the vibrations under your feet in the earthquake simulator, or, if wind is more your speed, try the tornado simulator.

Imaginations run wild in the Once Upon a Time costume workshop. Overflowing with splendid costumes for children (and matching ones for adults!), visitors transform into fairytale characters before heading into the play zone. Address your countrymen from a turret, ride a horse while brandishing a jousting stick, or slide into the soft play area. Be sure to verify hours before visiting, as this exhibit is currently only open on weekends and certain weekdays.

🌐 GOOD TO KNOW

Traipsing through the Old Town means walking up and down hills and across cobblestone streets. Leave the heels at home or risk twisting an ankle; opt for sturdy shoes and bring a robust stroller.

Though tickets for the Québec Winter Carnival are affordably priced, you can receive further discounts by purchasing online in advance at carnaval.qc.ca.

🍴 TASTE

Established in 1871, **J.A. Moisan** is the oldest grocery store in North America. In addition to produce, attractively merchandized in wicker baskets, this shop contains a snack bar, a deli, and an impressive selection of chocolate bars. With traditional French music playing in the background, it's oh-so atmospheric, and is a charming place to stop for a light meal or perhaps a pastry.

Poutine is one of the signature Québécois dishes—one you can't miss trying. Nobody said fries smothered in gravy and studded with cheese curds was healthy, but this gloopy mess is a delicious, hearty treat that's easily shared. Local favourite **Chez Ashton** is one of the best spots in the city to indulge.

Maple taffy is a sweet reward easily found within Québec City. This winter and early-spring treat is made from boiling maple sap and pouring it onto fresh snow before rolling it onto a wooden stick.

 ## NAP

You can't beat the location of the **Hilton Québec**. Less than a five-minute walk from Old Québec and across the street from the provincial Parliament Building, this hotel boasts breathtaking views of the St. Lawrence River and the Laurentian Mountains. The hotel check-in provides all of the supplies a family needs, from cribs to gifts for kids, and babysitting services are available. Better still, the property is pet-friendly, and has a heated outdoor pool and complimentary WiFi.

Just outside the city, **Village Vacances Valcartier** offers hundreds of camping spots, along with cute cabins fully equipped with the comforts of home. While it wasn't open at the time of writing, the site is launching a four-star hotel with 153 family suites, which will include access to their new indoor water park.

GETTING AROUND

Take a taxi from **Québec City Jean Lesage International Airport** to downtown for a flat rate of under $35. The public bus (No. 78) is more affordable, but only runs weekdays in the early morning or late afternoon.

Most of the touristy attractions you'll want to hit up in either the historic Old Town or Lower Town districts are easily explored by foot. Shuttle services are offered by Village Vacances Valcartier and Hôtel de Glace. Get from point to point along the St. Lawrence River, or take a sightseeing cruise, with **Excursions Maritimes Québec** (EMQ).

FUN FACTS

- Québec is the world's leading producer of **maple syrup**.
- Québec City was founded by **Samuel de Champlain** in 1608.
- The name **Québec**, comes from the Algonquin word *kebec*, meaning "where the river narrows."
- If you visit during Carnaval, you may notice many locals (and **Bonhomme**) wearing the *ceinture fléchée,* a woven arrowhead sash tied at their waist. The origin of the sash comes from the First Nations people, but it caught on with French Canadians. It became part of the traditional costume of Lower Canada residents around 1776, and has been kept alive through Carnaval.

GET EXCITED ABOUT YOUR TRIP

- Read *New France*, by Robert Livesey, to learn about the brave men and women who first settled in this part of the New World.
- Mid-elementary students should read *Samuel de Champlain*, by Elizabeth MacLeod, to learn about his exploration of the unknown lands of New France.
- For readers aged nine to twelve, *I Am Canada: Storm the Fortress*, by Maxine Trottier, reveals the siege of Québec from the perspective of a fourteen-year-old British sailor.

Miles of unspoiled wilderness surround the Saguenay–Lac-Saint-Jean region.

Take a break from paddling the Saguenay Fjord and play in the sand.

Saguenay Fjord

Where Whales and Wildlife Beckon

As the sun throws out its last rays and casts a dazzling spell of diamond light upon the river, a minke whale breaks the surface, gracefully rising out of the seaway mere feet away from our boat. Excited shouts of *"en regarde!"* can be heard as she pummels out salty water through her blowhole. Though slightly disappointed the spray didn't reach us, we're easily distracted seconds later when a pod of seals pop up to say hello, then just as quickly bob back down beneath the waves. We're on the St. Lawrence River, at the mouth of the Saguenay Fjord, one of Canada's best playgrounds for outdoorsy families and nature enthusiasts.

If you're on the lookout for whales, wolves, or caribou, you've come to the right place. Renowned for their scenic landscapes and abundant wildlife, Québec's Saguenay and Côte-Nord regions are filled with opportunities for adventure. Sea kayaking, wildlife observation, and easy hiking trails allow families to witness nature at her most glorious.

SAGUENAY FJORD NATIONAL PARK

Québec's Saguenay Fjord is a 65-mile (105-kilometre) inlet etched in stone and infused by the sea. What is a fjord? It's an inlet carved by a glacier and filled with sea water—in this case, the St. Lawrence seaway. This deeply cleaved glacial valley flanked by thick forests is ripe for discovery by ground, sea, or air.

Saguenay Fjord National Park bears witness to the receding of the icebergs that shaped this stunning landscape during the last Ice Age. Despite its English translation, Saguenay Fjord National Park is not a national park à la Parks Canada, but a provincial park that adjoins the Saguenay–St. Lawrence Marine Park for over 60 miles (100 kilometres) in a series of bays, coves, and jaw-dropping cliffs.

The uniquely protected marine park is home to thirteen species of whales, including beluga, minke, and fin whales. "Most places in the world, you have to take a boat to see the whales, but along this marine park it's easy to see them from shore," affirms Chloé Bonnette, partnership coordinator of Saguenay–St. Lawrence Marine Park. Indeed, the St. Lawrence is one of those rare places in the world where the blue whale, the largest animal on the planet, can be observed from land. Both parks offer a myriad of activities, from hiking to sea kayaking to backcountry skiing and snowshoeing during winter.

Baie Ste-Marguerite is the best place to watch beluga whales (mainly females and calves) from shore during summer months. It's a pleasant 1.8-mile (3-kilometre) hike to the bay from Le Béluga Discovery Center. The gravel trail is smooth enough to take a stroller and easy for littles to undertake on their own. Trek past Margaret River, which is filled with sea trout and spawning Atlantic salmon in June and July, and under canopies of maple providing refreshing shade above the trail. Expect about a forty-five-minute jaunt before arriving at Belvedere lookout, a pretty picnic spot with ample seating along the wooden deck with magnificent views of the fjord.

Tip
When on the hunt for blue whales, look for an explosive blowhole, blue-grey colour, and a small dorsal fin.

SOAR OVER TREETOPS

For a dramatic entry into Saguenay Fjord National Park, arrive via helicopter with Peak Aviation. The Cap Trinity Tour is thirty-five minutes of pure pleasure as you hover over a patchwork quilt of neatly parcelled farmland. Autumn is a particularly awesome time to take a tour over a spectrum of vibrantly hued leaves. A feast for the eyes, sugar maples are interspersed with birch and pine, spread

Fancy bedding down in a bubble? You can at Canopée Lit.

Children and parents reconnect with nature and one another at Village-Vacances Petit-Saguenay.

Contemplate all the possibilities for adventure while overlooking farmyards and the Saguenay Fjord region.

Beluga whales are abundant in the Saguenay Fjord.

out like a brilliant, textured carpet as far as you can see. From your aerial view, you'll spot picturesque villages, hidden lakes, and secluded chalets available to rent within the forest. Glancing down upon the fjord, you'll notice the effect the tide has. The banks will either be submerged or strewn with rocks coated in tidal mud, while in the centre white streams of current create a sharp visual contrast against inky black water. Keep your camera at the ready!

Tours leave from Bagotville Wharf, which merits a visit itself on a cruise day. Over fifty volunteer actors descend upon the port to welcome visitors. The region's history is depicted through period costumes, song, and dance. Fiddlers play merry tunes, square dancers do-si-do, and there's an abundance of maple syrup and blueberry treats for the taking. They haven't been awarded Best Port Welcome for nothing, so you'll want to take advantage of the spectacle if you're in Saguenay. For the cruise ship arrival schedule, check Saguenay.ca.

VIA FERRATA

Kids twelve years and older who get a kick out of freaking out their parents will want to tackle the Via Ferrata route inside Saguenay Fjord National Park. Via *what,* you ask? Via Ferrata is an assisted climbing route anchored into the cliffs that tower high above Eternity Bay. With a safety harness and carabiners, you clip into the metal rungs that are strung along the course, allowing adrenaline junkies all the thrills (not to mention endless panoramic vistas) typically reserved for elite mountaineers. A certified guide takes you along the three-hour course that'll have you clambering up the mountain face, tiptoeing across a monkey bridge (which is actually just thin metal wire), and crossing one of the fjord's deep chasms on a 272-foot (83-metre) suspension bridge. Climbers will need to pack their courage and sense of adventure.

JOURNEY BY BOAT

You'll see the same stunning vistas but avoid pricey boat tour costs by taking Les Croisières du Fjord, a marine shuttle offering several stops along the fjord. You may even reach your destination faster by boat than by car, so if you've decided to tool around on land by bicycle, throw those bikes on board, too.

The rhythmic pace of the covered boat lures babes to sleep, while guides detail the rich biodiversity that flourishes within this unique environment. Sail past the oldest formations on the North American continent; marvel at the sheer granite cliffs thrusting out of the fjord, teeming with marine life. Be on the lookout for belugas and seals, especially if you take the ferry from L'Anse-Saint-Jean to Tadoussac, where the Saguenay River meets the St. Lawrence.

Kayaking is another optimal way to get up close and personal with the marine life. Both Ferme 5 Étoiles and Fjord en Kayak operate family excursions with tandem and single kayaks. Even if you don't spot any whales on your trip, it's worth it for the sheer pleasure of making smooth strokes through the water while gazing at the brightly coloured cottages. Children as young as three years old can kayak with their parents.

EXPLORE TADOUSSAC

Perched on the edge of the boreal forest and at the mouth of both the St. Lawrence and Saguenay Fjord, Tadoussac is considered one of the most beautiful villages in Québec. It's also one of the most significant settlements in Canadian history. Visited by Jacques Cartier in 1535, this is the oldest European settlement in Québec (established eight years before Québec City), and it's here that the vital fur trade began.

Strike out on foot to explore the town, starting with Tadoussac Trading Post, established in 1600. It's one of the oldest First Nations trading and archeological sites in Canada. Another spot for history buffs is Chapelle des Indiens, the most ancient wooden chapel in North America, built by the French missionaries who descended upon Québec in the 17th century. Walk to Rue des Pionniers to find souvenir shops, a children's boutique, and plenty of cute restaurants. But, remember, despite the town's impressive history, that's not what draws in the tourists: this is, in fact, one of Québec's prime places for whale watching.

TAKE A WHALE WATCHING TOUR

Nine hundred belugas live year round in the Marine Park, but a dozen other species of whales join them as summer residents. "They come for the all-you-can-eat krill and plankton buffet," jokes local Suzie Loiselle. Brought in by the tides, the tiny crustaceans and organisms that congregate in these nutrient-rich waters make the Laurentian channel a massive feeding zone and a supreme spot for viewing a wide variety of marine mammals.

From May to October, families with children aged six and up can take a Zodiac whale watching excursion with Croisières AML. Out in the bracing sea air, you'll catch sightings of seals and whales, such as minke, humpback, blue, and grey whales—even belugas, their glistening white backs in sharp contrast to the moody grey water. Preteens and teenagers will laugh in wicked delight when their Francophone boat mates start shouting a word that sounds like "foc!" But, no, it's not profanity—*phoque* is simply the French word for *seal*.

Tip
Cruise to WhalesOnline.org to get an idea of the types of whales that will be in the vicinity during your visit.

HOWL WITH WOLVES

Parc Mahikan is an eco-adventure park where you too can become part of the pack. Families can view grey and Arctic wolves, while those over fourteen years of age can meet domesticated grey wolves with a wolf-contact experience. (And by meet, I mean get sniffed, licked, and possibly hugged inside a forested enclosure.) Do wolves really howl at the moon? Find out by extending your howliday with an overnight stay inside the park's ecolodge.

Another intriguing animal encounter can be found at Zoo

Sauvage de St-Félicien. Here the animals run free and the humans are caged! Boreal animals living in habitats as close to their natural topography as possible roam wild, while visitors view from a "caged train" or secure pedestrian sections. Close to 1,000 animals live within the zoo's natural, wide-open spaces, and include tigers, bears, moose, and farm animals.

INTERACTIVE MUSEUMS

Stepping through the actual jaws of a blue whale is your first clue that Marine Mammal Interpretation Centre is *not* a conventional museum. As parents of children with busy hands are well aware, most natural museums have strict do-not-touch policies. Not so here. Families are encouraged to handle all skeletons, baleen plates, and narwhal teeth on display at this Tadoussac facility.

Operated by GREMM, a marine mammal research and education group, this centre is the authority on all things whale. While display signage is in French, English guidebooks are available. But it's unlikely the language barrier will spoil your visit, since most of the exhibits are hands-on; bilingual naturalists (many of whom were directly involved in putting together the collections) are on hand and happy to share their expertise.

For a unique souvenir, consider picking up a baleinophone. This tube-like contraption gives off eerily accurate whale sounds. During the summer months, look for complimentary sessions that teach children how to sing like a whale. Certificates are awarded after training.

At Musée du Fjord, families dig deep into the captivating depths of the Saguenay River through exhibits and activities. A youth zone captures kids' interest with virtual exhibits, including a 3D animation game. The Fjord Aquarium is a large, live laboratory full of marine life, and includes a touch pool to get a hands-on feel for the fjord's wildlife.

SPA BREAK

The Nordic baths of Édouard-les-Bains are a terrific follow-up to a day of marine mammal exploration. Slip into the hammam before cycling through cool pools and funky relaxation chambers. The shock to the system produces adrenaline, which then turns into feel-good endorphins—perhaps a necessary pick-me-up when travelling with young children. Youngsters six years and older can chill with their parents for a specific two-hour window during the summer months, spring break, Christmas holidays, and on Sundays throughout the year. Massage therapy is available, and if you're up for it, dip your feet into the garra rufa tank, where tiny fish can eat away at your dead skin. It's pretty fun, if for no other reason than to gross out your family.

🌐 GOOD TO KNOW

All construction workers in Québec have the same two-week summer holiday, typically beginning at the end of July. If you want to avoid the crowds, it's best not to book your visit around this time. Mid-August is an excellent time to visit, as those pesky mosquitoes are usually gone. Children head back to school the week before Labour Day, yet family attractions remain open.

🍴 TASTE

This region is flush with seafood, game, and wild berries, particularly blueberries and cloudberries rich in vitamin C. You should also try moose sausage, cheese curds that produce a delightful squeak in your mouth, and tourtière du Lac-Saint-Jean. That's "*real* tourtière, not that meat pie," you'll hear many locals avow. While it's not easy to find this type of tourtière on menus, it is available at **Chalets sur le Fjord** in L'Anse-Saint-Jean and **Restaurant la Maison Marie** at Moulin des Pionniers. Traditional Innu foods such as bannock and Labrador tea can also be found for sale throughout this area.

🛏 NAP

Hotel Tadoussac is a pretty white lodge with green shutters and a cherry red roof, set upon sweeping grounds dotted with Adirondack chairs. It's the perfect perch from which to take in the majesty of the St. Lawrence. During the summer season, Club des Petits Mousses takes in children from ages five to twelve for late afternoon and evening crafts, treasure hunts, and movies. The hotel restaurant offers a children's menu, and cribs are available at no extra charge. Tadoussac Bay is just across the street, making it oh-so convenient to go beachcombing at low tide or play in the refreshing water (around 25°C [77°F]) on a hot summer day. You can also take a dip in the hotel's seasonally operated outdoor pool, or occupy your family with the tennis courts and shuffle boards.

Settle into the lodge or pitch a tent in the campsite at **Village-Vacances Petit-Saguenay**. During the day, children scuttle off to the kids' camp, while parents do as they please. Think: canoeing, wine and cheese tasting, or a fjord mud bath! Opt to have your meals included, or go the self-catering route and make them yourself. While it's a fun French immersion experience, many staff and camp counsellors are bilingual.

What child hasn't fantasized about staying overnight in a treehouse? At **Canopée Lit**, you'll find eight treehouses and five cozy bubble tents on 60 acres (24 hectares) of lush forest flanking the fjord. Children relish the sense of freedom they have with a stay here, exploring the woods and playing along the shallow stream. This is glamping at its finest, with wooden barrel tubs, mini-fridges, and breakfast delivered on your step in retro lunch kits.

As cool as the treehouses are, the bubble tents *really* wow kids' socks off. Faux grass serves as carpet, and two inflatable beds sit underneath massive skylights, allowing you to sleep under the stars while staying warm—an immersive nature experience that far exceeds any had by staying in a tent. Plus you'll stay much warmer. Whichever option you choose, you'll wake up to the sound of the wind rustling through the trees and the stream babbling away.

Tip

Pack lightly, as suitcase wheels will take a beating when walking down the gnarly rooted trail to your treehouse or bubble. It's a bit dark with the shade of the trees, but fortunately, flashlights are provided.

GETTING AROUND

From Québec City, Tadoussac is a three-hour drive, while it takes less than two and a half hours to reach Saguenay. Regional flights are operated out of the **Saguenay-Bagotville Airport**.

FUN FACTS

- Of the world's known fjords (all 2,130 of them), only thirty-eight are at least 62 miles (100 kilometres) long. Not only is Saguenay Fjord one of the world's greatest, it's one of the rare fjords that flows into an estuary.
- Did you know **peregrine falcons** are the fastest animal on the planet? Keep your eyes peeled for this threatened species. The rocky escarpment of the fjord is a perfect nesting ground for them. A single breeding couple was noticed in 1980, but there are now over 100 breeding bird couples in the Saguenay–Lac-Saint-Jean region.
- Canada has the second-largest grey wolf population in the world.

GET EXCITED ABOUT YOUR TRIP

- Read *F is for French: A Québec Alphabet*, by Elaine Arsenault.
- For animal lovers, pick up *Beluga Whales*, by Ann O. Squire.
- Immerse yourself in the mighty fjord with a copy of *The Children's Book of the Saguenay*, by Leonard L. Knott.

You won't believe how close to whales you can get in the Bay of Fundy.

St. Andrews by-the-Sea is a pretty town kids won't mind exploring. After all, there's more than one ice cream shop on the main drag . . .

New Brunswick's Bay of Fundy

Rise with the Tides

Coax a kid with chocolate milk and anything is possible. My daughter isn't that fond of boats, particularly if she has to use her own her muscle to propel them. Yet, as we carve our way through the Hersey-coloured waters of the Bay of Fundy, she exclaims delightedly, "Wow! We really are kayaking through chocolate milk!" Sea kayaking along the shores of Fundy National Park—a diverse landscape punctuated with towering sandstone cliffs and desolate beaches christened with fanciful names such as Squaw's Cap and Devil's Half-Acre—is just one of the incredible thrills found along New Brunswick's Fundy Coast.

It's not hard to persuade children to play in the planet's most massive, natural bathtub. The highest tides in the world flow in and out of the Bay of Fundy. With each tide cycle, over 100 billion tonnes of chocolate-coloured seawater surges through the claw-shaped bay. That's more than the combined flow of all of the world's freshwater rivers!

Parents, expect extra laundry duty on this trip: investigating this natural phenomenon means getting wet, muddy, and downright dirty—and kids will *love* it. Teeming with national historic sites and rich aquatic life, New Brunswick's Fundy Coast offers a myriad of options for families keen to dive into this fascinating seaboard.

SEA KAYAKING

Alma is a traditional maritime town and the departure point for family kayaking excursions. Dipping your paddle into the murky bay, you're apt to glide past seals and loons, while bald eagles soar over copses of cedar trees reaching up from the jagged coastline. Half-day trips often stop on remote sweeps of sand such as Hunt's Hole Beach, allowing paddlers time to rest, refuel, and, most importantly, explore. Rescuing periwinkle water snails and sampling fresh dulse seaweed that grows on the side of the rocks is equally as fascinating to kids as being on the water.

Expect an entirely different experience on your paddle back to shore: the vast energy and power of these tides is incredible. A few hours after your departure, the beach you set off from probably won't look the same. It could be flush with fresh water or strewn with thousands of algae-covered rocks, depending on what tide cycle you set out on. That's what makes kayaking on the Bay of Fundy so worthwhile—it's a new adventure with every tide.

Don't worry about keeping up with the group; tour outfitters realize most parents are new to this activity. Should you have any difficulty, your guide will attach your kayak to theirs with a nylon rope and give you a tow. (Not that I'm admitting I know this from personal experience.)

HOPEWELL ROCKS

Arguably the most famous spot from which to appreciate the vast range of these tides is found at Hopewell Rocks, less than an hour's drive from Moncton. The dramatic ebb and flow of the Fundy tides has caused continuous erosion at the base of these 350-million-year-old rock formations. The result is bizarre-shaped outcrops with evergreens sprouting from the tops. After seeing them for yourself, you'll understand why the Hopewell Rocks are nicknamed the flowerpot rocks.

Each tide cycle takes exactly six hours and thirteen minutes. Since they change daily, you'll want to consult a tide table before your visit. If you time it right (aim to arrive either three hours before or three hours after low tide to walk the ocean floor), you should be able to take in both high and low tide at this self-directed

Try to time your visit to the Hopewell Rocks so you can see the dramatic increase and decrease in tidal water.

It's almost hard to believe a grand hotel such as the Algonquin Resort is family-friendly, but it is!

Strolling along the shore in Fundy National Park.

Taking in the bountiful blooms at Kingsbrae Garden in St. Andrews.

Curl up with a good book or a board game at the Algonquin Resort.

park. You won't get very many chances in life to roam the ocean floor, and the kids will have a hoot frolicking amid the muck and seaweed while exploring these unusual rocks.

It's rare to have scenery change so quickly before your eyes, so you'll want to witness the extraordinary increase in water level—approximately 4 to 6 feet (1.2 to 1.8 metres) per hour. The difference between low tide and high tide can be as much as 46 feet (14 metres), and seeing these rocks partially submerged is awe-inspiring indeed.

It's easy to burn a few hours here between tides (though visitors receive a twenty-four-hour pass). Inside the Interpretive Centre, multimedia exhibits explain the tides, regional geology, and wildlife in the bay. If you're looking for more detail, interpretive staff located at key areas around the park can answer any questions. There's also an outdoor playground and picnic tables, and the High Tide Café dishes out tasty meals. Warning: you may be cajoled into purchasing a souvenir at Tidal Treasures Gift Shop, which is stocked with tourist trinkets and educational toys.

CAPE ENRAGE

Take the scenic driving route between Alma and Hopewell Rocks to hit Cape Enrage, a stunning viewpoint and light station that's been in operation since 1838. This side trip only adds twenty minutes to your journey, but going the extra mile is well worth it.

Local delicacies—from fiddleheads to dulse focaccia to lobster rolls—are dished out at the Cape House Restaurant, located inside the old lighthouse keeper's home. After feasting on both incredible views and maritime fare, adventurous families with children over 75 pounds (34 kilograms) can rappel down the waterside cliffs flanking these giant tides. Or get a glimpse of the spectacular currents from a zip line that's over 600 feet (183 metres) long—check in advance for age and weight restrictions. Anyone, however, can investigate the historic lighthouse or search for fossils along the pebble-strewn beach.

SEA CAVES AND SCENIC LOOKOUTS

St. Martins—known as the gateway to the Fundy Trail—is famous for its sea caves and arches. Thanks to the continual crashing of the waves against the sandstone rocks, erosion has revealed deep fissures and crevasses in the cliffs hugging the coastline. There's no need to plan this stop in too much detail; simply pull over and let little ones run wild (at low tide) as they suss out the impressive natural grottos.

Two lighthouses, covered wooden bridges, and a colourful fleet of fishing boats bobbing in the active harbour make the village of St. Martins a popular spot for photographers. Consider handing over the camera (or springing for a disposable one for each child) so you can relive the experience when comparing snaps after your journey.

Just outside the village, the forest meets the ocean along the Fundy Trail Parkway. Open from May until the end of October, this is one of the last remaining coastal wilderness areas between Florida and Labrador. The coastal road offers eco-experiences for bicyclists, hikers, and Sunday drivers. Scenic footpaths under 1.8 miles (3 kilometres) make for easy hikes; there's also a free shuttle service that drops you off at scenic viewpoints. Highlights include traipsing down a cable ladder to Fuller Falls, an Instagram-worthy waterfall; beachcombing along one of the four secluded beaches; and gathering bucketfuls of wild blackberries, which flourish in August.

ST. ANDREWS BY-THE-SEA

Nestled along Passamaquoddy Bay, a tiny nook in the Bay of Fundy, St. Andrews by-the-Sea is your quintessential seaside resort town and one of the country's most historic. Families have flocked here since the latter part of the 19th century.

The town boasts one the most spectacular playgrounds in the country. St. Andrews Creative Playground—a hop, skip, and jump from the downtown promenade—is well suited for babes, toddlers, and school-aged children alike. Reminiscent of a medieval fort, the wooden structure is comprised of towering turrets, rope ladders, and secret hiding spots that make games of hide-and-seek infinitely more interesting. You'll also find monkey bars, a climbing wall, and a treasure map engraved with images that little explorers can try to locate throughout the massive play site.

Need to calm the kids down? Engage their senses with a refreshing stroll through Kingsbrae Garden. Within this lush 27-acre (11-hectare) paradise lies an Acadian forest, a petting zoo, and several of the most beautiful playhouses you'll ever come across. Kids will no doubt want to plant their own flowers in the children's garden and meander through the labyrinth maze, so expect to spend more time here than you originally anticipated.

Ready for more action? Head down Water Street, where there might just be more than one ice cream and candy shop, in addition to quaint boutiques. To get up close and personal with the marine life that flourishes within the bay, book a whale-watching excursion with one of the outfitters along the harbour. Chances are high you'll spot minke whales and porpoises. Staff on board enthrall mini marine biologists by bringing out touch tanks for hands-on learning.

🌐 GOOD TO KNOW

Pack an extra set of clothes inside a plastic bag, so after your romp along the sea, what's wet and muddy can be sealed away. This is not the place to wear your tennis whites.

🍴 TASTE

It would be a shame to come to the Maritimes and not crack shells over a bowl of melted butter. Fundy lobster is said to be the tastiest in all the Maritimes. Keep your eyes peeled for billboards advertising community lobster suppers, or pick up a professionally cracked crustacean at **Alma Lobster Shop**.

The homemade sticky buns from **Kelly's Bake Shop** in Alma are quickly approaching cult status. Like cinnamon buns, but without any annoying raisins or nuts, these gooey morsels are the perfect pick-me-up for weary families.

🏨 NAP

A splurge-worthy stay can be had at the **Algonquin Resort** in St. Andrews. Set majestically upon a hill overlooking the bay, this Tudor-esque castle is sure to wow kids of all ages. Despite the external grandeur, the property is remarkably family-friendly, with its 3-storey indoor water slide, seasonal outdoor pool, twenty-four-hour sundry shop, and even a coin-operated washing machine. Parents can partake in a spa treatment or hit the links at one of Canada's prettiest golf courses.

Alternatively, you can camp in a tent or trailer at **Fundy National Park**. Don't have your own shelter? Opt to stay overnight in a yurt, a rustic cabin, or an oTENTik operated by Parks Canada.

GETTING AROUND

Fly into either Moncton or Saint John to begin your journey. This is a road-trip destination, and rental cars can be picked up at either airport.

💡 FUN FACTS

- The Bay of Fundy's diverse ecosystem has been compared to the **Amazon Rainforest**. Within its nutrient-rich waters are colossal amounts of krill and fish, which attract over twelve species of whales, not to mention dolphins, porpoises, and seals.
- It's not just aquatic animals that are attracted to the bay. Each August, **2 million migratory birds (mainly sandpipers) make a pit stop here** to rest and refuel during their epic journey from South America to the Arctic.
- The Bay of Fundy's **Old Sow Whirlpool** is 246 feet (75 metres) wide, making it the largest whirlpool in the Western Hemisphere, and the second largest in the world.
- Look for **balsam firs** and **purple violets** during your outdoor adventure. They're two of the provincial symbols.

- Young children can learn about Acadian history and culture with *ABC Acadie: An Acadian Alphabet* by Mary Alice Downie.
- *F is for Fiddlehead: A New Brunswick Alphabet*, by Marilyn Lohnes, shares fun trivia from A to Z.
- *The Town That Drowned*, by Riel Nason, is a coming-of-age story set in 1960s-era New Brunswick, and is suitable for both young adults and parents.
- Listen to the Les Hay Babies, a New Brunswick indie folk trio who make wonderful music with one guitar, a banjo, a ukulele, and powerful harmonies.
- Watch the *Amazing Places* video of the Fundy Biosphere Reserve by visiting fbramazingplaces.ca, or watch *Great Canadian Parks: Fundy National Park* at goodearthproductions.com.

Explore the Big Harbour aboard Theodore Tugboat.

Check out the kegs (formerly filled with gunpowder) at Halifax Citadel National Historic Site.

History made fun at Halifax Citadel National Historic Site.

Halifax

Play Soldier Inside a Historic Fortress

Redcoat soldiers in MacKenzie tartan kilts strut around the fort to the skirl of the bagpipes. They mark time, stand at ease, and ten-hut until . . . kaboom! A full pound of black powder explodes out of the mouth of a 12-pounder muzzle-loading cannon. Plumes of smoke billow in the air, the stench of gunpowder invades our nostrils, and the ringing in our ears takes a few minutes to subside.

We've just witnessed loading the charge at the Halifax Citadel National Historic Site by the 3rd Brigade of the Royal Artillery. The longest continual timepiece in North America, a cannon has been fired at noon every day for over 160 years. Got a kid (or spouse) who gets a kick out of things that go bang? The crack of rifles firing, the blast from the cannon, and the resounding beats spewing from the military band lure those leaning on the rambunctious side to this former military outpost.

Sure, you could walk through on your own and take a self-guided tour with kids, but that could be humdrum if you don't know what you're looking at. A better bet is to take the forty-five-minute guided tour, free with admission. Better still—enlist your children!

JOIN THE ARMY

No need to ship the kids off to military school. Instead, sign them up in the citadel's A Soldier's Life program (available daily during July and August), so they too can learn the skills needed to defend this important port. This Parks Canada program, suitable for children ages six to twelve years, is infinitely more interesting than anything a history book could teach you about life as a 78th Highlander. Suiting up in the iconic Highlander doublet, learning foot drills, and raising the flag to send a coded message—they'll step back in time to when Canada was evolving from a colony to a nation.

Cautiously we enter the Orderly Room, where our uniformed guide, Michelle Lehman, gets the children—now considered new recruits—to fill out their enlistment forms. Once they receive the Queen's Shilling, a soldier's pay, it's time to don infantry uniforms before reporting for duty. Even though it's close to noon on a 30°C (86°F) day, several "soldiers" make a beeline for the jazzy bagpiper's wool jacket. Apparently the price of fashion is worth the sacrifice, but they'll soon learn. It may be hot and humid, or it may be chucking rain, but suck it up one must when one is a soldier.

Now properly turned out, soldiers stroll into the parade square for foot drill lessons. "Left, right, left, right, and halt!" shouts Lehman. The children stop immediately in front of her with unsoldierly grins plastered on their faces. They continue marching to the beat of the pipe and drum band while Lehman regales them with stories of how certain tunes were played during battle to denote what maneuvers the soldiers should perform. They learn it's considered ungentlemanly to kill a musician in battle, so arms were hacked off instead. The recruits are impressed, though a tad disappointed this barbarism never happened in Halifax, as the fort was never attacked.

"Do you want to examine the black powder magazine?" asks Lehman. (The black powder magazine is the storeroom for kegs of gun powder.) Heads nod furiously. "Quick, then! Firm up your lines, and let's march out," she orders. We parents wonder why our marching orders aren't as quickly obeyed at home.

Inside, the children roll the wooden barrels so the gunpowder won't clump up, just as members of the infantry did when this room was filled over a century ago. Then, there's a cadence lesson on drum pads before graduating to historic snare drums. Matching the beat with their footsteps is a tricky business. Everyone, however, passes the grade inside the school room, where soldiers of bygone days learned how to count, write their names, and read maps.

Learn the ropes during A Soldier's Life program at Halifax Citadel National Historic Site.

It's a hoot riding the tidal rapids on the Bay of Fundy.

Pedal your way through the city with rental bikes.

Kids calm down and engage their senses at Halifax Public Gardens.

RAISE THE FLAG

Soon it's off to the signal post to send a coded message. There were no phones back then, so recruits had to raise the flag as high as they could to convey secret messages. Think this task is as easy as raising a blue flag at half-mast? Oh, no! Coded messages are military signals used to communicate with other forts and bases within sight of each other. Messages are chosen from a big book of message instructions inside the signal post.

Sadly, our message was quite boring: "I'm about to start sending code alphabet alert." It could've been much more glamorous, such as, "There is a desertion from the Navy!" Still, junior officers must learn to follow orders, and they lower the Dominion Flag with bolts, shackles, and rope (remember, we've been transported back to 1869). "This is complicated," admits seven-year-old Emmett from Owen Sound, Ontario. He and the other children solemnly fold the flag, and eventually it's squared away, and the coded message is sent.

After perfecting all drills, the kids stand down and suss out snacks in the Sergeant's Mess, also known as the Regimental Coffee Bar. At our leisure we explore the citadel's rooms, walls, and tunnels, which we didn't get to see while enlisted. Now we're at ease. We made it through.

MONUMENTAL MUSEUMS

Did you know Halifax played a key role in the relief efforts for the *Titanic*? While survivors were shipped to New York, those who perished were transported to Halifax. A permanent exhibit at the Maritime Museum of the Atlantic details how Halifax responded to the tragedy, and includes displays on the *Titanic*'s creation. Haligonians braved horrible conditions to recover the bodies and assist with relief efforts. Their personal stories, plus those of certain victims (many of whom were buried in Halifax), are highlighted in this museum. Some mariners kept pieces of the ship's wreckage, which were then passed down through generations until donated to this museum.

Is anyone in your squad fascinated by shipwreck treasures?

There are over 10,000 recorded shipwreck stories of vessels lost off the shores of Nova Scotia. The museum also details why the waters off this province are so treacherous, and showcases recovered bounty. Another exhibit you won't want to miss reveals how the 1917 Halifax Explosion reduced the thriving port city to ruins. Littles who can't get enough of Theodore Tugboat can meet their favourite characters while learning how a busy harbour works at a permanent exhibit dedicated to the perky entertainer. And no visit is complete without paying your respects to Merlin the Talking Parrot.

The Canadian Museum of Immigration at Pier 21 was once the gateway into Canada for 1 million immigrants between 1928 and 1971. It is Canada's equivalent to Ellis Island, and gives youngsters a sense of the uncertainty, hopes, and fears every new Canadian faces when immigrating to our multicultural country. While the topic of immigration may seem a bit heavy, the museum does a good job of keeping kids engaged with hands-on activities. There are suitcases children can pack, as they make tough choices between toys and necessary items for a new life in the New World, and inter-active displays where kids guess what items might be confiscated by customs officials. Train cars also showcase what cross-country trips must have been like with so little gear and space.

KICKING AROUND TOWN

Get your bearings with a city bike tour that showcases the best of Halifax within two hours. On tours with I Heart Bikes, you'll spin past historic monuments, public art installations, and charming parks. Cruise by the Titanic House and historic fort ruins in Point Pleasant Park, and meander your way into the inner city, where a swish new library abuts Dalhousie University. You can rent bikes (including carriers and kids' bikes) without a tour, too.

Stop and smell the roses at Halifax Public Gardens, an alluring Victorian garden set in central Halifax. Once a piece of swamp-land, this blossoming urban oasis and now national historic site has remained largely unchanged since opening in 1867, the year of

Canadian Confederation. Visitors can skip or roll strollers along the pathways that meander through 17 acres (7 hectares) of landscaped, Victorian-style gardens.

Ready for a Big Harbour adventure? Fans of the popular children's television series *Theodore Tugboat* can tour the Big Harbour aboard *Theodore Too*. This jaunty yellow tugboat introduces tots to his friends from one side of the Big Harbour to the other, while bringing the sights and sounds of this working port city to life.

Halifax has a lovely boardwalk that also begs to be explored. Along the waterfront, you'll find a number of museums, shops, and galleries, plus a playground with a sculpture called *The Wave*, which you're not supposed to climb, but everybody does. There are boat tours that range from sightseeing and whale watching to deep sea fishing. Refuel at one of the many snack shacks or patios anchoring the harbour.

BEACH TIME
About a half-hour's drive from Halifax lies Lawrencetown Beach, a provincial beach park set along the Eastern Shore. Some of the best surfing in North America can be had here, and if you don't surf, this lifeguard-patrolled beach is tops for swimming, too. Families can take surf lessons together, and some even include the surfboard rental for the rest of the day, allowing you to practise on your own. It's a pleasant spot, with change rooms and showers on-site.

¶ TASTE

The unsinkable history of the **Five Fishermen Restaurant & Grill** began after the *Titanic* slid into its watery grave off the coast of Newfoundland in 1912. Many victims' bodies were taken to John Snow & Co. Funeral Home, located inside what is now this fish restaurant. Reeking of history and ghost stories, the dining room is quite atmospheric, but it is also family-friendly with a children's menu for the twelve-and-under set.

Proper pub grub can be found at **Celtic Corner**, across the harbour and near the ferry terminal in Dartmouth. Families are welcome at this traditional, working-class pub that serves up unpretentious Irish fare. Feast on meat pies and lamb stews, or try a boxty, an Irish potato pancake that wraps around a savoury stew-like filling. While a kids' menu won't be presented, they do have one and can recite it to you.

Wedged in Portland Hills Centre, a Dartmouth strip mall, **Piez Bistro** is a small café that shouldn't be overlooked. Gourmet pizzas are made with locally sourced ingredients, and gluten-free isn't a problem. Don't leave without scoring a homemade peanut butter ball.

NAP

Perched upon the waterfront in Halifax, **Halifax Marriott Harbourfront Hotel** is steps away from city attractions. Rooms are spacious, and there's an indoor pool. The sixth floor has a lounge with breakfast, snacks, and appetizers, so what you pay in the room upgrade could be made up in food savings if you're strategic enough. Breakfasts are reasonably priced, and generous portions allow two people to comfortably share.

The pet-friendly **Atlantica Hotel** lies across the street from Halifax Commons, a vast green space that's home to the Halifax Oval, an Olympic-sized skating surface that offers complimentary roller skate and bike rentals all summer long. This hotel encourages guests to travel in style with a complimentary limousine service during the work week to downtown addresses. There's an indoor pool, and children under twelve years old dine for free. And there's no need to bundle into one bed: cribs, cots, and bunk beds are all on hand.

GETTING AROUND

Halifax Transit operates the public buses and four passenger ferries that service two routes along **Halifax Harbour**. Experience the oldest saltwater ferry service in North America by taking a ferry ride to Dartmouth from downtown Halifax. Ask for a paper "transfer": if you journey back within an hour, the return trip is free.

It'll take you at least thirty minutes to get from **Halifax Stanfield International Airport** to downtown Halifax. Halifax Transit operates its **MetroX** service to downtown Halifax on bus No. 320 every thirty minutes between 6 a.m. and 9 a.m. and between 3 p.m. and 6 p.m. Outside those hours, the bus departs hourly. From May 1 to October 31, **Maritime Bus** offers an airport shuttle service to Halifax and Dartmouth. Children under twelve ride for free, but require a ticket to travel. Taxis and limousines have the same set price from the airport, so if you're thinking of taking a taxi, ask for a limo instead. You can book these through the ground transportation desk at the airport.

 ## FUN FACTS

- **Halifax Harbour** is one of the deepest in the world, second only to Sydney, Australia.
- Open year round, the **Halifax Seaport Farmers' Market** is the longest continuously running farmers' market in North America.
- Halifax operates the **oldest saltwater ferry service in North America**. Since 1752, ferries have run between Halifax and Dartmouth.
- **The Halifax Explosion** was the greatest man-made explosion before the atomic bomb. Learn more about this disaster that occurred on December 6, 1917, at the **Maritime Museum of the Atlantic** or during a **Harbour Hopper tour**.
- The **Halifax Citadel National Historic Site** is one the most visited national historic sites in Canada.
- Taking place each summer, the **Halifax International Busker Festival** is the oldest and largest of its kind in Canada.
- Halifax is closer to London, England, than it is to Victoria, British Columbia.

GET EXCITED ABOUT YOUR TRIP

- For advanced readers and teens, *Blizzard of Glass: The Halifax Explosion of 1917*, by Sally M. Walker, is a gripping account of the devastating blast that killed nearly 2,000 people.
- For younger readers, pick up *Halifax Explodes!*, by Frieda Wishinsky.
- Many movies have been filmed in Nova Scotia, including *Titanic*.
- Nova Scotia is home to many Celtic musicians. Listen to music by Natalie MacMaster and the Rankin Family.

Picturesque Peggy's Cove is one of the province's top attractions.

Endless stretches of beach line the Lighthouse Route.

Nova Scotia's Lighthouse Route

Sandy Beaches and Shipwrecks Offshore

Hugging its way along the coast from Halifax to Yarmouth, the Lighthouse Route is all about the journey, not the end destination. This is a trip that begs you to slow down. Not only is this scenic roadway an affordable East Coast escape, it places you firmly in the driver's seat. If you're the sort who wants to tick every attraction off your list, go for it! Or simply pull out of the fast lane and make spur-of-the-moment decisions that will take you on adventures you never imagined. Whether you're looking for a laid-back beach break, a sensational Sunday drive, or to learn more about the first free Black settlement in Canada, you'll find it along Nova Scotia's Southern Shore.

PEGGY'S COVE

It's less than an hour's drive from Halifax to Peggy's Cove, but before visiting its famous lighthouse, I recommend stopping at Peggy of the Cove Gallery in Glen Margaret. Half a million annual visitors make a pit stop at Peggy's Cove, yet only a few intrepid tourists hit up this quirky historic house-cum-gallery a mere ten minutes away.

Local artist and character Ivan Fraser has written children's books based on a fictional character (Peggy) who was the sole survivor of a shipwreck near the famous fishing village of Peggy's Cove. Fraser has applied his artistic talents by making a Peggy's Cove mural on the side of his family's homestead house. Check out his wonderful art installations on the front lawn, with pieces such as a multicoloured tree and a super-sized lobster trap children can climb into. House tours are free, and kids are encouraged to choose a toy from the treasure chest upstairs. If you're lucky, Mr. Fraser will be on hand telling tall tales and describing the inspiration behind his lovely books.

Continue on to Peggy's Cove and spend a few minutes taking in the beauty of this iconic destination before scrambling over the craggy rocks for an obligatory family photo. A word of caution: Never walk on black, green, or wet rocks. People have perished after slipping on the rocks and falling into the ocean. Once this stop is crossed off your bucket list, drive to Paddy's Head Lighthouse in Indian Harbour, a much less visited yet equally attractive maritime site. After sightseeing, nosh on lobster or freshly shucked oysters at nearby Ryer Lobsters.

Before winding your way back to Halifax, stop at Terence Bay and the Interpretation Centre for the SS *Atlantic*. Prior to the sinking of the *Titanic*, the tragic end of this luxury steamship of the famed White Star Line was the world's worst single-vessel marine disaster; it sank off the coast of Nova Scotia in 1873. The centre details how local fishermen led the rescue, and you can view the impressive collection of items salvaged from the ship, or learn about the history behind the Nova Scotia Tartan, which was designed by a local resident. Outside, saunter along the board-walk through the SS *Atlantic* Heritage Park to take in views of the sea. This peaceful spot is located on the grounds of the St. Paul's Anglican Church cemetery, where hundreds of the unidentified victims of the SS *Atlantic* were buried.

LUNENBURG

A contender for the prettiest town in the Maritimes, Lunenburg is perhaps best known for building and launching the *Bluenose*, Nova Scotia's famous racing schooner. Despite its good looks, Lunenburg is an authentic fishing town with all the sights, smells, and quirky characters one would expect in such a place.

A colourful legacy has been left behind in historic Lunenburg.

There are so many bunnies to befriend at White Point Beach Resort.

Budget plenty of time for beachcombing when journeying down the Lighthouse Route.

Enjoy a beach bonfire at White Point Beach Resort.

There are only two urban UNESCO sites in North America, and Old Town Lunenburg is one of them; Québec City is the other. Back in 1890, it was the richest town per capita in Canada thanks to its booming fishery; the town ended up with an amazing architectural legacy as a result. Today it's one of the best preserved British Colonial towns in North America.

There's a lot to explore in Lunenburg, and your family will find it infinitely more interesting seen through the eyes of a local. Shelah Allen, co-owner of Lunenburg Walking Tours, is a seventh-generation resident who knows this town like the back of her hand. Delving into stories tourists don't often hear (unless they spend an awful lot of time in the pub), Shelah reveals more than the town's history as you stroll past the waterfront and vibrant-coloured houses. It's not uncommon for residents of seafaring towns to be a tad superstitious, and kids get a kick out of learning about these traditions. Just be prepared to spit on your thumb if you come across a single crow.

Before leaving, nip into the Fisheries Museum of the Atlantic. You can chat up a retired fishing fleet captain, learn how to shuck a scallop, and examine old fishing boats. If you're not squeamish, be sure to plunge your hands into the touch tank to get a closer feel for the creatures of the sea.

MAHONE BAY

One of the biggest joys found when travelling at your own pace is weaving in and out of charming coastal villages. The abundance of heritage homes and sailboats bobbing in the harbour make Mahone Bay an attractive community to to visit. Like many beautiful destinations in Canada, it's an artist's haven brimming with shops showcasing their skills, particularly pottery, pewter, and handmade quilts. Along Main Street, Amos Pewter offers a complimentary hands-on experience where you can personalize your own pewter sand dollar and take a tour of their workshop.

If you've heard about the mystery of Oak Island, made popular by the History Channel TV show *The Curse of Oak Island*, you'll want to investigate this private island off the coast near Mahone Bay. During the summer months, the Friends of Oak Island Society offers a two-hour walking tour that delves into the island's enigmatic history. Private tours can be arranged with Oak Island Tours.

BIRCHTOWN

Farther down the coast lies Birchtown, the first free Black settlement in Canada. In the late 1700s, United Empire Loyalists (those who maintained allegiance to the British Crown during the American Revolution) came up from the United States. The Black Loyalist Heritage Centre tells the stories of these brave immigrants and their ancestry. (If you enjoyed reading *The Book of Negroes*, you'll definitely want to visit.) Here you can search for ancestral roots, get a first-hand glimpse of what living in a pit house was like, and take a pleasant walk along the Heritage Walking Trail.

BEACH TIME

In the Hubbards and St. Margaret's Bay region, Queensland Beach, Cleveland Beach, and Hubbards Beach are local favourites. "They're not deserted by any means, but they're where we locals go. We were there every weekend last summer!" exclaims Helen Earley, mom of two and editor of the website Family Fun Halifax. Bayswater Beach, another Haligonian favourite, is nice and large, and across the highway there is a memorial site for the victims of Swissair Flight 111.

In the Lunenburg region, Rissers Beach Provincial Park boasts a sheltered beach, inland marsh, and two campgrounds, where many a family settle in for the summer. Popular Crescent Beach connects the LaHave Islands to the mainland, and hosts family-friendly events. Hirtle's Beach is another popular sandy enclave in the area, framed by drumlin cliffs. Carters Beach, near Port Mouton, is one of the province's most beautiful, and you're apt to find sand dollars the size of your palm.

Crack lobster shells alongside other visitors and friendly Maritimers.

Backed by sand dunes and an open salt marsh, Summerville Beach Provincial Park is as nice a spot for bird watching as it is for sunbathing. There are many reasons you'd want to stay at White Point Beach Resort, and its white sand beach is one of them. Not many tourists make it down to Crescent Beach in Lockeport. This well-kept secret holds many family-friendly events.

WORTHY SIDE TRIP

Since Nova Scotia is relatively easy to get around, it makes sense to visit both sides of the peninsula to experience the difference in the sea. For a rip-roaring good time, go tidal bore rafting along the Bay of Fundy with Shubenacadie River Runners. Located an hour's drive north of Halifax, this is one adventure you shouldn't go on unless you don't mind getting really wet. An ideal excursion for families with children over eight years old, they'll also take the younger set depending on their weight and stamina.

After a zippy ride in a Zodiac boat to where the incoming tide is at its best, you'll roll along with the eddy's gentle waves before doing an about face and crashing directly into them. At first you'll only get slightly wet, and then it really comes on, and on, and on. Hard and fast, the waves pummel the boat and go over your head. You'll be wearing full rain gear (supplied by the tour operator), but it won't matter. Soon you'll be soaked through to your unmentionables. It's possible you'll feel slightly concerned for the children on board, but the grins on their faces will confirm they're having just as much fun as you are.

After riding the waves to your heart's content, you'll peel off and motor farther down the river. At a certain point, participants are encouraged to jump off the boat and take a swim. You'll be soaked to the skin anyway, so why not properly finish the job? Kids cannonball off the raft into the water and are hauled back in by their life jackets. Expect to emerge looking like a drowned rat while feeling elated after experiencing these tides in a way most people never have.

Tip

Bring towels and a change of clothing. Wear warm clothes you don't mind getting wet and dirty underneath the rain gear and boots provided. (The mud in the river has a high iron content that can stain clothing.) There are showers and, blessedly, heated floors in the change rooms. Complimentary hot chocolate and cookies await after your adventure.

🍴 TASTE

Let tour bus passengers eat at Peggy's Cove (though I'm told locals are partial to the large square slabs of steamed gingerbread served up with soft ice cream, from the gift shop take-out window). Instead, it's a short drive from Peggy's Cove to **Shaw's Landing**, where you'll want to break for lobster rolls, chowder, and a children's menu.

Half the pleasure of **LaHave Bakery** is getting there. Peel off Highway 103 onto Route 331 for a scenic drive south of Lunenberg. The littles will have a hoot taking the LaHave Ferry, one of the oldest cable river ferries in Canada. It's less than a ten-minute trip, leaving at the top and bottom of the hour, and the bakery is located just before the ferry dock. The wheat used in their home-style baked goods is local and freshly milled, and you can also pick up readymade meals and groceries.

Even locals attend the **Shore Club** in Hubbards for lobster suppers (as did Prince Charles and Princess Diana in 1983). In addition to your freshly cooked lobster, dive into the unlimited salad bar, all-you-can-eat mussels, and dessert. They're not open every day of the week, so check their website in advance to avoid disappointment. Reservations are recommended.

In Lunenburg, sit on the patio at the **South Shore Fish Shack** for prime views of *Bluenose II* when she's in port. It's a tough call deciding between the fried clams, the fish and chips, or the lobster roll, but every portion comes with hand-cut fries, making no decision necessary on that front. Adventurous types ought to sample cod tongues, which taste similar to scallops.

NAP

Parents keen to recreate that laid-back summertime vibe they enjoyed as kids will want to book into **White Point Beach Resort**, one of Atlantic Canada's oldest seaside resorts. Set along a sweep of white sand on the province's South Shore, this well-loved family resort offers meal plans you can choose to opt into, plus several different types of accommodation, including seafront cottages with wood-burning fires. Rooms are kitted out with a kettle, microwave, and mini-fridge.

The Kids' Zone offers a dizzying array of activities to fill your stay, and complimentary children's programming holds attention from morning to night. The best part of this classic beach retreat isn't its family activities, which include marshmallow roasts and beach cookouts—it's the bunnies! Hundreds of adorable rabbits frolic freely around the property. The resort offers bags of bunny food; if you're patient, they'll eat right out of your hand.

GETTING AROUND

Fly into **Halifax Stanfield International Airport** and rent a vehicle from there to begin your South Shore road trip.

FUN FACTS

- *Bluenose* was both a fishing vessel and Canada's most famous sailing schooner. She's a provincial icon in Nova Scotia, and her likeness is commemorated on the Canadian dime. Eerily, every vessel that challenged *Bluenose* was later lost at sea.
- *Bluenose II* is a replica built in 1963 using the original plans for *Bluenose*. You can view *Bluenose II* and walk her decks when she's in port in Lunenburg.
- **Nova Scotians are referred to as Bluenosers**, but that's not just because of the famous schooner. One theory is that it's a reference to the blue-skinned potato that once grew in the Annapolis Valley. Another traces the nickname's roots back to fishermen wearing blue woollen mittens. Quite often they faced fierce Atlantic winds and would've wiped their noses with their mittens. The dye from these mitts would have left a blueish mark after contact.

- **Brook trout** is the provincial fish, while the **osprey** is Nova Scotia's bird. **Mayflower** and **red spruce** are the provincial flower and tree, respectively. Nova Scotia even has a provincial berry! It's the blueberry, which you may find growing wild.

✦ GET EXCITED ABOUT YOUR TRIP ─────────────

- Read *B is for Bluenose: A Nova Scotia Alphabet*, by Susan Tooke.
- Elementary-aged children enjoy *Peggy of the Cove*, written by local author Ivan Fraser.
- *Capturing Joy: The Story of Maud Lewis*, by Jo Ellen Bogart, is a lovely picture book biography of a talented Nova Scotia folk artist who suffered poverty and physical disabilities.
- *The Kids Book of Black Canadian History*, by Rosemary Sadlier, reveals inspiring stories about those who fought oppression, and the events they participated in. *Birchtown and the Black Loyalists*, by Wanda Lauren Taylor, recounts their incredible journey from Africa to the United States, and their struggles on Canadian soil.
- Fans of *The Curse of Oak Island* on the History Channel will want to read *Oak Island and the Search for Buried Treasure*, by Joann Hamilton-Barry.
- Listen to *Songs of the Sea*, a toe-tapping collection by Atlantic Canada's favourite recording artists that reveals what life is like on and at the edge of the sea.

Take some time to read on PEI, just as Anne of Green Gables would have.

There's nothing like tucking into a fresh PEI lobster at New Glasgow Lobster Suppers.

Prince Edward Island

Home of Anne of Green Gables

Canada's eastern seaboard is a magical place for a holiday on a budget. With friendly locals and postcard pretty villages, the Maritimes are ideal for family getaways—particularly Prince Edward Island. PEI is Canada's smallest province and also one of our loveliest. You can easily drive from one end of the island to the other in a day, but you wouldn't want to do that; visitors need to savour their time here. Whether you're taking in the haunts of Anne of Green Gables, digging for your dinner, or tapping toes at an outdoor music festival, this down-home destination is sure to remind you that good things come in small packages.

CAPTURE THE SPIRIT OF ANNE OF GREEN GABLES

Canada's most iconic fictional heroine, Anne of Green Gables, is a spunky red-headed orphan whose antics are beloved around the world. The novels, written by Canadian author Lucy Maud Montgomery, depict the lifestyle of many island families in the late 19th century. Though Anne's story is well over a century old, the inspiration remains alive and well.

Anne attractions are abundant throughout PEI, and a good place to start is along Green Gables Shore on the north side of the island; this particular landscape inspired the setting of the Anne novels. At Green Gables Heritage Place, families can explore the 19th-century gardens, farmyard, and, most importantly, the tidy green-gabled home the story was set in.

Would you believe that the Haunted Woods and Lover's Lane really exist? Indeed they do, and you can stroll along these Acadian forest paths while admiring the juicy raspberries that cling to the bushes lining them. Filled with canopies of red spruce and maple, low tree branches are ripe for climbing, and you can set the kids on a mission to try to find the Babbling Brook on Balsam Hollow Trail, just off Lover's Lane. After your romp through the woods, refuel with old-fashioned, homemade baked goods, such as butter tarts and that infamous raspberry cordial. Rest assured, the staff will not repeat Anne's blunder and confuse the cordial with Marilla's currant wine.

Avonlea Village in the town of Cavendish is another worthy stop for Anne fans. At this free-of-charge historical village, children can enjoy that immense sense of freedom we took for granted when we were their age. There are period shops to suss out and a schoolyard with old-fashioned play equipment. With several dining options, this attraction is a great spot for lunch or an early dinner. Conclude your Anne journey by going to the theatre in Charlottetown. According to Guinness, Anne of Green Gables: The Musical™ is the world's longest-running annual musical, and the popular production is a hit for all ages.

BEACH TIME

Beachgoers are spoiled for choice along this fishhook-shaped isle, with a selection of red and white sand beaches to sink your toes into. The island is famous for its red soil, thanks to its high concentrations of iron oxide. The result is fertile land, ideal for potato crops, and delightful red sandy shores that unfurl from the slopes of sandstone cliffs. There are loads of pristine sweeps of sand to choose from, and families do well when plunking their towels down at those that offer complimentary programming by Parks Canada.

Within the protected area of Prince Edward Island National Park, families can take a guided walk, chill out while listening to some lobster tales, or become beach detectives uncovering treasures along the shore. Perhaps the most entertaining activity is sandcastle building with a master sculptor at both Cavendish Beach

Dalvay by the Sea is a lovely seaside resort well loved by families looking to reconnect.

Search for giant bar clams in the ocean with Tranquility Cove Adventures.

Learn how to build a sandcastle with a master sculpture at Prince Edward Island National Park.

Feast on giant bar clams after harvesting them yourself.

and Brackley Beach. Children learn how to create impressive waterfront properties, borrowing tools and tricks of the trade from the sculptor-in-residence.

DIG FOR DINNER

Kids won't mind being stuck making a meal when they're in charge of digging for it. Clamming is one delicious activity everyone can participate in. Standing waist-deep in the cool Atlantic water might seem like an unconventional way to spend a summer's day—but, then again, so is throwing back a giant bar clam mid-morning. When clamming with Tranquility Cove Adventures, wade right in and heed their advice on how to best reap the bounty of the sea.

Skipper Perry, a third-generation fisherman, takes families out to Cardigan Bay on his spruced-up lobster boat. Before donning a wetsuit and plunging into the ocean, he offers instructions and a garden rake. "What you're looking for is belly buttons in the sand," instructs Perry. Once you spot these markers, rake the soft sand, and if you feel something hard beneath the surface, put a bit of muscle into it.

I find it takes two or three strong pulls before I uncover what feels like a rock. The reward: a hefty-sized bar clam. Perry patiently helps children spot the indentations in the sand, but there's no need to worry about the kids. On our excursion, they managed to haul in just as many clams as the adults.

After about an hour of foraging, wade over to a deserted island where the crew has set up a clam roast against the red sandstone cliffs. Do clams you've personally harvested and cooked along a beach taste better than what the world's best seafood restaurants serve up? I think so. Especially if you dip these meaty morsels into the warm broth of seawater and released clam juice they're boiled in. Our clams were savoury and buttery, not at all briny, and we gorged ourselves to the point of bursting.

After the clam bake, kids scamper along the shore, gleefully plunging sticks into the fattest of jellyfish. Then it's back on the boat for the return journey, as the crew hauls in lobster and crab traps for an interactive fishing lesson. Cruise past Panmure Island Provincial Park, where the island's most famous lighthouse (the one displayed on all the PEI postcards) stands guard. Near there, one can spot seals bobbing in the water and eagles soaring in the sky. "This area is good for storytelling," admits Perry. "It's not always about the fishing."

Clamming season runs each year from April 1 to December 31; you can score 100 clams per person per day without a licence.

VICTORIA-BY-THE-SEA

The storybook village of Victoria-by-the-Sea lies on the southern shore of the island, and couldn't be more charming. Stately Victorian-era homes and galleries line the streets laid out in a perfect grid. The working harbour boasts adorable shops, and an operating lighthouse showcases an exhibit on the town's seafaring history.

If you want to live out every child's fantasy, take the hands-on chocolate-making class at Island Chocolates, a family-run café and chocolatier that handcrafts Belgian chocolates. Lessons begin with learning about harvesting and the production practices of their suppliers in Ghana and Ecuador. Fortunately, this discussion takes place over frothy mugs of velvety smooth cocoa. Then it's onto swirling sugary concoctions through a silky sea of melted chocolate before plopping them onto a marble counter. At times it feels like finger painting as you create Jackson Pollock–like works of edible art, while learning how best to work the chocolate before it hardens.

After two hours of rolling, dipping, and molding, fantasies become reality when you're given the all-clear to reap your rewards. Even if you don't have time for a class, it's worth popping in for the homemade desserts, such as fresh PEI strawberries drizzled with warm Belgium chocolate and lashed with whipped cream. Vacations don't get much sweeter than this.

Historic lighthouses dot the coastline of the island.

▌ TASTE

One Maritime tradition not to miss: tying on a bib and tucking into a lobster supper. **New Glasgow Lobster Suppers** run from mid-May until October. They open early for dinner, which suits families with young children just fine. For a set price you'll chow down on all-you-can-eat mussels, a freshly caught Atlantic lobster, salads, homemade rolls, and a wide selection of pies and cakes. You'll sit with other diners at long banquet tables, but that Maritime hospitality is infectious and you won't leave a stranger.

There are some delightful eateries in Victoria-by-the-Sea, including **Island Chocolates** and **Landmark Café**. Hit up this café for hearty seafood entrées and children's portions.

▌ NAP

Dalvay by the Sea is a charming seaside enclave that was once a 19th-century summer home. You may remember it, however, as the White Sands Hotel from the *Anne of Green Gables* movie. Families can stay in the lodge or in a rustic three-bedroom cabin. Just as in Anne's day, there are no TVs or telephones (though there is WiFi). Afternoon tea inside the Queen Anne–style Victorian lodge is a must, as is taking a paddleboat out for a spin around the resort's lake. From the property you can cycle to the beach (rentals available) or walk across the dunes and go beachcombing along an endless stretch of sand. Because of its architectural significance, the hotel is commemorated as a national historic site.

▌ GETTING AROUND

You can fly into **Charlottetown Airport**, but many families combine a trip to PEI with other provinces in Atlantic Canada. If coming from New Brunswick, it's quite the experience driving over Confederation Bridge (which links PEI to mainland Canada).

From Nova Scotia, **Northumberland Ferries** offers several crossings a day, connecting Caribou, Nova Scotia, to Wood Islands, PEI. You can even access PEI from the Magdalen Islands in the middle of the Gulf of St. Lawrence via the **CTMA** ferry. Once on PEI, you'll want to rent a vehicle to get around.

☟ FUN FACTS

- PEI is the smallest and most densely populated province in Canada.
- Charlottetown, the capital of PEI, is known as the **birthplace of Confederation**, thanks to it having hosted the Charlottetown Conference in 1864. During this conference, our founding fathers discussed the framework for the formation of Canada in 1867.
- The **Confederation Bridge** is the longest bridge in the world spanning ice-covered waters.
- First published in 1908, *Anne of Green Gables* has sold more than 50 million copies worldwide.
- PEI's provincial symbols are the **blue jay**, **lady's slipper**, and **red oak tree**.

✦ GET EXCITED ABOUT YOUR TRIP

- *Chung Lee Loves Lobsters* and *I is for Island: A Prince Edward Island Alphabet,* both written by Hugh MacDonald, are fun picture books for young children.
- *The Summer of the Marco Polo*, by Lynn Manuel, will enchant slightly older readers.
- Lucy Maud Montgomery wrote many books besides *Anne of Green Gables*. Get the Anne series boxed set and plow your way through, or watch the TV miniseries.

Spot ships and icebergs from Cabot Tower at Signal Hill National Historic Site.

Head down Gower Street or Bond Street to see the jellybean-coloured homes.

Avalon Peninsula

Explore the Edge of a Continent

Looking over the steely grey waters of the Atlantic, we watch fishing boats carefully maneuver around imposing icebergs. Lingering longer, we spot mists of water spouting into the air, signalling the arrival of whales. Suddenly, dense fog swoops in and cloaks the indented coastline in a hazy embrace. There's a feeling of remoteness in Newfoundland and Labrador, like you've reached a secluded corner of the world. To some extent you have: this is the easternmost tip of North America.

This province's remoteness is part of the intrigue, and why many people think they'll get to Newfoundland and Labrador "someday." Once they do, they usually regret they didn't make the trip sooner. This is a place like no other in Canada, with a unique culture dating back thousands of years, absorbing Aboriginal, Viking, English, French, Portuguese, and Irish influences.

Long, harsh winters and the unforgiving sea have created warm, close communities and larger-than-life locals who, if you let them, will knit you into the rich tapestry of their lives; just be willing to listen to a story or three. No matter where you're from, it's hard not to enjoy the colourful fishing villages, live music, and even livelier characters found along the Avalon Peninsula.

TIP OF THE CONTINENT

Where to start your journey? Cape Spear Lighthouse National Historic Site is perched on the easternmost point of the continent, and is the oldest surviving lighthouse in the province. You can tour the lighthouse and the living quarters of its keepers, and during the summer months, interpreters portray the lighthouse keeper or his wife. Venture up the spiral wooden staircase to where the oil lamps (which needed to be cleaned, continuously filled with oil, and wound every three hours) shone brightly to protect vessels at sea. Cape Spear is a wonderful spot to witness dramatic weather. When the fog rolls in, you'll get a taste of the complete isolation the light keepers would've experienced. On a fine day you can see clear across to Signal Hill.

The site was also used as a temporary coastal defence battery during WWII to protect St. John's Harbour from attack. (German U-boats were known to skulk around Canada's coastline.)

Peer inside the cement bunkers that look menacingly like jail cells, but were actually used to store ammunition. Scramble over gun barrels that were too heavy to transport out after the war. Pretend you're on lookout for the enemy, although the only invaders you'll see are whales and icebergs.

Tip

Take an Xplorers activity book upon entry to better enjoy the site. Complete it and you'll receive a certificate and a special Parks Canada souvenir.

PETTY HARBOUR

Make your coastal connection more memorable by continuing on to the outport town of Petty Harbour, a few minutes' drive from Cape Spear. This traditional fishing village, with its pretty homes set on an outcrop of craggy rock, received a Tidy Towns designation, and is the hometown of famed Canadian singer Alan Doyle of Great Big Sea. Adventurous families can brave the zip lines, and there's a museum that may appeal to grandparents.

From June to October, stop in at Petty Harbour Mini Aquarium, one of the few catch and release aquariums in the country. Get an eye-level view of the sea from the thirty exhibits filled with local fish and crustaceans. Feel what lies beneath the ocean by plunging your hand into touch tanks filled with hermit crabs, starfish, sea urchins,

That Noon Day Gun at Signal Hill National Historic Site is a real blast!

Fresh cod is served up by Cod Sounds at their beach boil-up.

Sharing the chair at Cape Spear Lighthouse National Historic Site.

Petty Harbour is a pretty town close to Cape Spear Lighthouse National Historic Site and is worth popping into.

anemones, and sea cucumbers. At the end of the season, all visiting marine life are returned to the ocean from which they were collected.

ST. JOHN'S

St. John's may be one of the oldest English cities in North America, but it sure isn't tired. Stroll down Harbour Drive and admire mighty vessels along the dock. Walking around downtown is made much more fun when you're headed to Jellybean Row. Gower Street and Bond Street are good places to start, but throughout downtown you can view the candy-coloured Victorian homes.

Tip

Head to Moo Moo's Ice Cream on Kings Road to get your dose of design on the sly.

PARKS AND PLAYGROUNDS

There are many peaceful parks in which your family can burn off energy. Bowring Park is one of the loveliest, with a playground, outdoor pool, and ponds filled with ducks and swans. Stop at the playground at Bannerman Park en route to Signal Hill. In summer, you can take a dip in the outdoor pool, and there's an outdoor ice rink set up in winter. If you're headed to charming Quidi Vidi—set within the city and reputed to be the oldest fishing village in North America—Caribou Memorial Park on Quidi Vidi Lake has playground equipment.

SIGNAL HILL

Travel back to another era at Signal Hill National Historic Site as you cast your gaze over the ocean and imagine a time before ship-to-shore radio. Back then, signalmen communicated to townsfolk with flag signals from this strategic location. They'd scan the ocean for ships and then fly the flag of whichever merchant owned the ship coming into port, allowing shopkeepers to be at the ready.

That system, and the world of communication, changed on this spot in 1901 when Guglielmo Marconi received the world's first transatlantic wireless signal. Kids, this is a big deal—devices like iPhones wouldn't be possible without these milestones.

Next, step back a century inside Cabot Tower, which was built in 1897 to commemorate the 400th anniversary of John Cabot's "voyage of discovery." Wind your way up the wooden staircase for sweeping views of St. John's Bay and St. John's Harbour. You may even spot Cape Spear Lighthouse on a clear day.

Visitors can take part in the city's proud military history by firing the Noon Day Gun, a lasting tradition that continues to mark time. Don't miss the Signal Hill Tattoo performances in July and August. You'll be stirred by the pomp and circumstance as the Tattoo performs fife and drum music from 1795, plus infantry drills from 1812 and WWI training exercises.

Also located on Signal Hill is the Johnson GEO CENTRE, filled with fun, hands-on exhibits to foster children's curiosity in science and geology. Explore the evolution of the planet, learn about space exploration, or get an in-depth look into the *Titanic* tragedy through artifacts and iceberg models. Hibernia KidsPlace is a special exploratory zone where children under seven years old can travel through a time tunnel and unleash their creativity by designing and building to their heart's content.

CULTURE VULTURE

Bringing together three attractions under one roof, The Rooms, a cultural facility, houses the Provincial Museum, Provincial Archives, and Provincial Art Gallery. This is just the place to explore the province's vast landscape, filled with polar bears and woodland caribou, without having to leave the city. There are many treasures of the sea to behold, from a 9-foot (2.7-metre) squid to a Spanish olive jar, circa 1600 found in Ferryland along the Avalon Peninsula.

WWI had a profound impact on the province, and one of the best exhibits exploring this period is Beaumont-Hamel and the Trail of the Caribou. For those not familiar with the Great War, this gallery is an excellent introduction into the Battle of the Somme and the sacrifices made by local soldiers. While the subject matter is heavy, the exhibit is appropriate for children and offers much to look at and ponder.

TOUR THE IRISH LOOP
The Avalon Peninsula is the Irish heart of Newfoundland and Labrador. Thousands of Irish immigrated here in the 18th century, and their traditions live on through rousing music and quirky characters who are more than keen to swap stories. Hit Highway 10 and follow the signs emblazoned with shamrocks; weave your way through emerald parcels of farmland, painstakingly cleared by hard-working immigrants, before driving into quaint outport communities.

PUFFINS
Newfoundland and Labrador is the seabird capital of the Northwest Atlantic. Along the Irish Loop, you'll come upon the town of Witless Bay. Off its coast, the four islands of the Witless Bay Ecological Reserve are home to thousands upon thousands of nesting seabirds, including puffins—black-and-white seabirds with jaunty orange bills and legs.

Visit from August to October and you just might come across the Puffin Patrol. When baby puffins leave their burrows on the ecological reserve for their very first flight, which is always at night, they can become disoriented by the lights of Witless Bay (confusing them for the moon). These birds are at risk of landing on the road and being run over; locals and visitors participate in patrol drives looking for lost puffins, rescuing up to twenty a night.

While Witless Bay Ecological Reserve is set up for researchers not tourists, there are still ways to get up close and personal with these adorable seabirds. Head to historic Bay Bulls for boat tours May to October. Step aboard and cruise alongside Gull Island, home to 1.5 million seabirds, 250,000 of which are puffins—the largest Atlantic puffin colony in North America.

Once you get close enough, you'll realize those white dots on the grass are puffin parents standing guard at the same home they return to year after year. You'll glide past other islands within the reserve, home to razor-billed auks and common murre, who lay eggs right on the rocks without a nest. There are 30,000 of these birds sandwiched ever so close together. Miraculously, they come back to the exact spot—give or take a few inches—year after year for birthing. Along the way, you may spot humpback whales or even icebergs. Bring your singing voice: you're still on the Irish Loop, and no boat ride is complete without a few toe-tapping traditional songs.

FERRYLAND

Founded in 1621 by Lord Baltimore (the same gent they named the American city after), Ferryland is no sleepy fishing village. The coast surrounding the community is littered with shipwrecks, and over the centuries the town has seen epic battles. Raided by both the Dutch and the French in the 17th century, the Colony of Avalon survived to become one of best-preserved early colonial sites in British North America. Ongoing excavations have recovered over 2 million artifacts.

Visitors can tour the active archaeological dig, strolling down a 17th-century street to see what treasures have been uncovered, before admiring the bounty in the Colony of Avalon Interpretation Centre. Every day brings new discoveries, from bits of pottery to intact gold coins. In fact, thousands of artifacts are uncovered each year. Tours finish inside a 17th-century kitchen, where reenactments of daily life in that era take place.

LIGHTHOUSE PICNIC

A beacon to passing ships since 1870, the lighthouse at Ferryland Head is still operational, in more ways than you might think. Anchored on the precipice of the Atlantic, this is reputed to be Canada's best picnic spot. After all, how many chances do most people get to dine al fresco at the edge of a continent?

Find your spot along the grassy bluff, and within a few minutes a picnic basket will be delivered to you. Gourmet sandwiches made with home-baked bread and freshly squeezed lemonade are but a few of the delicacies packed inside. There's no rush to finish quickly; you have all afternoon to feast upon the views and homemade goodies. Explore the 150-year-old lighthouse at your leisure, and be sure to bring a ball for outdoor games and binoculars for whale watching. This popular experience books up quickly, so be sure to reserve your family's spot well in advance.

¶¶ TASTE

There are many ways to sample the island's traditional foods and, as you'd expect, fish is abundant on every menu. No visit is complete without sampling fresh cod—and, of course, fish and chips. The **Duke of Duckworth** pub welcomes families and serves up some of the best fish and chips in town.

A few blocks away lies the **Newfoundland Chocolate Company**, where you can order a sinfully rich hot chocolate so thick it coats your teeth. Their café, located at Signal Hill, is an ideal spot for lunch and a sweet treat.

Chafe's Landing in Petty Harbour is a casual seafood eatery featuring fresh-off-the-boat fish and shellfish. Moose is also on the menu, if you're so inclined.

It's one thing to try typical Newfoundland dishes in a restaurant; it's quite another to cook them up yourself using traditional recipes that have been passed down for generations. A combination of taste, education, and fun, the hands-on cooking classes with **Cod Sounds** will have you fashioning pork pies, frying up damper devils, and throwing scrunchions into lassy (molasses) buns. Sit down together to enjoy the fruits of your labour; leftovers can be packed up and enjoyed later.

Throughout this child-friendly lesson, you'll learn how generations were sustained by cod fishing and how families made do with few store supplies. Living off the land was a way of life, one that you too can experience. Visitors can forage for wild edibles (also with Cod Sounds) along a section of the East Coast Trail, and finish off the experience with a beach boil-up. Between courses, kids beachcomb for seashells, seaweed, and smooth worry stones.

This glimpse of life along the sea gives families a chance to detach from their busy schedules while reconnecting to past traditions—no easy feat in this day and age.

NAP

Ideally situated in the heart of downtown, children under six eat for free (half price for seven- to twelve-year-olds) at **Delta St. John's**. There's a mini-fridge in each room, plus safety kits with socket protectors. Night-lights are available upon request. The ocean is too cold to swim in, but that disappointment is tempered by the hotel's heated pool and hot tub.

Compton House has large comfy rooms, many with Jacuzzi hot tubs. Great for smaller families, this secluded B&B boasts an expansive front lawn and baked goods to which you can help yourself all day long.

GETTING AROUND

Sites are spread out, and you won't find public transportation to must-see stops along the Irish Loop or Cape Spear, so it's best to arrange for a rental car from the airport. No car? No problem! **Newfoundland Tours** offers walking and driving tours to the province's best attractions. In St. John's, the **Trolley Line** provides step-on, step-off buses around the downtown core and popular city attractions from the Delta and Sheraton hotels.

FUN FACTS

- Newfoundland was the first part of Canada to be discovered by European explorers, yet it was the last province to join Confederation.
- In 1949, Newfoundland became Canada's tenth province, but before then it was a colony and dominion of the United Kingdom.
- In 2001, the province was officially renamed Newfoundland and Labrador.
- The time zone here is set thirty minutes ahead of Atlantic Daylight Time, meaning the day begins before the rest of North America. Get going before dawn, and you can be the first person in the New World to spot the day's sunrise.

- Littles can learn more about the provincial bird by reading *Atlantic Puffin: Little Brother of the North*, by Kristin Bieber Domm.
- Based on a true story, *Dolphin SOS*, illustrated by Julie Flett, recounts how local children saved distressed dolphins.
- Read *The Great Ferryland Dig: Exploring the Colony of Avalon*, by Necie Mouland, before your visit to Ferryland.
- *Rhymes from the Rock*, by Bonnie Jean Hicks, and *Over by the Harbour*, by Dwayne LaFitte, are lovely storybooks for young children.
- Music is an integral part of the culture here. Listen to Great Big Sea and the Irish Descendants for a taste of toe-tapping Newfoundland and Labrador music.

It's amazing how close you can get to icebergs on boat tours out of St. Anthony.

Explore the Viking Settlement at L'Anse aux Meadows National Historic Site.

Western Newfoundland

Explore the Viking Trail

I t's a cold, blustery summer day, but we are oh-so cozy sitting beside the fire, nursing steaming mugs of mulled partridgeberry tea. Inside this sod settler's hut someone is plucking a lyre, but its chords are drowned out as we laugh at the lively comments of Bjorn, a merchant-adventurer. Along with his wife, Thora, and a blacksmith, Ragnar, these reenactors have brought the past back to life at L'Anse aux Meadows National Historic Site.

We're following the path of the earliest known European settlers in North America. Half a millennium before John Cabot sailed into Canada, other explorers recorded landfalls on the North American continent. Vikings established a base in Western Newfoundland, on the edge of a land they called Vinland. Their remains are the only known Viking settlement in North America, now a UNESCO World Heritage Site.

If you think your kids will get a kick out of playing Viking, hiking a toxic mountain, and beachcombing along a craggy coast, you've come to the right place. The Viking Trail, situated along Western Newfoundland, is filled with historic sites, easy outdoor adventures, and one impressive natural wonder after the next.

GROS MORNE NATIONAL PARK

There's something special about Gros Morne National Park, a UNESCO World Heritage Site. Yes, it's a geological and visual wonder, but beyond the ancient mountains, wind-lashed coastline, and dramatic fjords carved by glaciers, there's something more palpable going on here. In a word: space. Even in summer, at the height of tourist season, it's not crowded with people in the slightest. The

253

same cannot be said, however, for moose. With approximately 3,800 roaming through the park, Gros Morne has one of the highest densities in North America, with some areas of the park having four moose for every square kilometre.

The thing to do in Gros Morne National Park is walk upon the earth's mantle. And why not trek around a toxic mountain while you're at it? You can experience both while hiking the Tablelands Trail. The Tablelands is actually part of the earth's mantle, typically found far below the earth's crust (where we live). This rust coloured rocky trail is full of iron, magnesium, nickel, chrome, and copper—so much metal it's hard for plants to grow because the soil is considered toxic. Fret not, it's perfectly safe to walk on.

So how did this middle part of the earth end up sitting upon the crust? A collision of tectonic plates several hundred million years ago forced part of the earth's mantle to be pushed over the crust, just so you (and a few thousand moose) could traipse around on it.

"Climbing around the Tablelands mountain was rugged and gnarly, but magical," says Gillian Marx, St. John's mom of two. "My boys loved that there were carnivorous plants that grew in this mountain range that nourished nothing. There was still snow near the top, and my oldest remembers throwing a snowball in August!"

Though it's an easy 2.5-mile (4-kilometre) return hike around the base to Winter House Canyon, it feels like you're hiking on Mars. The orange rock you'll see is from the earth's mantle, and you'll notice that not many plants grow here. "Only a few do well in this environment," explains our guide, Park Interpreter Kris Oravec. Because it's hard for plants (like the provincial flower, the pitcher plant) to find the nutrients they need in order to grow, they've had to adapt, some by eating insects.

"It sucks up its food from the soup of the poop!" exclaims Oravec. Rainwater collects in the cup-shaped leaves of the pitcher plant. Insects drown or are eaten by hungry larvae and other things swimming around in the water. Happy larvae then have a little poop,

Families frolic along the shores of Shallow Bay Beach, near Cow Head in Gros Morne National Park.

It's so lush and green along the Western Brook Pond Fjord, you'll almost think you're in Hawaii.

Vikings lounging around the fire at L'Anse aux Meadows National Historic Site.

Hike along the Tablelands Trail in Gros Morne National Park.

which is when the pitcher plant does some sipping. Because kids are fascinated with all things super tiny, be sure to get a children's kit from the Discovery Centre that includes a pipette to scoop up water from pitcher leaves to inspect the ants and larvae inside.

BONNE BAY MARINE STATION

Peel off the Viking Trail here at Norris Point, and take some time to touch and marvel at the wide variety of indigenous marine mammals. This is a real, honest-to-goodness research centre, which means your tour (included with the price of admission) takes you behind the scenes to examine holding tanks housing research specimens. This is the spot to come face-to-face with the rare blue lobster—and yellow and green ones!

Admire the skeleton of a sperm whale that beached in the area, before trekking up to the touch tank. Plunge your hand into the icy cold North Atlantic water and gingerly pick up sticklebacks, sea urchins, starfish, snails, and scallops. You won't want to miss walking through the aquarium with a marine biologist, and every day there's a kayaking tour where you can catch jellyfish or other creatures for the scientists to study.

BROOM POINT

Betcha don't know what a yaffle of chores is! Find out at Broom Point, a small fishing community established in 1808 and now a national historic site. You can stop by anytime to see the summer cottage where three brothers and their families lived—just keep in mind that it's more interesting to visit when the yaffle of chores is offered.

Staff make it as traditional an experience as possible, though thankfully there's no emptying of the chamber pot. Don your apron and assist with old-fashioned chores such as washboard laundry, repairing a lobster trap, or salting and drying codfish as they did over fifty years ago. After all that hard work, you'll have earned your cup of tea with a lassie bun. As for the yaffle, you'll have to go on the tour to learn what this mysterious word means. Find out when the next yaffle of chores is being offered by checking the Gros Morne section of the Parks Canada website. Reserve your spot at the Parks Canada Discovery Centre at Woody Point.

WESTERN BROOK POND FJORD

One of the most stunning sights within Gros Morne National Park is the Western Brook Pond Fjord. OK, technically it's no longer a fjord, because it's been filled with freshwater for the past 8,000 years (a fjord is an inlet carved by a glacier, filled with seawater). Still, it's one impressive sight.

Lofty cliffs 2,300 feet (700 metres) high mark the front of the Long Range Escarpment; they were once used as landmarks by sailors, as they can be spotted from 30 miles (48 kilometres) away on a clear day. These are the roots of an ancient mountain chain that is part of both the Canadian Shield and the Appalachian Mountains. While geographical features may not thrill some kids, the two-hour boat tour into this billion-year-old marvel is sure to wow.

To access the boat, passengers must walk down a 2-mile (3-kilometre) interpretive trail. It's a pleasant forty-five-minute stroll strewn with irises and yellow buttercups, with frequent sightings of moose and even the occasional caribou.

Once on board you won't want to put your camera down. Towering granite cliffs shoot straight up from the pond. This land-locked, 1,968-foot (600-metre) fjord is so remote, it'll make you feel like you're headed to the end of the earth. Gaze upon the rock formations, watch hidden waterfalls melt into mist, and admire the lush hanging valleys that frame this postcard-pretty fjord. Toes will tap to the Newfoundland music that accompanies the 10-mile (16-kilometre) journey, and you'll get a good chuckle out of the fish tales told by the guides.

PLAY VIKING

You don't need to be told L'Anse aux Meadows National Historic Site is over 1,000 years old—it's something you feel. The Vikings didn't stay long (perhaps five to ten years over three or four decades), but they certainly left their mark. Children are taught how to live like intrepid Norse adventurers at this carefully preserved 10th-century Viking village. There are costumes to try on, heavy circular shields to carry, and even (play) swords for battle.

Trace the Vikings' journey inside the Visitor Centre, and marvel at how small the wooden boats were that brought them here across the sea, to the earliest known European settlement in the New World. Step into the reconstructed sod huts to hear tales of their exploits exploring Newfoundland and Labrador, told as though it was happening in the present day. These millennium-old stories are recited in glorious detail during Sagas and Shadows, an evening program that will leave you spellbound. After stepping back in time, explore the trails along the shoreline and see if you can spot an iceberg.

Viking fever doesn't end there. Norstead Viking Village is another worthy stop if you want to get a sense of how these warrior-traders lived day to day in the New World. "Norstead was totally interactive and engaging for my boys," recalls Gillian Marx. "They threw an axe at the woodpile (with a whole lot of guidance), traded beads, made necklaces with Vikings, and they played a Viking game similar to running around a maypole."

Here, you can step aboard *Snorri*, a full-scale replica of a Viking ship. Inside the Chieftain's Hall, Newfoundland delicacies such as toutons (a fried bread) are waiting for you, as are costumed interpreters keen to trade or tell your fortune. Animal lovers can't get enough of feeding the sheep in their pen, and you can take the lesson further by having the kids spin sheep fleece into yarn using ancient methods.

ICEBERG ALLEY

There's no better way to cool down in the heat of summer than by taking a boat tour along Iceberg Alley. As you drift along the northeast coast of Newfoundland, you'll spot icebergs that are up to 10,000 years old. Icebergs head downstream from Greenland along an ancient route, drifting by the town of St. Anthony (near the Viking settlements), continuing on to St. John's.

St. Anthony has the longest season for icebergs in Newfoundland (typically from spring until August), and boat tours allow you to come within a safe distance of these frozen skyscrapers. It's thrilling *and* unsettling to float by the icy giants as the crew plays the *Titanic* soundtrack—even more so when you come across icebergs similar in size to what took down that tragic vessel.

What you're seeing are chunks of Greenland glaciers that are continually breaking apart. Carefully, the crew reaches over the side of the boat to collect "bergy bits"—chunks of ice smaller than a car. Break off a piece and you'll notice how much slower it melts compared to refrigerator ice cubes. You'll also get to taste this ancient, pure water.

A WHALE OF A TIME

If icebergs are moving too slow for you, try spotting something more elusive. It's a two-for-one deal in St. Anthony as one of the world's largest populations of humpback whales head here for summer eats. Actually, twenty-two species of whales and dolphins migrate off the coast of Newfoundland and Labrador each year. The sea surrounding the province offers plenty of snacks that entice them to become repeat visitors.

"There's a dolphin coming our way," Captain Terry Simms announces over our tour boat's PA system. Turns out this is no dolphin. Just ahead of the boat, an orca surfaces. She dives back down, only to return for some bow riding, playing in the boat's wake.

Suddenly a humpback is spotted, then another and another. A dozen of these aquatic acrobats pop up beside our boat before arching back and showing off their tails as they dive deeper to munch on capelin. Other marine mammals to be on the lookout for include seals, white-beaked dolphins, and minke whales. Even leatherback turtles occasionally make an appearance in August.

Tip

May to August is the best time for whale watching in this region. Prime time for viewing both icebergs and whales is early May until the end of July.

NEWFOUNDLAND INSECTARIUM AND BUTTERFLY PAVILION

If you're prone to the willies, you'll want to get over that quickly so you can make the most of this attraction—the ever-present interpreters will be eager to place some sort of creepy-crawly in your hands. This is a safe place to explore a wasp's nest, and there's a fine selection of the biggest beetles in the world. Tarantulas and scorpions also mill about, but are safely contained within a see-through enclosure.

Over forty different types of butterflies are brought in every week from Costa Rica and the Philippines in chrysalis form (cocoons are what moths do). Watch them hatch right before your eyes, or step into the pavilion to be enveloped by 600 to 1,000 fluttering about. The beehive is equally as fascinating, with a bee highway teeming with troops returning from work with golden pollen attached to their legs. Kids get a kick out of watching bees shake their little bee-hinds, which is their way of communicating to the other workers where they found the nectar.

¶¶ TASTE

Try some of the local berries at the **Dark Tickle Co. Wild Berry Économusée**. This shop and production facility offers tastes of local partridge berry, cloudberry, blueberry, squashberry, and bakeapple. They're hand-picked by local foragers and transformed into jams, teas, syrups, pickles, and other preserves. The "wine" served at L'Anse aux Meadows is actually Dark Tickle Drinkable Wild Berries made with concentrated partridge berries.

Try a traditional Mug Up, a cup of tea with homemade bread and molasses at **Jenniex House**, a traditional saltbox house in Norris Point.

Near L'Anse aux Meadows, the **Daily Catch** offers traditional meals like fish and brewis (pronounced "brews")—salt cod and hard tack bread served with scrunchions (surprisingly delicious fried pork rind). The **Northern Delight Restaurant** in Gunner's Cove is popular with both tourists and locals.

Munch on moose spring rolls and fresh seafood as icebergs roll by while dining at **Lightkeepers Café** in St. Anthony.

For a traditional Jiggs Dinner with all the fixings, look to the **Big Stop** near the airport in Deer Lake, and at **Fisherman's Landing** in Rocky Harbour once a week.

NAP

Almost all campgrounds in **Gros Morne National Park** offer oTENTiks. A tent/rustic cabin hybrid, these roomy glamping accommodations sleep six and allow you to experience camping without the hassle. Bring your own bedding and food, and you'll be able to enjoy the great outdoors with ease. There are loads of regular camping spots within the park that accommodate tents and trailers, but check prior to booking as not all are fully serviced.

You'll find mostly three-star accommodation along the Viking Trail. Pools are hard to come by, but you'll find a heated outdoor one along with beachfront cottages at **Shallow Bay Motel** in Cow Head. **Holiday Inn Express** in Deer Lake has an indoor pool with waterslide. **Ocean View Hotel** in Rocky Harbour has recently been renovated, while **Grenfell Heritage Hotel** in St. Anthony offers rooms with kitchenettes.

Fantasies of staying on a deserted island come true at **Quirpon Lighthouse Inn**, situated a short boat ride away from L'Anse aux Meadows. Families can experience the exquisite privacy of lighthouse life, watching whales and icebergs drift by from inside the beautifully restored 1922 light keeper's home. All meals, including home-cooked traditional suppers, are included in your stay.

GETTING AROUND

Fly into Deer Lake from Toronto, Halifax, or St. John's. You can also fly into St. Anthony, but this airport services fewer cities. A vehicle is essential, and there are steep fees for dropping off a rental car in a different location than where you picked it up, so expect to spend five to six hours driving back to your point of origin.

FUN FACTS

- Approximately **ninety percent of an iceberg's mass lies underwater**. It takes icebergs two to three years to reach Newfoundland and Labrador from Greenland. By the time they get here, these icebergs have travelled 1,800 nautical miles and are a quarter of their original size!
- **Vikings** were the first European explorers to discover the American continent, a full 500 years before Christopher Columbus! They were excellent sailors, but also savvy traders who, according to legend, exchanged goods with early First Nations peoples.
- **Blue lobsters** are one in 2 million. **Green lobsters** are one in 60 million. Admire not one but *two* green lobsters at the Bonne Bay Marine Station.
- Naturally, **cod** is the provincial fish, while the **Atlantic puffin** is their bird and the **purple pitcher plant** their symbolic flower.

GET EXCITED ABOUT YOUR TRIP

- Pick up *Yes, Vikings!*, by Frieda Wishinsky, and *The Vikings*, by Robert Livesey, if you're en route to L'Anse aux Meadows.
- *The Saltbox Sweater*, by Janet McNaughton, and *Duncan's Way*, by Ian Wallace, both examine, from a child's perspective, what it's like to be part of a fishing family.
- *Around Newfoundland* and *A Newfoundland Year* are pretty storybooks by Dawn Baker, and are suitable for young children.
- Newfoundland music is rousing and hard not to sing along to. "I'se The B'y" and "Jack Was Every Inch a Sailor" are traditional Newfoundland folk songs worth downloading.

Glaciers look like rivers of snow and ice in Kluane National Park.

Who needs a playset when you have Kluane National Park for a playground?

Yukon

Land of the Midnight Sun

Wee ones excitedly race between the historic tents and the icy expanse outside. We're on a Northern Lights viewing excursion, yet so far none have come out to play. Just when we're ready to call it a night, a faint arc appears in the velvety darkness. Fingers crossed, we refill our hot chocolate mugs and wait ever so patiently. Within minutes we're rewarded with ribbons of green and white light unfurling across the night sky.

It may be the smallest of Canada's three territories, but the Yukon is most definitely larger than life. Nature calls the shots in this rugged frontier where natural wonders ravish the senses. Famed for its legendary landscapes and spectacular skies, the Yukon is the sort of place where, try as you might, it's difficult to contain your emotions. Humility, grace, and gratitude all bubble to the surface when you're surrounded by so much overpowering beauty. If your family likes wide-open spaces and deep forests populated by wildlife, consider this your cue to head north to the Land of the Midnight Sun.

KLUANE NATIONAL PARK AND RESERVE

Set in the southwest corner of the Yukon, Kluane National Park and Reserve borders British Columbia to the south and Alaska to its west. It's also adjacent to three other large swaths of protected land: Wrangell–St. Elias and Glacier Bay National Parks in Alaska, and British Columbia's Tatshenshini-Alsek Park, which together form the largest internationally protected area in the world and a UNESCO World Heritage Site.

Within Kluane lie the St. Elias Mountains spanning from Alaska to northern British Columbia. They are the youngest mountains in

Canada, and also the highest. Eighteen of Canada's twenty highest mountains are found here, and within this mountain range are twenty-four peaks that rise 12,000 feet (3,657 metres) above sea level. (Pretty impressive when you consider the Canadian Rockies only have three peaks that reach such a spectacular height.) Incredibly, thanks to tectonic uplift, the mountains in Kluane—including Mount Logan, Canada's tallest mountain—are still growing!

Whether you're standing on the edge of this rugged national park or gazing up from the middle, you're surrounded by nature's eye candy; taking in these staggering peaks and thick evergreen forests is one astounding moment after the next. Got a *Frozen* fan on your hands? Over eighty percent of the landscape is permanently draped in snow and ice up to 3,281 feet (1,000 metres) deep. That's right—even in summer (the park's high season), it's possible to see snow in this wild landscape.

Wildlife is abundant in Kluane National Park and Reserve. It is home to the most genetically diverse population of grizzly bears in North America; you'll want to chat with Parks staff about how to stay safe in bear country. During summer, keep your eyes peeled for wolves, moose, and snow hares, plus the lynx that hunt them. In spring and fall, you're most likely to spot Dall sheep with their curvy horns.

Help kids comprehend the enormity of it all by taking to the friendly skies on a scenic flightseeing tour. Flights aboard small aircrafts depart from Haines Junction, Silver City, and Burwash Landing, and whisk you over some of Canada's highest peaks. Glaciers look like highways, as they cut wide, textured paths along the deeply cleaved valley floor. Quite simply, it's a flight you'll never forget.

Most visitors come in summer, and there are a few day hikes well suited for families. Spruce Beetle Trail is a short drive outside of Haines Junction, and the 1.2-mile (2-kilometre) loop is made up of boardwalks in some sections, making it easy on strollers. Another popular hike is the Auriol Trail. This full 9-mile (15-kilometre) trail gets into the sub-alpine range, with pretty creeks to cross over. Budget approximately four to six hours to complete or simply trek

An ice sculpture competition is one of the many highlights of the Yukon Sourdough Rendezvous festival.

The Yukon Wildlife Preserve is a haven for northern Canadian mammals such as this Arctic fox.

Kids are happy to help their parents set up camp in Kluane National Park.

There's a whole lot of fun to be had in winter in Kluane National Park.

the first mile (2 kilometres) before it branches off into a loop trail.

Fortunately, you don't have to be totally granola and plan a backcountry trip to take in the epic views typically reserved for more hardcore hikers: Kathleen Lake mirrors the spectacular scenery. From here you can hike, boat, or camp a few minutes from the parking lot. There's a day-use area with a kitchen shelter, picnic sites, and a few different trails that are easy for little legs to handle. For a photo op, look for Parks Canada's Red Chairs and share your image on social media, using the handle #ShareTheChair.

The Parks Canada Visitor's Centre in Haines Junction is located inside the Da Kų Cultural Centre, and is open from late May until early September. Step inside and listen to audio stories told by First Nation elders or watch historic footage of the first mountaineers to scale Mount Logan. Active kids can engage in hands-on activities and cool digital exhibits to learn more about the diversity of flora and fauna that live within this park.

The gateway to the Kluane National Park and Reserve, Haines Junction is a small village along the Alaska Highway, located just outside the park. In winter, older kids (teenagers) can rip it up in the backwoods on snowmobiling adventures with Scott McDougall of Kanoe People. With the mountains as your backdrop, you'll fly through fat flakes of snow as you cruise your machine alongside the Alaska Highway. Once your confidence is up, you'll go through a cutline in the woods and power up, up, up onto a ridge where you'll be surrounded by exquisite silence.

WHERE THE WILD THINGS ROAM

With any luck you'll be able to see a variety of wildlife from the side of the road, on hikes, or perhaps during a scenic flight tour over Kluane National Park and Reserve. Unless you're headed to the Arctic Circle, however, it's unlikely you'll come face-to-face with musk oxen. Yukon Wildlife Preserve is a haven for these and other northern Canadian mammals. The 700-acre (283-hectare) property allows families to view and photograph wildlife in its natural habitat.

You can walk or cross-country ski along 1.5-mile (2.5-kilometre) and 3-mile (5-kilometre) loops, or opt for a bus tour led by an interpreter. During the tour you'll visit with mule deer, big-horned sheep, moose, and elk. Kids will learn why bucks fight and the difference between reindeer and the woodland caribou who live below the Arctic Circle. Musk oxen walked with woolly mammoths during last Ice Age. The musk oxen survived, while the mammoths did not. You're not going to see musk oxen on the side of the road, but a herd does live in this not-for-profit refuge.

TAKHINI HOT POOLS
Soothing sore muscles for over 100 years, Takhini Hot Pools is located less than a thirty-minute drive from downtown Whitehorse. Many tours include a visit to these hot springs, making it one of the most visited locations in the Yukon. When the sun sets, a dip in this odourless hot spring provides an excellent opportunity to view the Northern Lights. Even if the famous lights don't come out to play, the rich mineral water melts away travel stress, allowing you to reset before your next activity.

Keep the cozy, post-soak vibe going strong with a hot chocolate or crêpe inside Café Balzam, attached to the facility. The café also dishes out gourmet poutine, and almost everything is organic and locally grown.

NORTHERN LIGHTS
If you're able to glimpse the night sky as the auroras cast their ethereal glow, you'll witness the world at its most magical. As the lights dance across the sky, don't be surprised if the moment does something to your soul. Hearts glow as brightly as this natural phenomenon when you're able to view them, but that's the catch—you never know when the lights are going to come out and play.

Your chances of viewing the auroras are best when the sky is dark enough, typically from late August to mid-April. They're most active in the wee hours of the morning, shortly after midnight, which makes it tricky for young families. But if you've made it to the Yukon,

This porcupine is one of the many types of wildlife you'll come across in Kluane National Park.

it would be a shame to go home without at least attempting to witness the Northern Lights.

Making such attempts manageable for families are tours that offer comfortable viewing facilities. We went with Northern Tales, and though the aurora activity wasn't particularly strong on our night, it was still a memorable experience. Cozying up around the fire, roasting marshmallows, and telling tall tales inside a traditional trapper's tent will keep you occupied until the light show begins. Guides patiently walk you through all of the changes you'll need to make to your camera settings to capture the bright lights in the big northern skies, and they even offer tripods.

DOG SLEDDING

What could be more Canadian than driving your own team of huskies through the remote Canadian wilds? You're in good hands mushing along with Cathers Wilderness Adventures. This father and daughter team both competed in the famous 1,000-mile-long (1,600-kilometre-long) Yukon Quest, an international sled dog race from Fairbanks, Alaska, to Whitehorse, Yukon (the race-starting location alternates each year, with the 2017 start set in Whitehorse). They take novices, which most likely includes your crew, out on the frozen expanse of Lake Laberge.

Does Lake Laberge sound familiar? It will if you've ever read the poem "The Cremation of Sam McGee" by Robert Service. In this Canadian classic, Service writes:

> There are strange things done in the midnight sun
> By the men who moil for gold;
> The Arctic trails have their secret tales
> That would make your blood run cold;
> The Northern Lights have seen queer sights,
> But the queerest they ever did see
> Was that night on the marge of Lake Lebarge
> I cremated Sam McGee.

Fear not, nothing spooky will happen to you on your dog sledding adventure. "We tend to bring everybody back," owner Ned Cathers joked before we flew across the snow-clad landscape. You can enjoy the ride cocooned inside the sled pulled by a powerful team of Alaskan huskies, or drive the dogs yourself. This family company even allows children as young as five years old to drive their own sled—they'll just reduce it to a one- or two-dog team, and will take all the time necessarily so mini mushers (and their parents) feel comfortable. These are well-trained dogs that know exactly what to do, making it easy to soak up serene wintery scenes from either behind or inside the sled.

WHAT TO DO IN WHITEHORSE

Perched on the banks of the Yukon River and surrounded by mountains, the capital city of Whitehorse offers easy access to all the outdoor adventures that drew you here. There are well-kept walking trails along the river, but it's also nice to climb aboard the seasonally operated Waterfront Trolley to get your bearings. This canary yellow heritage streetcar is a fun, interpretive ride for families; the views are pretty, and the ride isn't too long for those easily bored. The SS *Klondike*, a national historic site, is a must for sternwheeler boat fans, and is open for self-guided tours in the summer.

Dedicate a few hours to wandering down Main Street. Old-fashioned period buildings contain delightful shops such as the Midnight Sun Emporium, where you can sign their clothespin guestbook. Stop by Mac's Fireweed Books for a wonderful selection of titles, and check out the children's section dedicated to books about the North. At the opposite end of Main Street lies Angelina's Toy Boutique; in addition to selling baby gear, quality wooden toys, and crafts, they hold events each spring for the younger set.

One of the highlights for families visiting Whitehorse is the MacBride Museum. Life-size Yukon mammals are displayed in the Wild World Gallery. Come face-to-face with massive wood bison, moose, lynx, bears, and caribou. In the Discovery Zone, children can feel the soft, fuzzy, and coarse fur of different animals. There are horns and antlers to hold, minerals to admire, and period costumes to dress up in. Most riveting for the younger set are the clear glass jars containing the poop of various animals, granting them many minutes of potty humour while they guess who dung it. Outdoor exhibits to explore include a coach house, an old-fashioned steam train, a North-West Mounted Police cabin, and the original cabin of Sam McGee, built in 1899.

Due to the climate, local hotels don't sport indoor pools, so you'll have to head to the Canada Games Centre for a swim, waterslide, or float down the lazy river. The children's play area is equipped with an indoor playground, plus there's ice for skating and even a soccer field inside this recreation facility.

Pop into the Yukon Beringia Interpretive Centre if you want to wow the kids. If the skull of a 400-pound (180-kilogram) giant beaver doesn't deliver, story time and family events uncovering the Ice Age should. And if you're lucky, you'll be in town for one of the Kids Kreate events, held one Sunday a month from September until April, at the Yukon Arts Centre.

In summer, there are a few different operators that offer half- and full-day guided canoe trips on the Yukon River from Whitehorse. You'll receive instructions, safety gear, and transportation, so all you need to worry about is wildlife spotting or slowing down your brain so you can fully appreciate this peaceful paddle.

GO FOR GOLD

You don't have to climb inside a time machine to discover what it must have been like during the Klondike Gold Rush, one of the most fascinating events in North American history. Simply head north of Whitehorse to Dawson City, the epicentre of action in the late 19th century. Gold was discovered in the Klondike region in 1896, which led to a stampede of prospectors hoping to strike it rich between 1897 and 1899.

History comes alive in this authentic gold rush town as you stroll along wooden boardwalks admiring the historic frontier buildings. Costumed interpreters roam the town and offer guided tours at the Klondike National Historic Sites of Canada from mid-May until early September. Pick up the complimentary kid's Xplorer Booklets at the Dawson City Visitor Information Centre. Let the kids guide you through the Klondike National Historic Sites and the Klondike Goldfields as they compete in fun activities along the way.

Got gold fever? Try your hand panning for gold with operators such as Claim 33 and Goldbottom Mine Tours. Additionally, geocaches have been placed around Dawson City and the goldfields.

GOOD TO KNOW

Consult sites such as AuroraForecast.com, so you know the best nights for viewing the Northern Lights.

Don't worry about purchasing snow gear especially for this trip. From boots to toques, all necessary winter clothing can be rented from several outfitters.

🍴 TASTE

At Whitehorse's **Wheelhouse**, it feels like you're dining inside a historic sternwheeler paddleboat. Families are most welcome at this restaurant set along the Yukon River, and children can play along the grassy bank while parents relax on the patio. The impressive children's menu offers delicacies such as Arctic char, elk bolognese, and bison shepherd's pie.

Baked Café & Bakery has a children's kitchen play set and serves up freshly baked goods, plus soup, salads, and pizza.

Open seasonally, **Klondike Rib & Salmon** receives rave reviews for its fall-off-the-bone ribs and local game entrées.

Earls is a popular upscale Canadian chain restaurant, and the Whitehorse location offers a children's menu, high chairs, and a baby change station.

🔑 NAP

Set on Marsh Lake, a thirty-five-minute drive from Whitehorse, **Inn on the Lake** is one of the few lodges where you can view the auroras right from your guest room. There are several choice options for families, including cottages that sleep seven and come with their own outdoor hot tub, and two-bedroom units with a full kitchen and living room.

Packages include airport shuttle, all meals, excursions, and cold-weather gear (snowpants, boots, jacket, mitts, etc.). You don't have to opt into the package, but their meals are a lovely treat. If it's good enough for Martha Stewart, who stayed here, you probably won't find fault with it. Stay here in summer and hop on complimentary mountain bikes, canoes, kayaks, and paddleboats. In winter, snowshoes are at your disposal. Throughout the year there's a fitness centre, sauna, and outdoor hot tub for guest use.

One block off Whitehorse's Main Street, **Westmark Hotel** isn't going to win any style points, but it's clean and cozy and perfectly suited for families. Thanks to its central location, you'll be able to get to all of the downtown attractions by walking. They have coin-operated laundry facilities and a restaurant.

Over fifty campgrounds are maintained by the Yukon government, operating on a first-come, first-served basis. These are quite basic, so if you're looking for amenities such as laundry facilities, internet, RV dump stations, and hot showers, privately operated campsites and RV parks might be the way to go. Parks Canada operates a thirty-nine-site campground at Kathleen Lake in **Kluane National Park and Reserve**, also available on a first-come, first-served basis. Another enticing option is found at **Takhini Hot Pools**. Open all year long, there are over 300 acres (121 hectares) of wilderness to explore on trails adapted for hiking, biking, snowshoeing, and cross-country skiing.

GETTING AROUND

Much of what you're going to want to see lies outside of Whitehorse, where you'll fly into. Before you rent a vehicle from the airport, ask your hotel if they offer a shuttle service. Many tour operators will pick you up from your hotel.

FUN FACTS

- At 186,661 square miles (483,450 square kilometres), the Yukon is similar in size to the state of California. The Yukon has a population of 36,000, while 39 million people reside in California—about 3 million more than the entire population of Canada.

- In the Athapaskan indigenous language, the word *Yukon* means "the great river" or "big river." At 2,300 miles (3,600 kilometres), **the Yukon River is the fourth longest in North America**, and the last major river on the continent to be explored in the 1800s.
- On June 21, summer solstice, the sun never sets in some parts of the Yukon. That's why this area (and many regions of the world close to the Arctic Circle) is referred to as the **Land of the Midnight Sun**.
- **Kluane National Park and Reserve** is home to Mount Logan, Canada's highest peak at 19,551 feet (5,959 metres), and the largest non-polar icefields in the world.
- **In 1904**, the Klondike region of the Yukon was the largest gold producer in Canada and the fourth largest in the world.
- The **common raven** is the territorial bird and **fireweed** its tree. **Lazulite crystals** are the Yukon's official gemstone. These and over thirty different types of rare phosphate minerals have been discovered in the Blow River delta. Samples of these minerals are on display at the **MacBride Museum** in Whitehorse.

✦ GET EXCITED ABOUT YOUR TRIP

- Read *Songs of a Sourdough*, Robert Service's epic book of poetry that includes "The Cremation of Sam McGee."
- Flip through colourful picture books such as *Children of the Yukon* or *Northern Alphabet*, by famed Canadian artist Ted Harrison, who resided in the Yukon for over twenty-five years.
- For children aged nine and older, *Fatty Legs*, by Christy Jordan-Fenton and Margaret Pokiak-Fenton, is a true story of a resilient Inuit girl who emerged from Canada's shameful residential school program.
- *Call of the Klondike: A True Gold Rush Adventure*, by David Meissner, is a non-fiction book that documents one of earliest expeditions of the Klondike Gold Rush.

Surviving Road Trips

If you believe that getting to your destination is half the fun, road trips are for you! For many, the journey is as memorable as the destination. For others, it's something to be survived. Whatever your inclination, road trips are an affordable way to get to your destination, but there's more to them than that, according to Laura Byrne Paquet, editor of OttawaRoadTrips.com. "It's almost certain that a plane trip will be a blur," she says, "but memories are made on road trips. Your kids may not appreciate it in the moment, but twenty years from now they'll still be talking about that time you saw a bear by the side of the road or stayed in a campground with a cool waterslide."

Road trips offer families flexibility by enabling spur-of-the-moment decisions to better suit the passengers. Rest assured, even if you're heading across the country, reenacting *National Lampoon's Family Vacation* isn't inevitable. With a little forethought, you can navigate a riveting road trip without being driven crazy.

PLANNING IN ADVANCE

Key to any successful road trip is having realistic expectations of all passengers, and scheduling the drive accordingly. Involve everyone when planning the trip by pulling out a map and a few guidebooks, and soliciting suggestions. What does your family want to see along the way? Where should you stop for breaks? How can you get from A to B within a set amount of time?

If you're not stoked to listen to a Disney soundtrack for eight hours straight, assign or agree to rotate DJ duties during your planning session. You trip needn't be organized with military-like precision, but the more buy-in you have up front the more pleasant it'll be. "By letting kids know the plan in advance, they feel they have some control over what's happening during the day. It's when they feel they have no control that they'll enter into power struggles with you during the trip," says Julie Freedman-Smith, co-founder of Parenting Power, a Canadian parenting consultancy.

Want to avoid the dreaded "how much longer" whines? Hand off responsibility to older children by asking them to help create the driving plan. Before your journey, set them up with Google Maps, and have them report back to you with a driving schedule. Once you're on the road, equip them with old-fashioned print maps so they can follow the trail with their fingers instead of draining your device battery. Most importantly, they'll be in charge of communicating exactly how much longer the trip is expected to take.

FINE TUNING

Your vehicle must be well prepared for the journey ahead. Schedule a maintenance check a week or two prior to your road trip, so there's ample time to make any necessary repairs. Consider buying a membership to a roadside assistance program. Even if you don't end up needing a tow or a boost, you're safeguarded in case someone accidentally locks the keys in the car.

Before hitting the highway it's a good idea to do the following:
- Top up all fluid levels
- Check lights and brakes
- Ensure all tires have appropriate air pressure
- Inspect air conditioning
- Test cooling system pressure
- Ensure the vehicle is capable of towing trailer weight if you're bringing a camper

WHEN TO BEGIN

Most seasoned road-trippers try to time their journey to coincide with at least one sleep cycle. For some that means starting before the crack of dawn and smuggling snoozing toddlers into the backseat before they're awake; others hit the road just before afternoon nap time. Then there are caregivers who have no trouble staying awake and are able to drive at bedtime and even through the night. There are obvious advantages to driving when children are sleeping—peace and quiet ranking number one. Know your limits, and have a backup plan in case you become sleepy during the drive.

PIT STOPS

Children will need to stop to get their wiggles out. With one set of relatives in Regina and another in Edmonton, Maria Schuba's Calgary-based family of four has logged plenty of miles. "We don't waste time eating at restaurants," explains Maria. "Stopping is for burning off energy." Their ideal pit spot is a green space for a game of tag. If it's raining, they hit up a mall to stretch their legs. Even if you decide to stop at a restaurant, consider a robust game of Simon Says in the parking lot to get the blood flowing before sitting down again.

Before the road trip, and at each pit stop, have everyone agree that they will try to go the bathroom. Nothing may happen, but at least your family will know what's expected of them. If the facilities at the roadside gas station don't look appealing, consider using a restroom inside a public building such as a library, recreation centre, or museum. If none of those appear, hotel chains often have washrooms off their lobbies.

PACK IT IN

No one can control traffic or accidents, but you can control how you deal with these situations. When the Freedman-Smith family was stuck in their car for several hours one summer, they were well prepared with food and hockey sticks. A bad situation turned into a pleasant afternoon of road hockey along the Trans-Canada Highway, thanks to strategic packing.

The added bonus of road tripping is that, in essence, your vehicle is one giant suitcase. Room isn't unlimited, but it beats having to worry about airline suitcase weight restrictions. Here are essential items to keep handy in your vehicle:

- Wet wipes
- Bucket lined with plastic bags for travel sickness or a make-shift potty
- Second set of clothes in resealable bag (what's wet, dirty, or smelly gets sealed)
- Coats, blankets, and candles in case you're caught overnight
- First-aid kit
- Soccer ball or hacky sack for break time
- Snacks and water

SNACK TIME

Set your family up for success by toting bite-sized healthy snacks. Keep your cooler filled with water and light-coloured drinks (who wants to deal with grape juice stains?). Avoid toting anything that could melt (chocolate), mush (bananas), or go off (mayonnaise and hummus). Best to skip sugary treats altogether unless you want to deal with the highs and lows that accompany them. Having said that, a few long licorice strands can keep kids quiet so long as their tendency is to suck or chew slowly. Options for road-trip munchies include:

- Pre-cut fruit and vegetables
- Slices of banana bread or other loaves
- Muffins
- Peanut butter and jam sandwiches
- Granola bars
- Trail mix
- Crackers
- Cereal

Keeping your food portioned and packaged inside small plastic containers or snack-sized bags makes for easy access and simplifies cleanup.

When you're stuck inside your vehicle for several hours, you'll want to have enough distractions to keep everyone occupied and out of trouble. Fortunately, you don't have to spend much money or energy to avoid a backseat mutiny.

Consider making a surprise bag with dollar store items for each child. Besides toys, goodie bags can contain handheld games, disposable cameras, and activity sheets. For the younger elementary school–aged set, an Etch A Sketch, pipe cleaners, and yarn for string games can pique their interest for longer than you'd imagine. Dole out these treats one by one, perhaps every half hour, so there's always something to look forward to.

A cookie sheet set across a car seat can be used as a food tray or lap-desk and for magnet play. Dry-erase markers also adhere to the tray with magnetic tape, so Mom and Dad don't have to climb over the backseat to hunt down lost markers. Attach a file folder to the back of the car seat to hold colouring sheets, slim magazines, and maps.

When it comes to entertainment, parents shouldn't set themselves up to be the main source of stimulation. "Kids can quickly get hooked on an adult as the entertainer," warns Kitty Raymond, a Calgary-based pediatric sleep and behavioural specialist. "This results in more demanding behaviour and the child not developing their own resources for self-calming and self-coping."

Remember, the worst part of the drive is usually the last few hours. Try to make it a habit to save electronics for later in the day, when nobody's fresh anymore. Is there bickering about who gets to control the movie or device? Come up with a strategy during your trip-planning meeting or decide on the spot to swap off hour by hour. Before your trip, sign out audiobooks from your local library or download a few podcasts to have as backup. If you're in the mood for quintessential Canadiana, *Vinyl Café* with Stuart McLean is a Canadian hit and can be downloaded for free from CBC Radio's website.

LET THE GAMES BEGIN

One of my sisters is a total games guru. Because she lives on a farm and drives lonely country roads every day, she makes the time pass with mentally stimulating games. These are her suggestions:

Start with the Alphabet Game, matching the letters of the alphabet (in order) to what you'll find at your destination. Switch to numbers and look outside your vehicle to find the numbers from 0 to 9 printed on road signs or licence plates. Make it more difficult by finding them in order.

The licence plate game is good in a city where there are lots of cars around. Find the licence plate that comes closest to your initials. Score bonus points if they are found in the correct order. Sneak in a little math and have the kiddos add, subtract, or multiply the numbers found on licence plates.

Simplify things by searching for vehicles that match a certain colour pattern. The pattern could be the rainbow (first find red, then orange, then yellow, etc.) or made up at random. Another option is having each person hunt down vehicles painted the same colour as the clothing they're wearing.

Car bingo is best when prepared and printed in advance. With enough paper, it is entirely possible to make up a sheet during your drive with squares for what you're noticing outside the car windows, and even words family members might say.

WHEN TO DISCIPLINE

When you stuff a group of people (even those who like each other) into a small space for a long period of time, don't be surprised if you get on each other's nerves, says Julie Freedman-Smith. "Rather than trying to fix a problem in the heat of the moment, make it work for the time being, realizing you can fix it later once everyone has cooled down."

Travel by Plane

Taking that first flight with tots in tow can be daunting. You've likely experienced a screaming baby on a flight or have been stuck behind someone in the security line who can't collapse their stroller. It all seems like such work. It is—and yet it isn't.

Going anywhere with young children requires a certain amount of prep. Flights quickly get you where you want to be, and there's no discrediting that value. While you shouldn't expect travel days with young ones to be relaxing, there are ways to make the experience less painful.

START SMALL

You'll hear a lot of stories—some of them worst-case scenarios—but that doesn't mean your first family plane ride is destined to be a gong show. Quite often what you expect to happen doesn't, which was the case for Calgary mom Robin Meckelborg.

She and her husband were keen to visit a relative who moved to New Zealand when their firstborn was six months old. Daunted by the prospect of a thirteen-hour flight, they decided to test the waters with a short-haul flight before committing to overseas travel. The excuse to visit family, and enough Air Miles to fly for free, was all the encouragement they needed to attempt a test run. Here's what Robin had to say about their experience:

> That first flight we learned our son is a good traveller. All that worry about having to nurse during takeoff or the trouble with ears equalizing—it wasn't our experience. During our quick flight from Calgary to Saskatoon, I was able let go of so much angst. It gave us the confidence to know we can travel with our children. I decided to stop listening to the horror stories.

You may be wondering, *Will everyone on the plane hate me?* This is a common fear when travelling with babies and young children. However, a good percentage of passengers are parents themselves; the majority of feedback you'll receive will be positive and understanding. Jerks that make flying miserable for caregivers are few and far between. I love what Colleen Lanin, editor of the travel and lifestyle site TravelMamas.com, shared with me:

> My advice? Focus on your child and ignore the haters. Pack oodles of toys, books, snacks, and other distractions. Dole these out slowly to avoid overwhelming your offspring and make the miles fly by. By putting all of your energy into your child, you'll not only keep them happier, but if there is a tantrum at 30,000 feet in the air, other passengers will be more likely to give you a pass.

Let's say your child does have a meltdown in the middle of a flight. What are you going to do? Simple: the best you can. Be prepared with food, distractions, and blankets to keep the little darling comfortable. And while keeping your cool can be a challenge, the calmer you are, the less agitated your child will be. All flights eventually end. Remember: this too shall pass.

WHAT TO WEAR

At the risk of sounding like someone's mother, I caution everyone to dress for comfort, not fashion, on travel days. If it's not your child smearing ketchup on your sweater, it's the flight attendant spilling cola all over your pants.

You'll want to be able to easily put on or peel off clothing, not just for those inevitable spit-ups and spills, but for airplane temperature fluctuations, too. Dress your crew in layers with easy-to-remove outerwear, and clothing without snaps, metal buttons, or studs; this will make going through security easier. Limit jewelry to small items.

Take a cue from school field trips and have your children wear shirts in matching colours. If they're young enough, they might even allow you to dress them in identical shirts. Not only is this adorable, it's so much easier to spot them running through the airport this way.

Colleen Lanin suggests removing children's shoes once they're seated on the aircraft. "That makes it harder for short legs to reach (and perhaps kick!) the seat in front of them. Even if they do, it'll be less jarring without shoes," she advises.

SAFETY FIRST

Even though it's free to fly with children under the age of two on your lap, you'll both be much more comfortable if you book them their own seat. While I've never opted for this route, I've appreciated the convenience of having an empty adjacent seat when travelling with my baby. It's also worth noting Transport Canada states the following on their website:

> Though a child who has not reached their second birthday may be held in an adult's arms, Transport Canada highly recommends the use of an approved child restraint for all phases of flight. The use of a child restraint system provides the greatest degree of protection for the infant or child and its use during flight will help in case of unanticipated turbulence. By using the child restraint on the aircraft, it will also ensure that you will have it available for use in the car at your destination.

Visit Transport Canada's website (tc.gc.ca) for their definition of an approved child-restraint system, and contact your airline for information on their specific policy.

Did you know that the Canadian Air Transport Security Authority (the group that runs and monitors airport security screening in Canada) has an online wait time indicator? Check it before you leave the house (by visiting catsa.gc.ca/waittimes); you'll feel more prepared.

Many Canadian airports also offer a family and special needs lane. This lane is for passengers who need more time or help with their belongings to get through security. If you're toting a stroller or travelling with very young children, you fit into this category. The lane isn't always available, but ask about it once you arrive at security.

Should you immediately board the plane when the airline announces that those with young children may do so? If you need the overhead compartment, by all means gallop through those gates. If your belongings fit comfortably underneath your seat, you may want to hold back. Boarding early means more time on the plane. It takes a good thirty minutes from the start of passenger boarding until takeoff, and frequent travellers know all too well it can take much longer. Don't put yourself or squirmy children in a confined space for any longer than you have to.

WHAT TO BOOK

Pre-booked seats are something you'll want when travelling with young kids. If you're not keen to pay extra for this privilege, be sure to complete your online check-in as early as you can (usually twenty-four hours before departure). While airline gate employees do what they can to seat families together, if a flight is fully booked there's little they can do. They may tell you the flight attendants will help, but this is not a guarantee.

I've been on flights where the onboard attendants were more than happy to assist and spoke to other passengers on our behalf. I've also been on flights where they were unwilling to help seat our family together.

One particular flight was filled with couples and had a three-seat configuration. Nobody was willing to swap seats. My daughter is not one to cry or get sick on airplanes, but the other passengers didn't know this. I instructed her seatmate on what to do should she become hysterical or throw up. Miraculously, he offered to change seats. Sometimes you've gotta do what you've gotta do.

If you can afford it, always book a direct flight when travelling with young children. The less time you spend in the air, the better. When that's not possible, Colleen recommends booking a longish layover. "This enables you to lug all of your child's paraphernalia from one end of the airport to the other as needed," she says. "You can also grab some non-airplane food, change a dirty diaper, and, most importantly for toddlers and bigger kids, let your child run free for a while to get some wiggles out!"

ENTERTAINMENT

Entertainment consoles on the back of the seats' headrests may very well be the best air travel invention ever. If you've had the misfortune of those blessed devices not working or not being available, you know the importance of having a backup plan. Some airlines offer entertainment channels free of charge when you download their app on your devices. Ensure you do this before departure on all devices you're travelling with.

Melissa Vroon, co-founder FamilyFunCanada.com, makes an activity kit for each of her children. "They ask for it as soon as they sit down on the plane," she says. "They're excited because they never know what's going to be inside, and the novelty keeps them busy for hours."

Dollar store trinkets are easy on the wallet, and you'll rarely regret packing a deck of cards. Printable colouring sheets (go double sided) take up less space than an entire colouring book, and reusable stickers can create wonderful fantasy worlds again and again. For more entertainment ideas, see the chapters "Surviving Road Trips" (page 279) and "Pack Like a Pro" (page 295).

Jet lag is one of the most dreaded aspects of long-distance travel. Unfortunately there's no magic formula for overcoming it, but you can take steps to mitigate its wrath. Lisa Goodmurphy, founder and editor at Gone with the Family, has taken several trips to Europe with her family, and tries to book overnight flights so everyone gets at least a few hours of sleep. She says,

> My experience has been that sunshine, fresh air, and exercise do wonders in helping everyone in the family adjust to a new time zone. Once we arrive we head outside to explore on foot. That first day is difficult, but we avoid napping and instead head to bed early. After ten or twelve hours of sleep we're all up the next morning and pretty much adjusted to the new time zone.

Not everyone is lucky enough to get a full night of sleep, so prepare to rise and shine earlier than normal. See if you can sneak in a daytime doze along with the little nappers in your crew, but try to keep your regular eating and sleeping times as much as possible. If there's little chance the parents are going to get any sleep, take it as an opportunity to sightsee by car while kids sleep in their car seats. Alternatively, you could encourage little ones to snooze in their stroller while you strike out on foot to explore.

Bedtime rituals signal it's time to go to sleep. If it's your practice to bathe your baby every night before bed, ensure you've booked accommodation with a tub, as not all hotel rooms offer them nowadays. Pack a few beloved bedtime stories, and don't forget their favourite cuddly toy.

Sleep props can be hard to tote, but they're worth it. Unfamiliar sounds can be unsettling, so a bathroom fan can sub in for a noise machine; alternatively, you can download a white noise app to your smartphone. Sometimes the light in a room can make it hard to settle down, so I packed the liner from a blackout curtain in my suitcase well beyond the years my daughter required it. Turns out I still needed it! Draping it over a curtain rod or securing it with duct tape to the walls ensured our room stayed pitch black when we needed daytime rest. Sleep masks and noise-cancelling headphones are two other sleep aids I never go without. I'm not a fan of ear plugs, but noise-cancelling headphones (though pricey) have been well worth my investment.

LUGGAGE LOSSES

In a single year, my luggage was either lost or delayed on no less than four flights. Take a picture of your luggage on your phone right before you leave. This way you won't have to rely on the chart at the baggage claim desk and can even email it to them. Ensure you've tagged your bag with your home address, and also throw in a business card on top of your clothing.

As an extra precaution, I attach one of those paper baggage tags available at the check-in counter with the address of my destination. Should your luggage not arrive with you, you'll be able to make do for a few days by packing an extra pair of socks, underwear, and a bathing suit in your carry-on bag. And forget the notion that your suitcase is for your clothes only: split everyone's clothing between all suitcases, in case one bag doesn't make it.

Pack Like a Pro

Packing takes on an entirely new dimension when stuffing suitcases for other family members, not simply yourself. Think lightweight and multi-purpose with every item you choose. While it's true that the more you pack, the more you'll be lugging around, peace of mind can outweigh any perceived inconvenience factors. I found it refreshing to hear what Corinne McDermott, founder of the website Have Baby Will Travel, had to say on this topic:

> Planning and going on that first trip is daunting enough without the added pressure of scaling down and worrying about packing light. If you think you'll need it, bring it. If you don't end up using it, you'll know better for next time.

SET YOURSELF UP FOR SUCCESS WITH THESE TRAVEL ESSENTIALS

Cash

You never know when a debit machine will go down. Save yourself hassle by stashing cash in various places. When kids are getting antsy, paying in cash also speeds up purchase time. It's also wise to bring an extra credit card in case of emergency. Credit card fraud happens all too frequently.

Copy of Adults' ID

Take a picture of your driver's licence and/or passport with your smartphone before your trip. Share it with another adult in case your phone and wallet are stolen. I've twice boarded domestic flights with the electronic version.

First Aid Kit

Bring any medications your family takes in their original containers, plus the prescription. Children's all-purpose pain relief and cold medications are good to have on hand, but please, don't dope your kid on cough syrup in the hopes they'll sleep through the travel day. Not only is that dangerous, it could cause the reverse affect, making them extra hyper.

Gravol is good to prevent motion sickness, and medication to treat ear infections is wise to bring if water time is heavy on the agenda. Antihistamines are needed for allergy sufferers, and they also work to reduce itchiness from bug bites. Rehydrating solutions such as Pedialyte are reassuring to have on hand should your child experience vomiting, diarrhea, or heat exhaustion.

Activities

Kids need easy amusement options to survive long journeys with lots of waiting around. Save your iPad as a last resort, and first try a deck of cards, colouring pages, magazines, or travel-sized versions of games. Stickers are a good option if re-stickable and not permanent. My favourite amusement items are wipe-off activity cards and books that can be used again and again. Bring an extra dry-erase marker, and two can play at the same time. Usborne Books has a wide selection of these types of products that will appeal to kids up to the teenage level.

Sunscreen

Even during a Canadian winter you may need sunscreen. The sun bounces off our dazzling white snow and can burn unprotected skin.

Thin Blanket

When no change table is available, this is worth its weight in gold. It also can be wrapped around anyone who is cold, or scrunched up into a pillow.

Casual Clothes

Canada is a pretty unpretentious country. So long as you're neat and presentable, you'll be welcome at most restaurants and attractions.

Change of Clothes

Whether you're travelling by train or by car, you'll want a backup outfit in case of spills or sickness. Keep a spare change of clothes stored in a Ziploc bag, so what's wet or soiled can be safely sealed away.

Bathing Suits

Even if you're travelling in winter or you don't think there's going to be a pool at your destination, pack a swimsuit. You may switch hotels, there could be a sauna for adults, or perhaps you'll come across a splash pad that you simply have to take advantage of.

Hats

Handy all year round, hats keep you warm in winter and cool in summer. They also protect faces if sunscreen wears off. If camping in the Rockies, you won't regret toting a toque, even in the summer.

Antibacterial Hand Gel

Proper hand washing is an art form. It also requires soap and water. When neither are available, squirt a little of this magic soap on your child's palms to ensure they're germ-free.

Wet Wipes

Whatever did we do without these all-purpose wipes? With them, your clothes no longer need to be used as napkins. They also disinfect surfaces, wipe up spills, and clean sticky fingers when a sink isn't accessible.

Multi-Purpose Soap

Found in camping and travel stores, these foaming agents are gentle enough to be used on your body and your hair. They can be used to wash dishes and act as a laundry detergent when hand-washing clothes. Some brands can even be lathered onto skin and used as shaving lotion.

Dental Floss
Floss can do triple duty—turn it into a makeshift clothesline, cut soft cheese and desserts when you don't have a knife, and take care of your dental hygiene.

Duct Tape
Travel with duct tape to repair ripped luggage, clothing, and pretty much anything else. Fix a broken toy, or childproof electrical outlets by taping over them. It can also act as a sink plug or Band-Aid (though if your child is allergic to Band-Aids, the glue in the tape might also cause a reaction). No need to bring a massive roll of tape: travel sizes are available.

Swiss Army Knife
Don't pack this handy tool in your carry-on baggage—it will pose a problem when going through security—but do consider adding it to checked baggage. Features can include a small blade, tweezers, corkscrew, nail file, mini scissors, and screwdriver.

Plastic Bags
Place shoes in plastic bags before packing so dirt from the soles doesn't rub off on your clothing. Throw in a few extra bags to store wet bathing suits and to keep liquid purchases from spilling over. At the airport, nab a few of those clear baggies from security to store food or smelly socks.

Eye Mask
You'll be able to sleep more easily on the plane, in your hotel room, or at the campsite when light is blocked out.

Noise-Cancelling Headphones

Proper headphones make watching movies or listening to music much more enjoyable. But you'll really see their benefit when you're trying to sleep while others make noise around you. White noise mutes external sounds to help you tune out noise distractions, and can even help you doze off. Consider ear plugs for a more economical solution.

Snacks

Wherever you go, have a few snacks on hand. Cookies, crackers, and fruits and veg will all help to manage energy levels. Consider bringing food that takes longer to chew such as beef jerky or bagels to pass the time on long car rides and plane journeys.

Diapers

Bring more than you think you'll need to get you through the first few days. It can take a while to locate a store that stocks your preferred brand.

That Special Something

Your child's favourite toy or comfort item is one thing money can't buy. Bring it and pay close attention to its whereabouts—or suffer the consequences.

Leave Out

Can you get away with taking only half the toys your children select? I bet you could take less. Additionally, most people don't need to pack as many clothes as they do. Allison Laypath, founder and co-editor of the website TipsForFamilyTrips.com, recommends packing only three outfits, plus the clothes on your back. "That should be enough to get most people through a week without laundry," she says. "If our trips are longer or dirtier, we throw a few laundry detergent pods and a roll of quarters into the suitcase." Canadian laundromats may take only Loonies or Toonies, so call your hotel ahead of time to see what's provided.

Wouldn't it be great to arrive at your destination without having to lug the stroller or car seat? Imagine being met at the airport with a breast pump or high chair or any baby equipment you need. Go a step further and envision having everything set up for you in your new digs. Yes, parents, all this is possible through baby equipment rental services across Canada. Simply type "baby equipment rental" followed by the destination you're visiting into your web search bar for a listing of local suppliers, or contact the companies listed in the Resources section of this book.

Making Mealtimes Manageable

Ensuring children are properly fed and topped up with all those essential vitamins and nutrients is challenging enough at home, let alone on vacation. While children are known to be picky eaters, it's still very doable to find and make meals that will meet the needs of your family when away from home.

You've got to expect the unexpected while travelling, so it's best to keep that blood sugar steady at all times to avoid meltdowns. Staying well-nourished and hydrated is the foundation for everything—I'm talking moods, energy levels, how your child sleeps, and their susceptibility to catching colds. And all this goes for parents, too!

But there's more to mealtimes than proper nutrition. Memories are made around the table (and campfire and picnic blanket, of course). While food may not be the central or defining memory associated with a trip, it certainly adds to it. I still remember the squished peanut butter and jelly sandwich I devoured during our family's first cross-country skiing adventure. (My dad had wiped out on our lunch bag.) I'd never tasted a sandwich so good! Here are some easy tips for making mealtimes not only manageable, but memorable.

FEEDING BABES

Finding food for babies isn't as difficult as it sounds. If travelling with Mom, breastfed babes are easier to accommodate than bottle-fed ones. In Canada, your right to breastfeed anywhere at any time is protected by the Canadian Charter of Rights and Freedoms. Nursing on the fly sure beats lugging around bottles and formula. If you've weaned, be sure to pack your baby's preferred brand of formula in case you don't find it at your destination.

For babies who've graduated to solids, it's easy to pick up an avocado, banana, or similar soft food. Just don't be surprised if your babe ignores this and wants to sample what you're noshing. My daughter didn't like the baby cereals we were instructed to serve when transitioning her to solids. The first meal she ate (at seven months of age) was risotto. Naturally, I freaked out when I noticed my babe licking a plate filled with a variety of ingredients that I was planning on introducing gradually. Fortunately, nothing adverse happened and the pressure was off. Still, I wouldn't experiment with new foods in an unfamiliar environment if I didn't know exactly where the nearest medical facility was in case of sudden allergies.

One tip I received from my cousin before taking my baby on her first overseas trip was not to rely solely on homemade baby food. Her rationale was that if you plan to travel together, baby ought to get used to different tastes. Though you can pack frozen cubes of homemade baby food and thaw them to room temperature, that's not a feasible option on a lengthy trip. Jarred baby food travels well and can save the day when experiencing unexpected delays. It also gets baby used to new tastes, which is never a bad thing.

FOOD THAT TRAVELS WELL

Food that keeps young children busy is always a winner. When packing food for travel, opt for foods that aren't too messy and that your children like. Cute Japanese bento boxes are ideal for separating food, but small plastic containers and Ziploc bags work just as well.

It makes sense to clean out your fridge before any trip longer than a few days. If perishable food won't freeze well, consider transferring it into something you can take with you. That's what Julie Van Rosendaal—published culinary writer and author of kitchen diary website Dinner with Julie—does before her family vacations. One of her favourite kitchen sink recipes is cold peanut noodle salad. It travels well, and you can add pretty much any veggies and leftover meat to it.

A few other tried-and-true suggestions include:

- RAISINS Picking up tiny dried fruits also helps work those fine motor skills.
- COOKED COLD PASTA Rotini and penne noodles can be looped onto little fingers.
- CEREAL Cheerios can be eaten one at a time and are ideal for occupying youngsters.
- BAGELS AND WAFFLES Both are sturdy and don't crumble easily. If frozen, these are great for a teething baby to gnaw on.
- CHEESE As long as it's consumed within a few hours of being unrefrigerated, cheese is safe to eat. Firm cheese that holds its texture is your best bet for little eaters, and cheese string will keep them entertained.
- BEEF JERKY It's difficult to find protein options that are easily transportable, but this fits the bill. Be sure to mind the sodium content.
- SANDWICHES Cut sandwiches into strips or fun shapes with a cookie cutter to make them more enticing.
- KALE OR BRUSSELS SPROUTS SALAD Both salads travel well and taste better the longer they're in their marinade. (Note: You may wish to avoid mayonnaise-based dressings if your dish can't be refrigerated.)
- COOKIES Julie recommends spiking homemade cookies with red lentils. They mimic oats, so it's unlikely they'll be detected as an enemy agent. Lentils contain heaps of protein—and fibre, too. Feel free to add in nuts, oats, and chopped chocolate. When you make such a robust cookie, you'll feel less guilty about eating it for breakfast.
- WATER Take a filled water bottle for each person when travelling by car or train, and at least one empty water bottle on air flights.

EATING HEALTHY ON THE ROAD

Is it possible to eat healthily while travelling? Sure it is, but just like at home, it takes discipline and forethought. Like many things in life, it's all about moderation. If fast food is the best, quickest, cheapest option, go for it. Food shouldn't become an issue that prevents you from doing wonderful things on your travels. Even at a gas station convenience store you can find healthy choices. The challenge lies in selecting the healthier option, not the cleverly marketed, tempting one.

While portion sizes in Canada aren't as large as those of our neighbours to the south, they're still generous. Most folks eat the entirety of what's on their plate. Ask your server to split your entrée onto two plates. Sharing meals not only saves money, but also prevents overeating.

Try to arrange it so your fruit and veg intake happens early in the day. Fruit is easy to keep, even if you don't have a fridge, and veggies make great snacks. A few years ago, the UK launched an effective marketing campaign to encourage people to get enough fruit and vegetables into their diets. The idea is that if you calculate your fruit and vegetable consumption and aim to hit five portions a day before dinner, you're sure to feel good. Constipation and other tummy woes are common maladies among travellers, so aiming for these portions makes sense. The better you eat, the better you feel—so keep in mind a five-a-day goal.

"But we're on vacation!" you say. I get it. I sit here writing this chapter in our apartment rental in Vancouver with a bowl of potato chips wedged between my daughter and I. But here's the thing: we almost never eat potato chips outside of school holidays. Dinner was sushi, and there's fresh fruit waiting on the counter for breakfast. It's all about choices. Keep in mind, if you regularly roll through drive-thrus at home, that's a pattern you'll probably repeat on your vacation.

SAVING MONEY

Eating out quickly adds up when travelling. There are still ways to trim this expense without sacrificing your experience. For our family, that means eating one meal out a day. We usually have enough leftovers for another meal the next day, and it's easy to stock your hotel room with snacks.

If your brood needs to eat quickly upon waking, search out hotels that include breakfast or at least offer a mini-fridge to stash milk for cereal. If you don't mind cooking the odd meal, self-catering is the way to go. For some reason, grocery shopping in a different city doesn't feel like a chore to me. It's fascinating to see the foods of other cultures, and you'll be able to pick up a few familiar foods at prices more reasonable than what you'd find at a restaurant.

If you time it right, it's possible to eat two full meals a day and subsist on snacks in between. Brunch works if your kids are happy to nibble until 10 or 11 a.m., and that late-afternoon snack can easily be turned into an early dinner. Happy Hour fits this bill quite nicely, too. If it's not a huge disruption to eat between 3 and 5 p.m., search out family-friendly happy hours to stretch your pennies even further. Coffee shops are also good options for meals; many sell soup, can customize sandwiches, and offer muffins the size of your head.

Groupon-type deals are abundant. Besides attractions and spas, you're sure to find a few restaurants running deals you can purchase ahead of your visit. Talon Windwalker, editor and publisher of the website 1Dad1Kid, recommends eating outside of the main tourist zones. "Even just walking five minutes away can make a big difference," he says. "You'll save money and have a better meal."

Theme parks are notoriously expensive. Consider packing sandwiches so you won't mind splurging for the popcorn or cotton candy or whatever it is you know the kids are going to demand they eat in the park.

Antipasto platters are easy to whip up at home and replicate on the road. At two years old my daughter became hooked on capers, garlic-stuffed olives, and prosciutto, thanks to a platter we devised with ingredients from a Belgian grocery store. Picnic-type snacks can be made into a meal when you've got a bit of protein, some veg, and crackers or bread. These fresh appetizer plates are fun and easy on the wallet.

Inga Batur, founder of the blog Cool Kidz Cool Trips, is also a huge fan of picnics. "We'll either prepare the food or buy a pizza and eat it on a beach or up in the mountains—no restaurant can top those views," she avows.

HOW TO GET PICKY EATERS EATING

When we lived in London, one of our neighbours had a son who was a notoriously picky eater. He desperately wanted to go to Italy, and his parents agreed to an Italian holiday on the condition he begin eating Italian food. Suddenly he started trying plain pizza and a few simple pasta dishes. They went to Italy and had a wonderful time. The expectation was set and met, and I daresay their family is better for it. Last I heard, he was still eating Italian cuisine.

Trying vivid new tastes often takes time. If your child has never tried Indian food before, you can't really expect them to tuck into chicken curry and naan bread. Holidays aren't the best time to experiment with big changes. That includes when and what you're eating. Boomer parents often demanded their children eat what they were served, but that's no longer the norm.

If you suspect you're going to encounter new tastes on your trip, it's in everyone's best interest to become familiarized with them before you hit the ground running. If your child is accustomed to getting chicken nuggets every time they eat out, you're probably going to struggle if those aren't on offer.

Claire Tansey, owner of the website Claire Tansey's Kitchen, believes food shouldn't turn into a power struggle when you're on vacation. Her thoughts:

> It's my job to provide nutritional food at predictable times. It's my son's job to decide what he wants to eat and how much. That said, I make it easy for him. There's always bread and butter, yogurt, nuts, fruit, and cereal. If we have those around, I don't worry. It's about balance.

Remember, children are resilient. If they're hungry enough, they'll often eat what's been served up. One bad meal, or even a few days without much variety, isn't the end of the world. Combat any potential off-food days by finding a few items you know your child will eat, and keeping them close at hand for backup.

BEHAVIOUR

The more familiar children are with dining out, the better they know what's expected of them. It's unreasonable to expect more from children than they're capable of delivering. Babies cry. Toddlers have loads of energy. You want to set your kids up for success. As such, Claire Tansey advises leaving multi-course dinners for the grown-ups. "We want our child to have happy memories of going to restaurants. That way, he won't dread going there."

Children (and adults) can get overwhelmed by new experiences. If they're tired, waiting in line for a seat is tempting fate. Likewise, you never want to arrive anywhere too hungry or else hangry behaviour is sure to erupt. Julie recommends searching out food trucks on your vacation. "Food trucks often offer good quality, and they're much quicker than waiting at a restaurant," she advises. "Depending where they are, you may find several grouped together offering lots of choice."

Even if you've timed the meal perfectly and there are several options that are interesting to them, kids may still act out. Discuss with your partner ahead of time how you'll handle any outbursts. It's one thing to have a battle of wills at home, but it's quite another to do so in public. Some kids may even be betting you won't follow through on consequences because its more work to enforce them on holiday. It's up to parents to set expectations. Just don't threaten something you're not 100 percent sure you'll be able to follow through on. Kids remember if you're inconsistent.

It's common these days in restaurants to see families more engaged with their screens than with each other. If you don't want your children to associate going out to a restaurant with watching cartoons on an iPad, don't offer it. Just don't. There are plenty of games—like I Spy or Hangman or even just colouring—that can occupy youngsters. Consider keeping a few conversation starters in the notes section of your smartphone. The Family Dinner Book website has wonderful suggestions on games and how to connect with your family during mealtimes. Check those suggestions out at thefamilydinnerbook.com.

Even adults can get overwhelmed when eating out all the time. And since it's all up to you to make sure everyone is properly fed, facilitating nutrition can seem daunting. But by mixing it up, planning ahead, and having a few different ways of getting healthy food into you and your family, you'll be able to nourish yourself, keep up your energy, and make some sweet memories when on the road.

Money-Saving Tips

It's a common misconception that only the wealthy can afford to travel. That's certainly not the case in my family. It comes down to what you prioritize in life. (Looking over your calendar and receipts will give you a pretty clear indication of your priorities.) Our family drives secondhand vehicles and doesn't have cable TV, and our sporting gear is well past its expiration date. We're still living in our "starter" home fifteen years after purchasing it. For us, less stuff equals more life.

To make travel dreams a reality, some families pay themselves first and have money siphoned off into a separate bank account on a monthly basis. Others earmark their tax return towards their family vacation. I've heard of some who keep a stash of cash they receive from odd jobs and designate this as their travel spending money.

It's a matter of priorities, really. You can choose to buy a new suit or have a regular housecleaner, or you can put your money towards new experiences shared with your family. The choice is yours.

MAXIMIZING REWARDS

If you focus your efforts on loyalty reward programs, you'll find that they can really add up. Our family's main credit card offers air mileage points for every dollar spent, so we put most purchases down on this credit card—as long as we're able to pay off the balance at the end of each month. (Nobody needs to go into debt for travel.) Even our mortgage gives us mileage points that match the interest owing; at the grocery store, our reward points transfer to an airline points program.

Magalie Boutin, a Montreal mom of four, takes collecting points seriously. She makes a point to go shopping on weekends when triple Air Miles are offered. She travels frequently for business and is a member of every hotel's loyalty program. "Everything I buy goes on the credit card that provides flight rewards," she says. "With four kids, it's worth it to pay the higher credit card fee and accumulate the miles."

TIMING

You'll pay more when travelling during peak season, which unfortunately often coincides with school holidays. Travelling during shoulder or low season is not only easier on the wallet, but more pleasant because popular attractions are less crowded. Luckily, just because your children are off school doesn't mean everybody else's are. Spring break varies across the country, just as professional days vary by school division.

Some schools give parents a hard time when pulling kids out of class for travel, but most are reasonable and recognize that education lies beyond the classroom. Book a meeting with your child's teacher well in advance of your trip to discuss ways to keep them from falling behind. Offer to photocopy any worksheets the class may be working on, and make a point to check in with the teacher during your trip if you're gone for an extended period of time.

ATTRACTIONS

There are free things to do everywhere you visit. Check your destination's local tourism website before your trip, as it will likely have listings of free attractions in their event calendar. Some tourist boards offer package deals combining popular activities with local hotels at a discounted price. Many attractions offer discount days, where one day a week it's free for the last couple of hours or entry is offered at a significant price reduction. Usually these take place on weekdays, which also means less crowds. Check the attraction before visiting, so you can schedule your trip accordingly.

More and more attractions offer discounts for groups, but even if you're not a family of four, you can still take advantage. "If you're travelling as a single parent, you can often join another parent or family to acquire the group discount, which can be a big savings," recommends Talon Windwalker, editor and publisher of 1Dad1Kid.

Accrued reward program points can be used for activities and entertainment. Put your points towards dining out or towards the most expensive attraction to save yourself a bundle. If you don't have enough points, you may find discounts if you purchase your tickets in advance instead of on site. Even the Canadian Automobile Association (CAA) offers travel discounts for members, in addition to roadside assistance.

I often find the first trip to a new destination is more about information gathering. You don't have to do absolutely everything on your trip. Naturally, you'll want to hit a few must-see attractions, but purposefully plan your days so you're not schlepping the family around from one wow moment to the next. Pace yourself and save both money and energy.

TRANSPORTATION

It's almost always more affordable to drive instead of fly. If your destination is less than a two-day drive away, you'll probably end up spending less money than you would on flights, even when you factor in a hotel stay. A money-wise move is planning your fill-ups based on general gas prices. "Gas is usually cheaper in Eastern Ontario than in Western Québec, for example," says Laura Byrne Paquet, editor of OttawaRoadTrips.com, "and it is usually cheaper in the US northeast than in either province. Check sites such as GasBuddy.com for up-to-date prices."

You'll want to stick to the speed limit, and not just for safety's sake. According to Mr. Lube, you use twenty percent more gas when you drive at 75 miles per hour (120 kilometres per hour) than when you go 62 miles per hour (100 kilometres per hour). You can also maximize your fuel economy by eliminating roof carriers that increase aerodynamic drag, and by not being so reliant on the air conditioner.

With flights, it's best to begin shopping well in advance. You can set up alerts with online travel agencies and receive daily or weekly notices about the best fares. The more flexible you are with your dates the better. Once you find a good deal, you'll want to jump on it, as discount fares don't last long.

Families shouldn't discredit taking the bus, or even the train, if available. You'll want to spend some time researching the best options, weighing the convenience factor with the amenities offered. In Canada, our public transportation—consisting of subways, buses, trains, and light rail transit systems—are safe and affordably priced. Many resort towns offer free shuttles that get you into the town center and to its main attractions.

HOTELS

If you like the amenities offered by hotels, you can save money by booking through discount travel sites or checking out the specials advertised on the hotel's website. Staying in small towns is also a more affordable way to go. Not only are they typically cheaper than their big-city equivalents, but they usually offer free parking and WiFi.

And don't be afraid to ask for a lower rate, especially if you're dealing with an independent property. Allison Laypath, founder and co-editor of the blog Tips For Family Trips, found this out accidentally during a spring break road trip. She shares:

> We hadn't made any reservations and were looking for a new place to stay every night. We found that most hotels and inns were happy to give us a better rate to fill a room that would have been empty otherwise. One desk clerk dropped the price from $120 to $70 to keep us there!

Paying a little extra for a hotel that offers a mini-fridge and microwave can save you money when factoring in dining out costs. Amber Mamian, founder of GlobalMunchkins.com, has found that it can be worth paying more for the perks. She writes:

Some hotels have large spreads that include full break-fast, snacks, cocktails, appetizers, and treats for dessert. If you ask to be upgraded at check-in, I've found many times (during the off season) that they have rooms available on their concierge level, and the added last-minute fee is much cheaper than booking it in advance.

ALTERNATIVE ACCOMMODATION

Of course, there are so many more options nowadays besides a traditional hotel or camping out to save some cash. If you'd like to make your own meals and are looking for separate bedrooms and more space in general, self-catering is the way to go. Renting a condo or a vacation home also offers the opportunity for a more authentic experience in a less sterile environment. Renting a home allows you to get your own groceries, hang out at the community coffee shop, and chat up locals to get recommendations for what to do in the area. There are plenty of vacation rental sites to consider, as well as online travel agencies that have self-catering categories.

Even though your carefree backpacking-around-the-world days may be a thing of the past, you may want to revisit staying in a hostel. They aren't just for backpackers anymore. Some have dorm rooms divided between men and women's quarters, while others offer private rooms—even private cabins in some cases. Hostels almost always have a kitchen facility and usually a manager on site to guide you through the process.

"It's more comfortable than camping, especially if you're travelling early or late in the season," says Tanya Koob, a blogger who's reviewed most of the wilderness hostels in the Alberta Rockies on her site, Family Adventures in the Canadian Rockies. Look for options through Hostelling International or the Alpine Club of Canada.

Finding affordable accommodation that meets your comfort needs *and* is in a killer location isn't a pipe dream—not if you arrange to do a home exchange. Swapping your abode for someone else's gives an insider's glimpse as to how locals really live, and you can even negotiate to swap vehicles.

For some, it's a conscious decision to adopt a slow travel mentality. House swapping allows you to become immersed in the local community and shrug off the fast-paced sightseeing mentality that plagues many tourists. But if the thought of strangers poking their way through your cupboards sends shivers down your spine, house swapping probably isn't for you. The same concept can apply to friends and family who might be happy to hand over the keys to a known and trusted housesitter.

Beyond those you know, formal housesitting has become more popular in recent years. It's an effective way to keep your travel costs down, especially when visiting more expensive locales. This isn't like going on a no-cares holiday, though. There is always some kind of responsibility involved. Housesitting duties typically include picking up the mail, lawn maintenance, and caring for pets.

Dalene and Pete Heck are a Canadian couple who sold everything to travel the world; they blog about their adventures at HeckticTravels.com. They've housesat at over a dozen different properties and find housesitters to be "a community of like-minded travellers. There's a level of trust there to invite someone into your home for weeks. As much as you respect their things, you need to be sure you're going to be happy in that space as well. It's a reciprocal arrangement. Key is being flexible and adaptable."

They recommend interested housesitters ask the following questions of the house owner before entering into an agreement:

- What maintenance is expected?
- What is the pet schedule? Can you leave the house and the pets for the day?
- Are there any rooms that are off limits?
- Will a vehicle be at your disposal?
- Who can you contact locally if something goes wrong?

- Can you schedule a FaceTime or Skype chat with the owners before committing? You'll want to make sure the property is indeed as described.

TrustedHousesitters.com and Nomador.com will give you a good indication of what's available, and the Hecks' ebook *How to Become a House-Sitter and See the World* is an invaluable guide.

GO ONLINE

Looking for free activities? Plug "free things to do in [the place you're visiting]" into your web browser and see what comes up. It's not uncommon for local parenting websites and bloggers to offer deals or coupon codes on their sites. Many have listings of free or less-expensive activities at your destination. Not only will you save money, you'll gain a local's perspective.

While online, find discounts for local tours, attractions, hotels, and restaurants on sites such as Groupon and Living Social. Because you pay in full when you purchase these types of vouchers, you'll want to carefully read the fine print to ensure there are no restrictions for when you plan on using it. There's no returning vouchers that aren't used, which means money down the drain, defeating the purpose.

Couple Time

Picture this: You've just had an epic day out with your family. The kids went to sleep easily, and you've got a date with your partner and are enjoying a glass of wine on the hotel balcony . . . but you can't keep your eyes open. Or have you ever been looking forward to a night of romance, only to have your spouse get a second-degree sunburn that afternoon? That was my girlfriend Michelle's experience, only to be topped by the time her hubby got food poisoning on their next family vacation.

When travelling with children, making time to connect with your partner often gets neglected. With all the logistics, new attractions, and energy spent ensuring nobody gets hangry, romance is often put on the back burner. Yes, you're on a family holiday; the point of these trips is to connect with your kids while they still want to hang out with you. Still, that doesn't make meaningful moments with your partner less of a priority.

GET THE RIGHT ACCOMMODATION

Mom and Dad enjoy their vacation so much more when there's a separate bedroom. Not only does everyone sleep better, but a door that locks also provides parents the same level of privacy enjoyed at home (or at least close to it). Hotel suites are notoriously pricey, but one-bedroom apartments on vacation rental sites are an affordable option.

If you're staying at a hotel, aim for one that runs a complimentary kids' club, which were invented so parents could snag a little down time. Many resorts offer them, and you'd be surprised by the number of city properties that do, too. At a minimum, most hotels offer babysitting services, or should be able to provide you with contact information for a local certified babysitting or nanny service. If guaranteed time alone with your partner is a must on your holiday, be sure to budget for this expense.

Another advantage hotels offer is proximity. Depending on the age of your children (and the laws in each province), it's feasible for parents to go on a date within the hotel, as Allison Laypath, founder and co-editor of TipsForFamilyTrips.com discovered:

> My kids are pretty responsible, so once my oldest turned ten, we felt comfortable leaving them in the room while we enjoyed date night at the on-site restaurant. We typically get pizza or room service for the kids, find the Disney Channel, and leave them with a mobile phone. They enjoy the alone time as much as we do!

MAKE IT MULTIGENERATIONAL

Travelling with grandparents or other adults in your family does double duty: not only do you get to spend quality time together creating shared memories, but the other adults can usually be counted on to watch the children at least one night during your vacation.

Barbara Orr has taken numerous trips with her children and grandchildren and is happy to give her grown kids the gift of free time. Still, she cautions grandparents not to become the live-in nanny at the expense of enjoying the vacation themselves. "That just leads to resentment," she warns. "The duties should be shared. Maybe one day Nanna gets up at six with a little one, and Daddy does it the next day so Nanna can sleep in. My kids are very good about that, and would never impose or take us for granted, but that isn't true for all families."

Parents, remember: while having grandparents along on vacation is great, they shouldn't be expected to be at your beck and call. Perhaps Grandma would like a little break from not only the kids, but also Grandpa (or vice versa). See how you can accommodate their needs, so it's a mutually beneficial arrangement.

Another option is to bring along a teenage niece or nephew. If they are mature enough, you'll feel comfortable taking advantage of the freedom their presence provides. Your kids are sure to enjoy bonding with their cousin, and it's probably a nice change of pace for the cousin, too. Their parents might even offer to pay for some of their expenses, but this shouldn't be expected. If you're bringing along a relative on a working holiday, you'll want to hash out the terms of the agreement prior to booking their flight.

MANAGING EXPECTATIONS

If you feel frustrated with the lack of time alone with your partner, try to remind yourself that you're on a family holiday, not a couple's getaway. Also, be aware that even if you do manage to find some privacy, you may find it difficult to shift your attention away from your children and to each other. Be assured, this gets easier over time. Once you've secured reliable childcare, you can relax knowing that your kids are well taken care of—and could likely benefit from a break from Mom and Dad.

If private adult time just isn't in the cards during your holiday, here are a few suggestions:

- Take the kids out of the room to let your partner sleep in. Bonus points for returning with coffee and breakfast.
- Surprise with a souvenir. It needn't be tacky! A Christmas tree ornament that reminds you of the destination is a lovely memento of the good times you shared as a family.
- Pick up a local magazine or newspaper to read together.
- Offer to watch the kids while your partner has a few hours to themselves to do whatever they wish.
- Purchase a specialty pastry to share (be sure to buy extra for your offspring).
- Sip a bottle of wine together on the patio.
- Give a shoulder or foot rub—easily done if the kids are watching TV.
- Wait! Are the kids glued to a screen? Run to the washroom and draw a bath for the two of you. See where that leads . . .

PARENTAL SELF-CARE

Everyone needs downtime. Don't feel guilty about carving out a little alone time for you and your partner—or even just for you. If you take time to yourself, be sure to reciprocate the favour, so each adult has time alone to recharge. It's actually quite fun at the end of the day to meet up and compare your adventures.

There's a lot of talk about setting kids up for success, but what about setting *parents* up for success? First and foremost, make sure you're getting enough sleep. If not, perhaps nap time is in order for you too. If you find yourself getting overwhelmed with trip logistics, or are getting short with your family, give yourself a time out and step away from the group. By nurturing yourself, you'll be able to give them your best.

Maybe you can't manage to sneak in much couple time during your family vacation. So what? It's not the end of the world. Perhaps you can schedule a date night a week or so after you return home. How about bringing in a mobile massage therapist to the house right after you get back? Not only will the massage help to unravel those travel kinks, it'll put both parties in a relaxed mood.

Sharing Spaces

Benjamin Franklin famously said that guests, like fish, begin to smell after three days. Whether you're visiting relatives over the holidays or renting a lakefront property with friends, it's not hard to see where he was coming from. The older we get the more entrenched we become in our routines, and when disrupted it's not always pleasant.

Yet there are many advantages to sharing your travel experience with others. For starters, it's a great way to share expenses. It also relieves a lot of work for caregivers. "It's like having a built-in second mom," says Stephanie Holmes, editor and owner of How to Survive Life in the Suburbs. "Travelling with other families cuts the workload in half. Suddenly I'm not the only one in charge of making dinner!"

One of my girlfriends, whom I lovingly call "the IBMer," is, like me, a tad tightly wound. Yet we're able to straight-up chill when we merge our families together. It feels surprisingly similar to a girls' getaway, even though our spouses are still kicking around. Both families return home feeling refreshed and full of ideas (nothing wrong with copying best parenting practices). OK, I'll admit it: I find shared parenting so much easier. Perhaps it's because I have an only child, or maybe it's because I dislike cooking and cleaning by my lonesome. Whatever the reason, bring on the shared spaces, I say.

BE INDEPENDENT

As much as you likely adore those you're staying with, you probably don't want to do absolutely everything with them. When a group of children spend day after day together, downtime can be rare, and disputes can all too easily erupt.

Cabin fever loves close quarters, so plan an activity at least once a day when your family can snag some alone time. When the Schuba family split a house in Naramata, BC, with three other families, they communicated their wish for alone time in advance so nobody's feelings would get hurt. Here's what mom Maria Schuba had to say about their experience:

> I was concerned our friends would take it the wrong way, but talking about it prior helped. Nobody even questioned it. If I didn't do that before our trip, people might have taken it personally or wondered if there was a problem. Because I laid the groundwork, our friends knew what to expect, and some even followed our example. Sometimes we just went for a drive or took a walk. It was basically a chance to have some quiet time together as a family and connect with our kids. Going off alone allowed us to do that.

RULES

Pick your travel partners very carefully. You'll want to know the other family well, and make sure your schedules jive, advises Stephanie Holmes:

> Ensuring similar sleeping schedules is not quite enough— make sure that the families have the same idea of travel, too. One family might want to sit around the pool all day, while the other wants to go, go, go. You have to prepare to compromise, especially if you're sharing a vehicle.

Shared spaces are no one's exclusive territory. And each family is going to have their own rules and differing opinions regarding bedtimes, discipline, and what to feed the children. Ground rules should be discussed ahead of time. Some questions to ask: Can people eat anywhere? Will you be limiting sugary treats? When is bedtime? The rules don't have to be the same for all kids, but getting your child used to the idea that there might be different rules sets you up for success.

Melissa Vroon, co-founder of FamilyFunCanada.com, ran into this issue when vacationing with another family:

> We don't let our kids have pop at suppertime, but the other family did. They questioned this, and we felt pressured into letting our kids have it. I felt strongly about it, so I told them, "This is a family rule. My kid's behaviour is affected by it. This isn't up for negotiation."

When you're as confident as Melissa was, you won't worry much about what anyone else is doing or their opinion of you and your guidelines. Certainly you'll want to allow some flexibility, especially if children are too young to understand that different families have different rules. Determine which rules are non-negotiable in your family and stick to them. The rest you can evaluate on a case-by-case basis.

When families share accommodation, housekeeping items are best hashed out before the trip. Figuring out who will make meals or be on clean-up duty is something that needs to be worked out to ensure no one feels resentful. When it comes to costs, many assume they will be split down the middle, but how far do you take that? If one family isn't allowed sugar and loads of treats have been bought, do you still split groceries fifty-fifty? Do you divide the fridge in half? Some people are quite happy to share everything equally, regardless of use; others not so much.

Then there's the rental contract. Typically just one person signs, but it makes sense to have one representative from each family sign it. That way if the landlord comes back to you afterwards (for example, if someone didn't take out the trash), the repercussions don't fall squarely on one family. Everyone sharing the space will have to deal with it.

HELPFUL HOUSEGUESTS

Having lived in England and Japan, I've entertained my fair share of houseguests. As a budget traveller, I've also made myself quite comfortable in the homes of dear friends and relatives around the world. Good guests are always welcome back, and the very best guests don't make assumptions. They follow the lead of their hosts and are not an inconvenience.

I appreciate it when guests don't expect to be waited on, but others take issue when guests rummage through their fridge. Just how much do you make yourself at home? Ask. Inquire as to whether you can commandeer the kitchen for a day or rearrange their spice drawer. If your host wants mealtime under their control, respect that and offer to take them out for dinner, or at least pay for groceries. And you rarely meet a host who doesn't appreciate being off dish duty.

Cleaning up after guests can be a tiring. Stripping bedding and throwing it in the wash before you leave goes a long way. Some travellers bring their own sheets and towels and take them home so they're doing the laundry, thus sparing the host.

If staying with grandparents, try not to revert to childhood behaviour. Make sure you pull your fair share of the workload. Your mom might be genuinely happy to do your laundry—or she may complain to your sibling how much work it was having your family over.

Good old-fashioned manners sometimes fall to the wayside when close friends or family share time and space together. Nothing is worse than spending a glorious summer day waiting for guests when you could be out hiking (which, unfortunately, I know from personal experience). Putting your life on hold because guests haven't yet flown the coop is also a drag. If you're a guest, don't be flaky about your arrival and departure times.

Bringing a thoughtful hostess gift can also go a long way. A bottle of Aussie plonk won't endear you to your hosts if they're Old World oenophiles. Figure out the host's preferences and gift accordingly.

MAKING THE ROUNDS

A visit to relatives is often one of the first trips a new family takes. You want to show off your baby, and staying with family is an easy way to trim costs while test-driving family travel. Just like when vacationing with friends, you want to make sure your family doesn't get overwhelmed with visits and activities. This can be tricky, especially if you've moved away from home and feel the need to see several people.

The solution is to combine activities with visits and organize group outings. As much as you'd love to catch up with all of your high school friends individually, that's better saved for a solo trip. Instead, set up a group brunch or a "meet the baby" tea, so you can see several folks all at once. Close friends and family members will understand your predicament and will likely be OK accompanying you to attractions or even while you run errands. Before your trip, suss out the local event calendar and invite friends and family to join you on the outings you want to take.

As much as you may feel obligated to fit everyone in, the worst thing you can do is overschedule your family. Expect that you're going to feel pressure and may even get guilt-tripped into doing something you really don't want to do. But remember, you have a family of your own; they are now your first priority.

If too much stimulation equals meltdowns, be firm about your family's needs. And don't forget to carve out time for just your unit so it actually feels like a break. "Go in with an idea of how you're going to relax, and build that into your plan," recommends Jes Watson, an Ontario mom of three. Having something daily for each family member to look forward to, coupled with time alone, helps shore up energy reserves so you're better able to enjoy the trip.

Sometimes (dare I say, oftentimes) going cross-country to make those obligatory visits isn't a holiday. It may be necessary, but don't fool yourself into thinking this is a family vacation just because you've taken time off work. Call it what it is and plan a more appropriate family getaway another time.

Can't afford to go? Consider whether you really need to schlep your entire brood along for the duty trip. If you can't go alone, see if you can tack on a few days at the end of the trip for your immediate family to have some fun.

Camping Made Easy

Camping is one activity that's both low-cost and a lot of fun. It's a fantastic way to spend quality time with your family, and research shows time in nature helps reduce anxiety and strengthens the immune system. Camping means you're outside, usually in a picturesque spot getting crazy amounts of fresh air, while working together towards a common goal. From putting up the shelter to making a fire to cooking dinner without modern conveniences, camping encourages families to work together before reaping the rewards of their efforts.

Sadly, many children, particularly those brought up in cities, are nature starved. According to Richard Louv in his bestseller *Last Child in the Woods*, "Direct exposure to nature is essential for the physical and emotional health of children and adults." In 2014, the Canadian Parks Council produced *Connecting Canadians with Nature*, a report that estimated Canadians spend ninety percent of our time indoors—much of that tethered to a screen. People protect what they care about, and the current trend of not offering children regular access to unstructured play in nature is disturbing on so many levels.

Camping offers an easy introduction into the natural world. It's not only a tonic to your senses, but also provides the basis for so much education. Listening for bird calls, observing animal tracks, and learning what constitutes good kindling offer teachable moments that kids eat up. Better still, camping provides children with a freedom rarely granted these days. Not only is it liberating for kids to roam outside without being helicoptered over, but it gives them the opportunity to see what they're capable of.

TIPS FOR SUCCESS

Camping (especially your first time out) can be hard work. There's a certain amount of necessary prep work, and it's not like a hotel where someone is paid to pick up after you and make your meals. The key is to make it easy on yourself. Camping ought to be low stress for parents and fun for kids, or else nobody's going to want to go. One family I know manages to camp in their tent trailer with their six kids. Instead of getting frustrated backing the trailer into its designated camp space, Dad simply unhitches it from the truck and has the kids grab the hitch post and maneuver it into the spot. Dinner the first night is always pizza picked up on the way out of town. They arrive at the campsite with enough time to build a fire and have s'mores before bed. Everyone arrives happy, and the more challenging aspects of setup are eliminated.

Leigh McAdam, founder of the popular outdoor adventure blog HikeBikeTravel, recommends involving kids in the process as early as possible. "Teach them how to put up the tent—every time," she says. "Make it fun by turning it into a race or timing it. By the time they're eight years old, kids could be setting up the tent on their own. It gives them such satisfaction."

Most importantly, you want to make camping comfortable for everyone. Choose warmer months and warmer locations, so you don't have to pack your gloves or a winter hat. Many a camping trip has been saved by camping close to amenities. Camping close to town gives you options. Should something horrible happen (like forgetting ketchup), you can easily sort that out by running into town. If the kids are up all night, make it easy on yourself by going to a restaurant for breakfast.

If you need a little time to yourself, set the kids up inside the tent while you and the other adults take a breather around the campfire. Kids love being on their own, and it gives parents peace of mind knowing they're safely contained, within eye sight.

GROUP MENTALITY

Busy parents know how challenging it can be to get together for dinner parties, much less an evening on the town. Camp with friends and you'll get to spend an entire weekend (or longer!) with those you cherish without having to spring for a babysitter. And let's face it, doing anything with friends makes parenting easier; camping is no exception. Teaming up gives you another set of hands during the all-important set-up and take-down portions of your trip, and an additional set of eyes to help monitor what the littlest campers are getting up to.

Tanya Koob, owner of the website Family Adventures in the Canadian Rockies, manages up to forty nights of camping a year with her husband and young son. She believes camping with families has other benefits as well. "You can learn so many skills from the people you camp with," she says. "I've also found it helpful to share gear. Quite often somebody will forget something, but when you're with other families, somebody shares or provides you with a duplicate."

Koob recommends joining a group to meet other likeminded families. Camping and outdoor groups can be found on Facebook and through Meetup sites. Of course, camping with other families brings bonuses to children as well. Kids have a ball running wild with others their age. For only children, it gives them a chance to interact with other kids in a way they don't often get outside of recess and playdates.

CAMP EATS

Half the fun of any camping trip is what you're eating. Who can deny the simple pleasure camp cuisine brings? Food cooked outdoors just tastes better. When camping with youngsters, the food ought to be something they like (especially if you're not close to a grocery store or restaurant), but easily prepared by you.

Julie Van Rosendaal, nutrition columnist with CBC Radio and founder of the recipe blog Dinner with Julie, likes to get cheesy on her camping trips. She recommends wrapping brie in foil and setting it into the coals, or making fondue by tossing chunks of meltable cheese into a cast iron skillet. Crackers or hunks of bread are used as vessels for dipping. Another recent winner was chili cheese fries. Cut-up potatoes (or frozen fries) are topped with prepared chili and shredded cheese.

If you're car camping, many meals can be pre-made and frozen. The frozen food helps keep your cooler cold, and you can gently thaw your meal in a soft cooler the day of. Some memorable camping meals that have performed well for Canadian families include:

- Pasta
- Souvlaki skewers
- Premade pizza that's set on the rack over a grill or campfire
- Bush pies (made with a pie iron)
- Bannock bread
- Foil dinners: Wrap meat, slices of potato, and a few veggies inside heavy duty tinfoil. Be sure to dot liberally with butter and double wrap before setting into the fire.

If you're camping with other families, consider communal dining as the Koob family does. They occasionally have theme nights, which sounds like a lot of fun. "We make camp margaritas, and one mom chops the ice with a machete when we don't have power for a blender," says Tanya. "Then it's tacos, fresh guacamole, and a batch of shredded chicken, made ahead, that can be put over nachos or into wraps."

For dessert, s'mores are the quintessential camping treat. Sandwich a piece of chocolate and a roasted marshmallow between two pieces of graham cracker. Banana boats are also winners. Cut a long rectangular strip off the banana peel (but leave one end of the skin attached). Scoop out about half the banana and fill with chocolate chips and pieces of marshmallow. Wrap in foil and roast either in the coals or on the grate. For the more ambitious, pour brownie or cake batter into a hollowed-out, intact orange peel. It'll take longer to cook than most camp desserts, but the results are worth it.

GATHER ROUND THE CAMPFIRE

Rituals are huge for kids, and there are few experiences more sacred than gathering around a fire. Fire teaches children many things. There's learning how to build a proper fire—a skill they'll have for the rest of their lives—as well as the all-important safety aspect. Children should know and respect fire boundaries. Establish a fire perimeter kids are not allowed to cross, and enforce consequences if they do. Tanya recommends putting lawn chairs around the fire pit and instructing children not to enter that circle. Explain the concept of stop, drop, and roll and other fire safety tips before striking the match.

Make it the children's job to gather kindling. If mature enough, they could easily be taught knife safety. Many nature schools teach children as young as six years old how to properly handle knives. With patience and proper supervision, it's entirely possible for elementary-aged children to whittle their own sticks for marshmallow roasting.

Cooking over open flames is one of the most treasured aspects of camping. Show kids how much fun it is to cook your own food over the fire, be it a sausage or a skillet of potatoes. If you involve kids in the process, they'll want to stick around for the outcome.

PLAY IT SAFE

The outdoors carries different risks than cities do. Make sure you've established firm guidelines with your children before they're let loose to play. Some suggestions for children:

- Tell a grown-up where you're going and get their permission before venturing off into the woods.
- Always explore with a buddy.
- Stay close to the trail.
- Hug a tree, stay put, and blow a whistle if lost.
- Leave wildlife alone.
- Avoid prickly plants.
- Leaves of three, let it be!

Camping is certainly made more challenging with toddlers in tow, but it's not impossible. When they're crawling around and getting into everything, caregivers need to be vigilant not to leave out anything that could be harmful. To combat this, some parents bring a playpen to their campsite, while others block off an area with baby gates. I've even witnessed jolly jumpers fixed to a tree.

Choosing the right campsite is also something to consider. As picturesque as it may be, setting up camp directly beside a lake or river may not be the best idea for families with little ones who like to wander off. Likewise, you'll want to stay away from cliffs or busy roads. Proximity to the bathrooms is also paramount. A ten-minute walk to the outhouse isn't ideal when you're in the midst of potty training—especially when you know they've probably been holding it for the past half hour!

Be courteous. Don't leave axes or dangerous equipment lying around. Instruct children not to touch or go into the campsites of others. Be sure to clean up after yourself, especially if partaking in a few beverages around the campfire. Nobody wants to cut their finger on a can or stumble over a bottle when making an emergency trip to the outhouse in the middle of the night.

RELAX ROUTINES?

To keep the routine or ditch it? Many treatises have been written on this very topic. It can be tricky to figure out if it's best to keep bedtime routines or if giving your child unlimited freedom in the great outdoors means letting them decide when to go to bed. Making the decision more difficult is camping with other families, who may operate differently than yours.

For many, camping is about breaking up routine—whether it's bedtime or mealtime. Others worry that if their children stay up too late or eat too much sugar, everybody will suffer. If camping with other families, you'll want to talk to the other parents ahead of time. Try to find common ground, or at least find out how they intend to roll, so you can set expectations for your family ahead of time. It's crucial to make compromises you feel comfortable with.

Lack of gear prevents many people from camping, but you can easily rent, borrow, or opt for an equipped campsite before you decide to invest in equipment. Keep in mind, it's a good idea to include children in the packing process. Let them take ownership by packing their own bag. You can double-check it, of course, but try not to let them see you doing that.

You'll need a tent (or camper), sleeping bags, pillows, and a sleeping pad to cushion yourself from the hard ground. As for clothing, comfort is key. You'll look out of place if dressed in nice clothing, and you're apt to ruin it. Dress in layers, bring rain gear and extra socks, and keep in mind that you don't need a lot of clothes. Most campers end up wearing the same old stuff day after day. Here's a list of some items you may consider bringing along:

- HEADLAMP Not only do headlamps beat flashlights for size and efficiency, but they make it possible for children to be in the tent by themselves with a deck of cards, game, or book, allowing parents a few minutes to themselves.

- BACKPACK Children enjoy hiking so much more when they have their own water bottle, snacks, and perhaps some small wildlife brochures they can pull out from their own backpack any time they wish.

- TOYS Bring along a few of your child's favourite small toys and their clutch item, be it a blanket or stuffy. They'll be happier having something familiar from home, and it helps to calm kids no matter what their age. Pulling out a new, small toy during a traffic jam or inclement weather has also been known to work wonders.

- ZIPLOC BAGS You'll want these to separate items, and if you pack clothing in larger plastic bags, it helps to keep them dry.

- HAND SANITIZER You may not have clean, running water nearby, or soap in the outhouse; antibacterial lotion helps keeps hyper parents calm about germs.

- TOILET PAPER There may be toilet paper in the camp wash-room facility, or there may not. Either way, this is easy to stash in your pocket.
- WHISTLE A whistle should be mandatory for all children playing in the woods. They should know to blow it loud if they are lost or in danger.
- EYE MASK Anyone who doesn't necessarily want to wake up with the early morning sun would benefit from blocking it out.
- NOISE-CANCELLING HEADPHONES OR EARPLUGS These allow people to mute noise from other campsites and possibly keep sleeping despite those stirring around you.
- PORTABLE POTTY If you're in the midst of potty training, set a potty (or a bucket lined with a plastic bag) inside the vestibule area of the tent. This will help prevent accidents if the toilet isn't convenient.
- SAND TOYS Even if there's no beach, children can play in the grass and dirt using their beach toys. Toy cars and trucks are also big hits.
- TARP AND ROPE Two of the most essential camping items, these allow you to make a roof over your campsite and stay dry. They're also particularly handy when trying to block out your camp neighbours.
- EXTRA LAWN CHAIRS There never seem to be enough chairs around the campfire. You may have surprise visitors, or a friend may have forgotten theirs.
- SWISS ARMY KNIFE You don't need a lot of gadgets, but this all-in-one contraption really comes in handy. Try to get the one that has a knife, scissors, and toothpick. You probably don't need the one with the fish scaler.

What to leave at home can be as important as what to pack. Electronic devices distract from the outdoors. If you want your children to have a fully immersive experience in nature, you'll need to leave the cell phones and iPad at home. Give your kids the opportunity to find joy in simple things. Send them on a nature scavenger hunt, look for tadpoles, watch the clouds float by in the sky. Even a game of hide-and-seek in the woods taps into many of our senses. Children will survive and are quite likely to thrive when left to their own (non-device) devices—off the grid.

RAINY DAY ACTIVITIES

You'll surely check the weather forecast before your trip, but rain can sneak up on you, threatening to ruin even the most carefully constructed camping trip. So long as you make like a Girl Guide and come prepared with a few boredom busters up your sleeve, camping trips can be salvaged. The key is to stay busy and not dwell on the weather.

"There's no such thing as bad weather, just bad clothing," goes the old Scandinavian saying. If you have appropriate rain gear, you can still play outside; when you're active, you won't notice inclement weather as much. Go for a hike along a forested trail. The tree branches overhead will provide a bit of shelter, and you'll feel so much better for getting out. Tarps are wonderful for having overtop your campfire area, allowing you a dry place to gather outside while still enjoying a fire. (Be sure to store wood under the tarp so it stays dry.)

Poor weather is also an excellent opportunity to take advantage of naturalist programs and learning experiences offered by Parks Canada or provincial parks in their campgrounds. Check in at the Visitor Information desk to see what's scheduled during your visit. These interpretive programs are interesting for kids, and you're sure to learn a whole lot, too.

Books, cards, and board games can engage all family members in a warm, dry spot. When all else fails, don't discredit driving to the nearest town. Remember, the point is to spend time together as a family outside of your normal environment. This can be accomplished a number of different ways. There's no shame in sussing out the local attractions, grabbing a hot meal, or spending the afternoon at a community pool or library.

It's safe to assume that you're going to get dirty when you go camping. If you're the type that has to sterilize a soother every time it falls on the ground, camping might not be your thing, warns Nadine Silverthorne, a Toronto mom of two. "You have to see all that dirt as building immunity. What doesn't kill you makes you stronger."

Parents also need to expect that their children could wake up early—really early. Those accustomed to sleep props such as blackout blinds, noise machines, and a nightlight might have some adjusting to do. Best to negotiate with your partner who takes the early shift, unless you don't mind possibly waking up the entire campground.

These early mornings, however, often have a silver lining, as Silverthorne found. Taking her tots and a few granola bars along for good measure, they tiptoed to the lake on the edge of their campsite. "We called it 'watching the lake wake up.' Once there we stayed still, and it felt almost meditative. There was a certain raven that would show up, and if we were really quiet the loons came out." Having the lake all to themselves in the early morning hours turned into a tradition—so much so that even now, when her children are at the sleeping-in stage, they still ask to be woken up early so they can watch the lake transform.

DON'T GIVE UP!

If your first experience camping isn't a pleasant one, you're not alone. Not that it can't be great—it's just that most of us have survived camping trips where it rained the entire time or the children wouldn't sleep or the baby kept trying to eat rocks. Despite a few hardships, there are usually many nice moments in any camping trip. Try to focus on the good, and realize you'll know better for next time. We learn as we go, and modifications are often needed for each and every trip. For some, that might mean bringing along an older cousin to supervise the preschoolers, or upgrading to an air mattress, or even calling it quits a day early. If you truly think you're done, know there's an entire world of comfort camping out there. Yes, you'll pay more to have your sleeping quarters all set up for you, but you won't have to lug as much, and you'll probably be way more comfortable.

LEARN TO HOW-TO

Not everyone was brought up backpacking in the backcountry. In fact, most of us weren't. Newbie campers and those of us who haven't spent much time recently in the great outdoors do well taking courses to get back up to speed. These classes are often complimentary or offered at a nominal fee, and allow you to quickly get familiarized with what to expect. Mountain Equipment Co-op (MEC) offers a wide variety of courses at their stores across Canada. Topics range from Backcountry 101 to canoe trips to bear awareness and wilderness first aid. They've even partnered with Parks Canada to present Learn to Camp events that offer planning tips and teach necessary skills, so your family has a safe and enjoyable camping trip.

If you're staying at a Parks Canada campsite, be sure to check online before you go for their wide range of programs and activities. Families can learn how to build the perfect fire, cook bannock, or take a guided hike with an interpreter to learn more about the natural wonders in the national park you're visiting.

Resources

This resources section, accurate at the time of printing, is meant to be used as a directory. The companies listed are not personal endorsements. Offers will vary from one organization to the next. Since many of those listed are small businesses, some may fold and others may emerge over time.

BABY EQUIPMENT RENTAL SERVICES

Make your travels smoother and lighter by picking up what you need from these rental services located across Canada.

British Columbia

BABY'S ON THE GO! Services Whistler and Vancouver. babysonthego.com

WEE TRAVEL Canada's first baby equipment rental company supports the Vancouver and Toronto markets. weetravel.ca

TRAVELING TIKES Offers free deliver in the Vancouver area with no minimum order. travelingtikes.com

TINY TOURIST This Okanagan region service offers rental pick up or personal delivery of baby and toddler products. thetinytourist.ca

Alberta

ONE TINY SUITCASE Offers a wide variety of rentals, including breast pumps and toys, in Edmonton and Calgary. onetinysuitcase.ca

LITTLE TRAVELLER Serves Calgary and the surrounding area. littletraveller.ca

SNUGGLEBUG BABY GEAR Delivery in the Alberta Rockies to Canmore, Banff, Lake Louise, and the Kananaskis. snugglebugbabygear.com

Saskatchewan

HERE FOR YOU BABY EQUIPMENT RENTALS Operates out of Regina, Saskatchewan. Facebook.com/BabyEquipmentRentals

Manitoba

MOXLEY'S RENTALS Rents baby and toddler gear for the Winnipeg market. moxleysrentals.ca

Ontario

BABY GETAWAY Supplying the Greater Toronto Area, they deliver to Pearson Airport for free. babygetaway.com

TRAVELBUG BABY Offers a wide variety of brands and equipment in Toronto and its surrounding areas. travelbugbaby.com

WEE TRAVEL Canada's first baby equipment rental company supports both Toronto and Vancouver. weetravel.ca

BABY TRAVELS Services the Niagara Region, Greater Hamilton, and Burlington. babytravels.ca

Québec

MINI NOMADE Supplies Québec City, Mont-Sainte-Anne, Stoneham, Île d'Orléans, Levis, and Beauport, with service in both English and French. mininomade.com

TRAVEL-BUGGY This Montreal-based company delivers and sets up the products for you. travel-buggy.com

Nova Scotia

TINY TRAVELLERS Based in Halifax, they will deliver to the airport, or locations in Halifax, Dartmouth, Bedford, and Sackville. tinytravellers.ca

Newfoundland

GO BABY RENTALS Offers free delivery to the St. John's airport in Newfoundland. gobabyrentals.ca

With so many apps out there, it can be hard to know which are worth downloading. Here are a few travel apps that can improve your travel experience:

HERE Maps
Shows you the fastest way to get around, be it by foot, bus, or car, with live traffic information and voice guidance. This app works without an internet connection in more than 100 countries, with maps saved to your phone.

Mom Maps
Find family-friendly spots like museums and playgrounds (including reviews and directions) in over 28,000 locations.

CAA
Allows you to search all of the gas stations in your area to find the best price and which ones offer CAA Rewards. If you need roadside assistance, you can get a quote before submitting your request so there are no surprises.

Fast Camera
If you want those holiday snaps to have professional quality, this app is excellent for capturing action and interval-timed shots on your phone.

Google Translate
Canada is a bilingual country. Type or use your camera to translate text. Download your target language to use it offline.

Headspace
A meditation app that shares mindfulness techniques to help calm nerves and (in my case) induce sleep on flights.

Mad Libs

This fill-in-the-blank game is a fun way for families to pass the time.

GateGuru

There's no need to run down the terminal to find a monitor with your flight status. This app updates your itinerary with flight delays, gate changes, and security wait times. An amenities list displays your options for a play space or family-friendly restaurant, based on your terminal.

Airline

Download the app for the carrier you're flying with to receive check-in reminders and complimentary in-flight entertainment.

Museum

Many museums have apps to make the experience more interesting for children (and parents) with scavenger hunts and in-depth details of what you're viewing.

CANADIAN TOURISM BOARDS

Get the scoop on the destination you're visiting by spending some time on the tourism websites prior to your visit. On their sites, you'll get the low-down on events, travel deals, and scenic drives. Some even allow you to design your own discount passport for city attractions, accommodations, and restaurants.

British Columbia

- hellobc.com
- tourismvancouver.com
- exploresquamish.com
- tourismvictoria.com
- tourismvi.ca
- visitparksvillequalicumbeach.com
- visitpenticton.com

Alberta

- travelalberta.com
- visitcalgary.com
- calgarystampede.com
- banfflakelouise.com
- exploreedmonton.com
- dinosaurpark.ca

Saskatchewan

- tourismsaskatchewan.com
- visitcypresshills.ca
- tourismregina.com
- tourismmoosejaw.ca

Manitoba

- travelmanitoba.com
- tourismwinnipeg.com
- everythingchurchill.com

Ontario

- ontariotravel.net
- ottawatourism.ca
- seetorontonow.com
- bluemountainvillage.ca
- niagaraparks.com

Québec

- quebecoriginal.com
- quebecregion.com
- tourismeoutaouais.com
- saguenaylacsaintjean.ca
- quebecmaritime.ca

New Brunswick

- tourismnewbrunswick.ca
- bayoffundytourism.com
- discoversaintjohn.com
- tourism.moncton.ca
- tourismfredericton.ca

Nova Scotia

- novascotia.com
- destinationhalifax.com

Prince Edward Island

- tourismpei.com

Newfoundland and Labrador

- newfoundlandlabrador.com
- gowesternnewfoundland
  .com
- destinationstjohns.com

Yukon

- travelyukon.com

Parks Canada

- pc.gc.ca

Destination Canada

Canada's national tourism marketing organization offers travel guides that can be easily searched by topic or location. Find out more: canada.travel

TOUR OPERATORS

This is not a comprehensive list of all the tour operators in each province and territory. The tour operators I have worked with, and who are mentioned in this book, are listed below:

British Columbia

- Kayaking tours in Victoria: oceanriver.com
- Caving in Parksville: hornelake.com
- Eagle viewing and rafting in Squamish: sunwolf.net/eagle-tours
- Via Ferrata, hiking and outdoor adventure in Squamish: mountainskillsacademy.com
- Paddleboarding in Penticton: pentictonpaddlesurf.com
- Kayaking tours in Penticton: hoodooadventures.ca
- Bike tours of the Okanagan Valley: monasheeadventuretours.com

Alberta

- Segway tours in Edmonton and Calgary: rivervalleyadventure.com
- Guided hikes, wildlife tours, and outdoor adventure in and around Banff National Park: whitemountainadventures.com, banffadventures.com, and banfftours.com

Saskatchewan

- RCMP Academy tours: rcmpheritagecentre.com
- Orchards tours: overthehillorchards.ca
- Moose Jaw's underground tunnel tours: tunnelsofmoosejaw.com

Manitoba

- Churchill boat and Zodiac tours, beluga snorkelling, and kayaking with Sea North Tours: polarinn.com
- Churchill polar bear viewing via tundra buggy: frontiersnorth.com

Ontario

- Toronto City Sightseeing bus: citysightseeingtoronto.com
- Pirate ship cruises on Centre Island: piratelife.ca
- Boat tours of Niagara Falls: niagaracruises.com
- Foodie adventures in Ottawa: cestboncooking.ca
- Tours of Parliament: lop.parl.gc.ca/Visitors
- Haunted tours of Ottawa: hauntedwalk.com
- Ottawa bike rentals: rentabike.ca
- Hop-on, hop-off double-decker bus tour of Ottawa: grayline.com

Québec

- Helicopter tours of Saguenay Fjord National Park: peakaviation.ca
- Kayaking Saguenay Fjord: ferme5etoiles.com/en and fjordenkayak.ca/en
- Whale watching along Saguenay Fjord: croisieresaml.com/en

New Brunswick
- Kayaking the Bay of Fundy: freshairadventure.com

Nova Scotia
- Halifax city bike tours: iheartbikeshfx.com
- Lunenburg Walking Tours: lunenburgwalkingtours.com
- Tidal bore rafting along the Bay of Fundy: tidalborerafting.com

Prince Edward Island
- Giant bar clam dig: tcapei.com
- Chocolate making: islandchocolates.ca

Newfoundland
- Iceberg, whale, and puffin viewing near St. John's: obriensboattours.com
- Iceberg and whale watching from St. Anthony: discovernorthland.com
- Zodiac boat tours and Quirpon Island lighthouse stays: linkumtours.com
- Cooking classes, foraging, and beach boil-ups: codsounds.ca
- Irish Loop, St. John's, and around the province walking and driving tours: newfoundlandtours.com

Yukon
- Flightseeing: rockingstar.ca
- Northern Lights tours: northerntales.ca
- Snowmobiling: kanoepeople.com
- Dog sledding: cathersadventures.com

Acknowledgements

They say it takes a village to raise a child, but I say it takes a village to produce a book. There are many people and organizations who helped make this book a reality, and I'm indebted to you all.

Thanks to my husband, Dan, for your continuing support—and for giving me the freedom to do the job I want to do, not the one I have to do. Eve, thank you for becoming such a resilient traveller. Sharing these experiences with you has meant more to me than you'll ever know. (I won't thank our dog, Buddy, because he has been an enormous pain in the butt with our frequent comings and goings. But he is awfully cute and did keep me company during those early morning hours of writing, so perhaps he deserves a tiny shout-out.)

I'm forever grateful to Marlene and Barry Bannister for so graciously supporting our family when work trips collided. Thank you also to the Laigos and the Oliver family, plus the staff at MESP for providing reassuring childcare.

Michelle Kohl, you're a beta reader extraordinaire. Your advice and friendship are invaluable. Leigh McAdam, those impromptu dog-walking brainstorming sessions have benefitted me so much!

Thank you, Andrea, for your friendship and candid comments. And Dianna Campbell-Smith, thank you for telling me the things I don't want to hear, I guess.

Adrian Brijbassi and Jane Usher, you both took the time to help me become a better writer. Your constructive criticism is always welcome. Nadine Silverthorne, thank you for taking a chance on me. Julie Van Rosendaal, you've always been so gracious in sharing your expertise and contacts with writers and bloggers who aren't quite as far along the path as you are. Tom Babin and Leanne Shirtliffe, thanks for your candid advice about the publishing world and how best to navigate it.

I'm proud to be a member of both the Travel Media Association of Canada (TMAC) and the Society of American Travel Writers (SATW), two dynamic organizations that assist professional travel writers. Without the hard work of these volunteers, I wouldn't have been able to carve a career out of travel writing.

I'm grateful to have been welcomed into so many wonderful writing and blogging communities. Thank you to the Housewives, and to all the bloggers, writers, and editors who shared their expertise with me for this book. Thank you for your time and tips: Kathy Buckworth, Sarah Deveau, Helen Early, Tamara Elliot, Colleen Lanin, Lisa Goodmurphy, Claudia Laroye, Allison Laypath, Stephanie Holmes, Corinne McDermott, Melissa Vroon, Tanya Koob, Pete and Dalene Heck, Claire Tansey, Amber Mamian, Lesley Carter, Inga Batur, Talon Windwalker, Barbara Orr, Laura Byrne Paquet, Jes Watson.

To my good friends who also shared their family travel experiences with me: Maria Schuba, Robin Meckelborg, and Magalie Boutin, thank you!

A heartfelt thanks to the lovely team at TouchWood Editions. Taryn Boyd, I'm so glad we didn't break up! Renée Layberry, I don't think I've ever clicked with an editor so well. You've made this book sparkle! Also thanks to Pete Kohut, Tori Elliott, and Cailey Cavallin for making this book (and me) look polished and enticing (but not in a creepy way).

So many destination marketing organizations went above and beyond the call of duty. Thank you for not instantly deleting emails from me with the subject line "Urgent Last Minute Request!" I'd especially like to thank:

Destination Canada

and

Parks Canada: Jennifer Burnell, Guy Thériault, Eric Magnan, Lori Bayne, Nisha Tuli, Krista Lingley, Nadine Gauvin, Justine Hunse, Victoria Delorme, Kris Oravec, Kimberly Thompson-Vokey.

British Columbia: Josie Heisig, Carla Mont, Holly Lenk, Luba Plotnikoff, Amber Sessions, Sauchie MacLean, Heather Kawaguchi, Heather McEachen, Sonya Hwang, Elyse Mailhot, Brian Cant.

Alberta: Rose Bolton, Jessica Harcombe Fleming, Ashley Meller, Meredith McLennan, Jeffrey McDonald, Lindsay Jardine, Jennifer Booth, Noelle Aune, Angela Moore, Tara Gaucher, Jonny Bierman, Andrea Visscher.

Saskatchewan: Jodi Holliday, Shane Owen.

Manitoba: Gillian Chester, Jillian Recksiedler, Tamara Soroka, Tricia Woikin.

Ontario: Helen Lovekin, Jantine Van Kregten, Judy Hammond, Kristin Ellis, Chelsea Tobin, Tracy Ford, Vanessa Somarriba, Karly Melo, Deneen Perrin.

Quebec: Magalie Boutin, Gillian Hall, Anne Chardon, Steve Hutchison, Nancy Donnelly, Suzie Loiselle, Paule Bergeron, Kathy Leclerc, Patrick Lemaire.

New Brunswick: Allison Aiton (miss you!), Denise Bradbury.

Nova Scotia: Regis Dudley, Pam Wamback, Shelah Allen, Katie Conklin.

PEI: Isabell McDougall.

Newfoundland and Labrador: Gillian Marx, Laura Walbourne, David Walbourne, June Alton, Tracy Byrne, Darrin Steele, Loyola O'Brien.

Yukon: Jim Kimshead AKA Yukon Jimmy. Adventures with you are surprisingly good.

Index

Photo credits
Cover:
Top left: Canada's Wonderland
Top centre: Tourism Calgary
Top right: JP Danko, Stocksy United
Bottom left: Parks Canada/Eric Magnan
Bottom centre: Tourism New Brunswick/
    Alison Aiton
Bottom right: Village Vacances Valcartier/
    Stéphane Audet/Quebec City Tourism

Interior:
Aaron Cohen/Canadian Museum of Human
    Rights, 103
Andrea Hamlin Photography at Blue Mountain
    Resorts, 140
Assiniboine Park Conservancy, 100, 103, 104
Banff Lake Louise Tourism, 44
Banff Lake Louise Tourism/Paul Zizka
    Photography, viii, 47

Calgary Stampede, 59, 60
Canada's Wonderland, 120, 123
Canadian Museum of Human Rights, 104
Capilano Suspension Bridge Park, 27, 28
Charles-David Robitaille, 189
Charles-David Robitaille/Tourisme Saguenay-
    Lac-Saint-Jean, 186
Chelsea Hotel, 120, 124
Destination Halifax, 212, 218, 222, 225
Destination Halifax/Len Wagg, 208
Doug Ross, 112
Edmonton Economic Development
    Corporation, 79
Garry Kan, 201
Hamid Attie/Vancouver Aquarium, 28
Hornblower Niagara Cruises, 130
Jody Robbins, 4, 7, 8, 14, 17, 18, 24, 36, 68, 71,
    72, 76, 91, 92, 153, 154, 221, 240, 243,
    244, 252, 255, 256, 267, 332
JP McCarthy, 112